Packing Up Without Looking Back
A 36/365 Memoir

MAUKTIK KULKARNI

Packing Up Without Looking Back

A 36/365 Memoir

Cover design and illustrations by Leslee Lazar

DEDICATED TO

The circle of life which made me go through the pleasure and
pain of writing a book all over again.

ALSO BY MAUKTIK KULKARNI

A Ghost of Che: A Motorcycle Ride Through Space, Time, Life
And Love

CONTENTS

PREFACE

My first solo backpacking trip started on a whim, without any coherent reason. I didn't even keep a diary for the six weeks I was on the road, riding a motorcycle in South America. I just wanted to escape. Since I didn't speak any Spanish and was traveling through the small towns and villages of South America, where nobody spoke English, I ended up traveling in silence and internalizing almost every little detail of the trip. So much so, that it was easy to write a book about my experiences even without having taken any notes.

However, this book is different. Unlike the first book, which got published before I turned thirty instead of sixty, to my utter surprise, this book was not meant to be written. I did not know I had a second book in me. But then, we are not born with "Number of books to be written – X" etched on our foreheads. It all depends on the kind of life trajectory we choose, or that gets chosen for us, or somewhere between the two. The story of this book, from its genesis to its completion, has several twists and turns. Let me start with the trip itself and peel off one layer at a time.

My motorcycle trip had a well-defined start and end because I had an offer letter from an exciting start-up with a start date. In the larger scheme of things, it was also quite a short trip at just six weeks. However, the seeds for this longer, round-the-world trip were sown during the motorcycle trip, when I met a few Aussies and Kiwis who had quit their jobs – or "normal" lives – and decided to travel indefinitely. For a small-town, middle-class Indian with serious goals in life, this was as outlandish as it could get. How can you waste time like that? Sure enough, after a life-changing six weeks on the road, and four years in a live-wire start-up back in the United States, I was ready to waste time, just like that. The perimeters of my academic and professional worlds started to feel small and restrictive once I was bitten by the travel bug, knowing well that there was an organic world out there waiting to be explored.

After a rather enjoyable four years in start-up America, I was ready. However, taking the actual leap of faith was not that easy. My job had given me thousands of airline miles and a decent bank balance. The day I put in my papers, I still had three weeks of transition period to hand over my responsibilities and wrap up work before I bid my final good-bye. That evening, the only thing on my mind was celebrating my newfound freedom. As exciting as my job was, I knew that the time had come to take the plunge and spend a year bumming around. Time flew quickly as I wrapped up work and my then-current life, selling all my possessions, and bragging to my friends about my upcoming adventure. It really hit me on the last day of that three-week transition period, coming home to realize that there would be no more playing office and no more paycheck coming my way. It made me restless and sleepless, forcing me to wonder whether I should postpone the whole adventure for another time, when I was older and wiser and instead, find another job for the moment to save some more money. It seemed like the safer and saner thing to do, although I couldn't put a number to that "some more." I was clearly getting cold feet. *I am still in my early thirties and there is a long way to go. I can do this some other day.*

This restlessness lasted for a week, after which I finally woke up one morning, called the airline agency, and booked my round-the-world itinerary. April 28, 2012, I was taking a flight from New York to freedom. The clouds of anxiety eventually cleared up and the planning began. The clock was ticking. I had no time to waste.

The trip was successful beyond my wildest imaginings. I am not sure whether traveling to 36 countries in a year made sense. Given another year, I would probably not pack in so many countries again; twelve, or maybe ten, or fewer. However, that doesn't mean I regret any moment of this trip, getting high on wanderlust steroids. When I completed the trip, the physicality of it all made me realize I had done it at the right age and stage in life. There is that joke about freedom, money and health. At any given age, you only have two of the three. I managed to find that tiny little sweet spot in my life when I had all three and pounced on it.

Other than the crazy range of experiences, from scaling Kilimanjaro to exploring the Great Barrier Reef, there are three ingredients without which this book would not have been possible. One is named Jorge Campos. A colleague in the start-up where I worked, Jorge and I used to talk routinely about science, sports, and a round-the-world trip. Quiet, introverted, and insightful, he was the first one to realize I was about to quit my job and start this trip. Jorge forced me to start writing a blog before I started my trip. Now, I had never been a fan of regular journaling or blog writing, and I had never kept a diary in my life. I wrote sporadically, and at length, but only when something truly inspired me. A 500-1000 word blog post seemed too restrictive, but Jorge insisted. And he was right. Without this journaling, it would have been impossible for me to remember all of these events, places, and people from around the world. At times, it was excruciatingly painful to write. Lack of time, exhaustion, better motivation to stay outside, and inertia, the reasons were endless. It was a tough task to keep noting down events from every country, but I am glad I did it. My musings about the countries I visited are not meant to be in-depth analyses of the local cultures, histories, or societies. Given the frantic pace of the journey, that would have been a near-impossible task. Rather, these are thoughts that go through an aimless traveler's mind when his abstract ideas about the countries – shaped primarily by popular media – meet the slices of reality on the ground. The book is presented mostly in chronological order, with a few chapters moved back and forth for geographical continuity or ease of reading.

Jorge also wanted me to make money from my blog while traveling, but that was another layer of marketing and coordination I was not willing to deal with. So, by the time I finished the trip, the raw material for this book was ready. As an interesting side story, Jorge quit the same company six months after I did, with the intention of doing the same trip in the opposite direction. We made some grand plans to meet up somewhere, but it was not meant to be. Plus, while I stuck to my round-the-world flight itineraries like clockwork, Jorge went straight south from the United States at a snail's pace, covering about 6 countries – instead of 36 – in two and a half years!

The second ingredient is Devasmita Chakraverty. It probably sounds poetic that we met in person for the first time one day before the last chapter of this book. It was as if the universe was telling me, "Now that you have finished the trip, here is someone who will help you finish the book." Growing up, I never harbored any burning desire to become an author. I still don't consider myself one. Before publishing the first book, the concept that most human experiences are shared, which is why readers connect to writers, was alien to me. I wrote my first book for friends and family, most of whom had a fairly predictable and not too critical stance about my work. However, the book slowly started reaching people outside friends and family, people who did not know me or had never met me. Their responses were quite fascinating. Who knew there were so many people wanting to do a motorcycle trip in South America, or at least get out of their comfort zones? I am not sure how I came across the review Devasmita wrote after reading my book. Perhaps a common friend sent it to me. It was intriguing at first and downright scary after a moment's reflection. In my book, I was talking about getting rid of the cobwebs of social influence in my life, and here was someone being deeply inspired by my book and thinking about how to travel more, and travel independently.

I still had a couple of months to finish my round-the-world trip when I read Devasmita's review of my book. I reached out to her and we decided to meet in the United States after I completed my trip. For the first time in my life, I was meeting someone who knew me only because of my book. Given our shared passion for traveling, we had a blast.

After I wrapped things up and left the American shores for good, Devasmita kept insisting that I convert my blog into a book. There were several obstacles to this endeavor. The first one was why. My first book was published in 2009, when smartphones were new and expensive. Not everyone had one and not everyone who had one was addicted to it. I recently read an article in an Indian newspaper citing a new study claiming that the average attention span of humans has dropped below that of goldfish. Yep. Goldfish – 9 seconds, humans – 8 seconds. If this is the situation in India, a country where smartphone penetration is still not 100%, imagine the situation in developed countries. Given this, who the hell is going to read this book? But for most writers – the non-commercial ones at least– the answer is simple: Writing gives them a sense of catharsis. While the post-publication dialogue with readers is interesting, that is not my motivation for writing a book. Rather, it is to get a sense of completion for my year-long adventure. Devasmita believes that most of the girls in India who have ever wanted to travel will fall in love with me after reading this book. I am not sure how many of them will even open it!

My other challenge was time. I finished the year-long trip, wrapped up my life in the United States, and moved to India. I had spent my childhood and college days in India and, after a long absence of 13 years I was living in India again. By then most of my friends had plush jobs, were raising families, and were visibly happy with their life trajectories. Here I was, practically fresh-off-the-boat in my own country, with no work experience and no professional network in India. Having spent a significant portion of my savings traveling around the world, I needed to focus on making some money and establishing myself in the Indian professional arena. I continued occasionally writing on my blog because, after an absence of 13 formative years, I was rediscovering my own country. It was not possible to set aside a chunk of time for converting the blog into a book.

For the first book, it was my aunt, Sheetal Kulkarni, who kept pushing me to write it. For this one, it was Devasmita. After our first – and still only – meeting, we kept in touch while living our own lives. Devasmita was insistent on my writing the book. I kept shoving it on the backburner, finding one excuse after another, until I accidentally entered the world of film-making. My foray into the film world is an evolving story and perhaps my third book in the making. The only upside of embracing film-making, as a career option, is that any semblance of a 9-to-5 day goes out the window. There are weeks when the work goes for 150 hours straight, and there are weeks when you just sit on your ass, waiting for others to complete their work. Embracing film-making as a career path gave me chunks of time to conceptualize this book and start the process of compilation.

The third and biggest challenge was finding the right editor. When I wrote my first book, my mentor, Paul Fitzgerald, guided me through the maze of the publishing world. He also recommended that I go straight to self-publishing. The traditional publishing world has consolidated significantly and become risk-averse. I followed his advice and did not waste much time chasing literary agents or the big publishing houses. For the second book, I thought the traditional publishing houses might be more receptive, since I am not a first-time author. I was wrong. A huge majority of them did not respond. A handful of them said it was not their genre. In one interesting exchange, an editor wrote back, saying she had gone through the rough draft and the manuscript had too many "I"s. I reminded her that this was an autobiographical work, something people are historically known to relate to because of the nature of shared human experiences. How else am I supposed to say "I was walking around aimlessly in Prague, turned a corner, and saw this beautiful, majestic Gothic church?" Convert it into passive voice and say "The roads of Prague were being traversed by me when all of a sudden, a left turn was taken and a beautiful, majestic Gothic church made a lasting impression in my heart?" I never heard back from the editor.

I quickly gave. I realized I had to find a collaborator who has lived a similar life, or at least tasted the backpacking life. It could not be an editor sitting at a desk, buried under piles of dusty manuscripts. And Devasmita was the first name that came to my mind. She shared my cultural background – middle class, conservative Indian family that heavily stressed academic success as a gateway to achieving what one desires in life, until getting married and raising a family takes precedence. She had dared to step out of this mindset, moved to the United States singly, travelled solo in many countries, and thrived in spite of rejecting the socio-cultural norms of the Indian expats in the United States. Instead of choosing a predictable trajectory of life in American suburbia, she chose to live and work in different countries, hike a live volcano in Sicily, tried rabbit meat for the first time in Malta, and grilled a physicist on string theory after getting high in Amsterdam. I enjoyed reading about her travel experiences and, especially, her style of writing.

It may sound like a perfect team, but we had never worked together. People can get closely attached to their work when it comes to writing and editing. Devasmita had never edited a book before, something she confessed to me on the first day. However, I was not worried. In my professional and traveling life, I had worked with people from all kinds of backgrounds, and enjoyed challenging myself, as well as others, to do things we had never done before. All said and done, this was my journey. I was not writing the next bestseller. Who cares what the outcome is as long as we enjoy the process of working together?

We had a blast working together on this book. When Devasmita is traveling, she writes about what people eat and wear and speak in different countries. I am virtually oblivious to these details of life. I love politics, history and sports, which she is mostly clueless about, especially the last one. Just like challenging myself and my editor, I also like to challenge my readers to learn more about world history or culture. She instinctively loves to simplify experiences for the readers. She is an activist, but I am mostly a dispassionate observer. She does not like to swear, but I curse like a sailor. All in all, we have had our skirmishes and also learned a lot from each other in the process.

The third ingredient was Leslee Lazar, the graphic designer. It is a strange coincidence that he is also a neuroscientist and has given up the high-octane research world to pursue other hobbies in life. It would have been very easy for us to drift back into the world of neuroscience, create some geeky illustrations unrelated to the theme of the book, and congratulate ourselves for a job well done. Leslee's visual art IQ is too high to do that. I am grateful to him for working closely with Devasmita to design the book cover and the sketches for each section of the book.

Nancy Wall, an experienced copy editor, ensured that we stay humble and realize that we have a long way to go before we can write without making mistakes.

In a nutshell, that is the story of the birth of this book. However, a preface cannot be just about that, right? In the end, what is this all about? Catharsis and closure, primarily. And, of course, being a part of a myriad of shared human experiences. Listening to Jorge's advice and working with Devasmita made my journey engaging, enlightening, and fun. The curious reader might even find a few nuggets of wisdom tucked away in the pages of this book. However, I have reached a stage in life where I am more of an observer and less of a preacher. Being a techie, I am aware of the millions of distractions these days that prevent people from picking up a book and finishing it. I am sure things are only going to get worse. In this day and age, other than "Bravo!", I would have nothing to say to whoever shows the fortitude to open – and complete – this book. However, let me briefly summarize how this entire experience of traveling without a purpose and then writing about it has changed me. At the highest level, it has brought me closer to my roots of Eastern philosophy, but not in the sense that I am willing to call myself a Hindu or a Buddhist. I am an atheist and do not consider myself affiliated to any particular religion. However, I have a newfound respect for certain concepts of life, such as the world being an illusion or the idea that life – and the world at large – keeps moving in circles. Growing up in India, I was introduced to the concepts of reincarnation and cycles in life quite early in my childhood. I had to go around the world to internalize them. If you have not been introduced to Eastern philosophies, perhaps you have heard Pink Floyd sing

"And you run and you run…
to catch up with the sun…
that is sinking…
racing around…
to come up behind you again."

There's gotta be some truth to that cycle business!

With a whole lot of backpacking experience under your belt, it is easy to get haughty and smug about it. But I have realized that travel is not for everyone. Aniket Ketkar, another one of that rare breed of middle-class Indians who have quit their so-called normal lives to travel far and wide, was asking travelers along the way what travel meant to them. One backpacker gave him a fitting reply. She said traveling taught her that she could have learned, within the comfort of her four walls, everything she learned on the road, but she did not care to.

There is another mythological story in Hinduism in which Lord Ganesha's brother Kartikeya, in a bid to impress his parents and establish his physical superiority over his overweight brother, challenges Ganesha to a round-the-world trip. Kartikeya dashes off, thinking that Ganesha will be nowhere near him when he finishes his trip. When Kartikeya returns, he is surprised to find out that Ganesha has been declared the winner. When he asks his brother, Ganesha tells him he had just walked around his parents once and that was his round-the-world trip. Leaving aside the excessive parent-worship in the story, it is quite clear that traveling means and does different things to different people. It's my poison, but it doesn't have to be yours. Try it out. If you don't like it, find your own.

Most importantly, this trip has helped me become an observer of my own life more than anyone else's. In my first book, I wrote "...life is way more beautiful when you can take the backseat and watch yourself drive." Back then, since I was riding a motorcycle, it was perhaps more of a clever metaphor than a life lesson. Over the years though, I have started feeling like that was a moment of epiphany that did not sink in all the way. I think it has now. You remove your emotions, desires, and vested interests from the scene and start understanding people for who they are. Then, in the next stage, when you become an observer to your own life, you start asking

"Who am I?"

"What twist of fate has brought that guy here?"

"What does it mean to be that girl?"

"Beyond my memory, and if I am lucky, her memory, what does first love mean? Does it have any meaning at all?"

Before, during, or after completing this book, if you start asking yourself questions like these, I would love to hear from you.

EDITOR'S NOTE

Mauktik and I first met in the virtual world under interesting circumstances.

2009

I was in California, visiting a childhood friend whose husband had friends in common with Mauktik (most Indians in the United States are interconnected that way; someone is always someone else's friend's friend). She told me about coming across a book cover with the cutest baby picture.

"And what is the book about?" I asked her, out of curiosity.

"I don't know. Some motorcycle trip he did in South America," she shrugged.

I needed no more nudging. I came back to Seattle and looked him up. True to what was said, Mauktik's book cover had the cutest picture of him, as a child, that had probably appealed to the motherly instincts of my friend. To me, what appealed more is reading about an Indian man who had done a solo motorcycle trip in South America and written about it. Most Indians I knew were busy traveling in herds in time-tested places and taking selfies at Niagara Falls and the Golden Gate Bridge.

I read his book, loved it, wrote a review highly recommending it, and forgot all about it.

2012

I was living in Virginia. It was November, and I had spent my entire day glued to the news channels that were reporting Ajmal

Kasab's hanging, reflecting on issues around the death penalty. I knew I should be working on my comprehensive examinations, but I was unable to focus. It was late at night when I got an email from Mauktik, thanking me for writing a book review and telling me that he was on a yearlong trip around the world. Although I welcomed the distraction, I did not believe him.

Once again, the idea of an Indian taking a year off from work and traveling around the world was so alien to me that I thought someone was impersonating Mauktik and writing me fake emails. The Samaritan that I am, I looked up Mauktik's Facebook page and sent him a message, warning him that his account had been hacked and someone was impersonating him and telling everyone that he was on a yearlong trip.

I heard back soon enough, from the real Mauktik, letting me know that he was, indeed, the one who had sent the email and thanking me for reviewing his work and that his account had not been hacked.

And the rest, as they say, is history.

I was in awe that a person from my background could actually do what he was doing. As someone who grew up in a highly protective, middle-class family in India, the last thing I could imagine was to leave whatever I was doing and go globe-trotting on my own. Education was very important. Career was equally important. Family was very important, too. Traveling, not so much. In my limited travel experience, I had mostly seen white backpackers go on round-the-world missions, teach English in foreign countries, live on limited budgets, embrace yoga, and see the world.

After that, I closely followed Mauktik's journey, as he documented it on and off in an online journal. I earnestly hoped he would write about it and publish it someday. That was also the time I had recently discovered the joys of traveling solo. Although not as prolific as Mauktik, I had done a solo-trip in Europe, for my thirtieth birthday, hiking the mountains of Switzerland, marveling at the beauty of Portugal, discovering the alleys of Paris for myself, and hiking Mount Etna, an active volcano in Sicily. It was a happy coincidence, indeed, that I now had a new friend – a traveler friend.

2013

I really wanted to meet and interview Mauktik at the conclusion of his yearlong trip. He was back in the United States for a few weeks before moving to India. We tried meeting a couple of times, but our schedules conflicted. I was preparing to defend my PhD, and Mauktik's constantly changing coordinates were not really close to mine. After a number of unsuccessful attempts, Mauktik was visiting Baltimore one last time before leaving for India in two days, and was planning to drive down to northern Virginia from there. That was the closest he had come to where I lived. However, there was a little problem. Northern Virginia was almost a two-hour drive from my place, and my PhD defense was scheduled the next day.

Naturally, I was in a dilemma. After thinking it over, about a hundred times, I said, "Let's do it!" I was really inspired by his travels and, if I had not prepared enough for my defense in three years, one extra day was not going to make a difference.

Mauktik and I met for dinner somewhere at a non-descript restaurant that summer evening. The dinner was fantastic. The conversation was even better. He talked for hours about his travel experiences. I drove home enthused and inspired about traveling some more, the weight of my impending dissertation defense momentarily forgotten.

2015

Mauktik moved to India. And I moved to Germany. I started pursuing my travels more seriously than ever, and had already visited some thirty countries. I had had some interesting experiences under my belt by then – being robbed of hundreds of Euros and my passport in Athens in broad daylight, being chased and almost killed by a mad donkey while hiking on an island in Greece, riding the biggest cruise ship I have ever seen from Helsinki to Estonia, doing pot for the first time in Amsterdam, and logging 8,000 miles on a solo road trip, driving to all four corners of the United States in 3 weeks. Moving to Germany made me embrace strange life choices. After driving extensively for five years, I no longer own a car. I do not even own a cell phone anymore, and love every bit of this liberating experience of not being connected to the world every moment. Mauktik asked me if I would like to work on the book you are currently reading. I was skeptical, since I had never edited a book before. However, Mauktik managed to convince me, and I knew that this was exactly what I wanted to put my time and energy into.

Traveling is a privilege for many reasons. One needs a basic level of physical fitness, economic stability, and the ability to be open to the uncertainties that come along. Unfortunately, the window when physical fitness and economic stability are at their peak also coincides with the time when most people are busy writing exams, building careers, buying homes, raising children, and striving to climb higher up the social ladder. Although a person from a very humble background and limited resources, I have realized, with experience, that traveling does not require a whole lot of money. What it needs is a mindset.

My travel journeys started like most, traveling in groups to destinations pre-determined by others, doing things that were touristy and mostly restricted to showing up in group pictures and selfies, eating pre-planned meals, usually cooked and carried with us during road trips (I once traveled with someone who carried a rice cooker to Las Vegas!), and hanging out with the same group of people based on language or ethnicity. Though it was fun while it lasted, it isolated me from the more local experiences. I was traveling for the heck of it, just to check places off my list. I soon outgrew this mode of travel and started to venture out alone or in small groups of ones and twos. I started living in hostels and hanging out with the backpacker crowd. I embraced poverty while traveling. I began interviewing people I met during my travels, and started picking up words and phrases in Spanish, German, and other foreign languages. And what my traveling did was open up an entire new world for me, a world I had been insulated from. I once met a Taiwanese lady in Latvia who told me she was a nanny. She worked for six months every year and traveled for the rest of the time, using all of her savings. "Don't you fear the uncertainty?" I asked her. Her response was profound, and is something I will never forget: "Time is my currency, not money. I get to decide what I do with my time, not the others." I had never before thought of time as a currency. I am sure I was financially better off than that lady, yet her bravery told me about my time-slavery. Despite my inherent desire to travel, I do not think that I could be brave enough to let go of my job, embrace poverty and uncertainty and, in the process, become the master of my time. Traveling taught me who I am, and also, who I am not. Despite everything I received or achieved, learning to travel independently, fearlessly, and tirelessly is the biggest gift of my life. Traveling changed my life.

2017

I am back in the United States. I am now an assistant professor, and I think I have found my sweet spot for traveling. Summers offer me a three-month window during which I can be in any part of the world. I have adopted a minimalist mode of living, so that my travel budget is healthier. I am still car-free, and I take the bus to work every day and immensely enjoy the social experience of watching people. More importantly, my philosophies around travel have evolved. I no longer see travel as tourism. I see it more as a way of living. I have extended my travel philosophies to foster professional relationships with colleagues from other countries around the world, finding ways to write grants that would fund trips for me anywhere I can go and get to know the people, their educational systems, their aspirations, their mindsets, and their ways of living. It is more of an intellectual endeavor for me now. Mauktik and I have managed to complete the book and, surprisingly enough, we are still good friends. We continue planning to someday meet in some obscure country in the world, and I am curious to see when and where that will happen.

Chances are you will read this, nodding in agreement until you close the book and forget all about it. Or you will read, nod in agreement, close the book, and go plan your next trip. Whatever you decide to do, I can tell you something based on my limited life-experience. Time, money, a demanding job, family responsibilities, internal fear, anxiety about traveling alone, whatever is holding you back right now, will all melt into nothingness once you hit the road. You will be truly grateful and humbled by what you learn in life outside the confines of your classroom, office, or home. And Mauktik's journal, his high-spirits, and rich travel experiences will act as a catalyst in this journey of yours.

- Devasmita Chakraverty

INTRODUCTION

1

1. CHASING DEATH AT THE EDGE OF HEAVEN

June 22, 2012
Tromso, Norway

Have you ever seen oxygen masks dropping when in a plane that is flying at 30,000 feet? Today, I did. I do not even know where to begin. Statistics might be a good place to start. Given that I clocked more than 300,000 airline miles before starting this trip, the same miles that are fueling this round-the-world adventure, it was about time for the odds to catch up with me. I remember my first flight as an adult, flying from India to the United States in the year 2000. Back then, every time I got on a flight, I marveled at this amazing feat of human ingenuity and imagination. How on earth does this gigantic, complicated piece of engineering work so reliably? Ironically, these thoughts were always followed by the thought of death. Even if only for a brief moment before take-off, I would always wonder, "Is this how it will end?"

The sense of awe evoked by human engineering faded over the years, perhaps, in part, because of the list of "100 ways to screw up air travel" I had personally experienced. Things nobody has ever imagined have happened on flights I have booked. Missing nuts and bolts, the airport not having the mechanical expertise to fix a particular airplane model, leaving the gate and realizing halfway down the runway that an airspeed indicator has failed – I could go on and on. Everything that could go wrong on the ground

3

probably has gone wrong, chipping away at my initial sense of awe and wonder. These damn airplanes, their manufacturers, and their mechanics are no better than those of cars or trains. However, that brief moment of "Is this how it will end?" never went away. Like clockwork, whenever the plane approached the runway and the captain fired up the engines for take-off, thoughts of death always crept into my mind.

I had spent just over twenty-four hours in Norway, although I'd been in Scandinavia for a few days now. You are in Scandinavia when you are standing in a metro and are not able to hold the overhead rails comfortably, along with feeling like there is a hole in your wallet. People here are tall, Viking tall. Also, things are exorbitantly expensive, even by European standards. In Oslo, a 5-6 kilometer public bus ride from the airport to the "Airport Hotel" costs $12. A breakfast of eggs, ham, and toast costs $25. A bland, cold sandwich and a can of coke are $10. I had just left Oslo to spend a day in a tiny little town called Tromso, which is just north of the Arctic Circle, to see the midnight sun. As we reached cruising altitude, I was debating whether I should order a small pizza with a coke or a sandwich with orange juice. I wondered if I should spend a few extra bucks on flight food and call it my lunch, or if I should wait until we landed at the Tromso airport.

All of a sudden, it felt like the plane had gone over a major air bump. In my row of six seats, three on the left and three on the right, I was at the left window seat. A girl sat at the extreme right, the seats between us empty. We instinctively exchanged worried glances. Before we could look away, we felt another air bump. This one was bigger, and scarier than the last one. I have experienced a lot of air turbulence in the past. I was on a flight that was the last one to land in the middle of crazy thunderstorms in North Carolina before they had to shut down the entire airport. However, I could tell right away that this was different. I looked at the girl across the aisle again, and she was still wearing that worried face. My first thought was that we had hit an air pocket. A friend once told me how his flight dropped 5000 feet in a matter of seconds after hitting an air pocket. Maybe it was just that.

Even before these thoughts left me, the ceiling spit out oxygen masks that dropped in front of our faces without preamble. *Holy shit! Is this it?* I grabbed the mask in front of my face, fumbling with shaky hands to secure it tightly, symbolically grabbing on for dear life while helplessly looking around. There was a curt announcement by the captain, in Norwegian, that consisted of exactly one sentence. What followed was, no, not an announcement in English, but stunned silence. Have the wings broken down? Do I smell smoke or fire coming from somewhere? Have the engines stopped working? What the hell do I know about airplanes anyway? Come on, captain, please say something...in English! Please!

Suddenly, the plane tilted to the right and started losing altitude very rapidly. *This is it. This is how it is supposed to end, suspended at 30,000 feet over the middle of Norway, with absolutely no explanations. Just like that!* I looked over at the girl across the aisle. She had tears streaming down her cheeks, stained from her mascara-lined eyes, holding onto the seat next to hers for dear life. Her face was ashen. I looked out the window, but there were still no visible signs of smoke or broken parts. Just the wing lights blinking amid a thick layer of clouds that made it impossible to find any answers outside. *Are we going to die without knowing what happened to our plane? If we are dying anyway, maybe it does not matter.*

The next few minutes seemed like an eternity, as the flight continued its rapid descent, still tilted right at a precarious angle. I tightly clutched my seat with one hand until my knuckles hurt, holding the oxygen mask with the other, my mind drawing a complete blank. In a dazed and confused state, I had forgotten to tighten the straps of the oxygen mask around my nose and mouth and was holding it with one hand instead. At some point, I even tried to pull the elastic strap hard and make two rounds around my head, a completely desperate but unnecessary and futile attempt on my part. After a few moments of deadly silence, I let go of my seat for a few seconds and briefly gestured with my hands to my panic-stricken, mascara-streaked fellow passenger to calm down. Other than that, I mostly stared out the window with a mind completely gone blank. I wondered what the possibilities were of a wing flying off, smoke coming out of somewhere, or the plane ripping apart into pieces and disappearing in the sky. *Should I get ready for the last seconds of my life, witnessing my entire life flashing in front of my eyes, regretting the things I never did or the people I could never say good-bye to?*

A baby started crying somewhere. Was this another omen, a sign of impending doom? Animals can sense an approaching earthquake or natural disaster, an evolutionary programming of an extra-sensory perception that prepares them to face danger. Perhaps adult humans have lost this extra-sensory perception after spending too much time in a technology-driven, industrialized world away from nature. Babies might be different, though. Damn it! Where was the announcement of assurance when I so needed it? Living in a world overloaded with information, it was surreal to bear this pause, this stunned silence of about ten minutes that felt like a lifetime, with absolutely no clue about what was going to happen next. We were all up there, 50-odd people on board, suspended mid-air over the Norwegian Sea, flying in choppy weather, floating in the puffy, white clouds, and hanging onto our seats for dear life. I felt utterly helpless as we stared straight ahead at the possibility of death.

After ten minutes that seemed an eternity, the plane straightened up a bit. The captain made an announcement, this time in Norwegian, as well as in English. We could let go of our oxygen masks now. Did it mean that things were getting better, or were we going to die anyway, just without our masks? There was another announcement informing us there had been a sudden loss of cabin pressure, but that it was all fine now, and we were still going to land in Tromso around the scheduled time. However, within the next few minutes, the crew appeared from somewhere and informed us that we were flying back to Oslo. The confusion between Tromso and Oslo persisted for awhile, and seemed a welcome change from the confusion of life and death. Finally, we were told that we would be flown back to Oslo, and that, after landing, the captain would make an announcement about the technical problem.

I was still not sure about what we were dealing with. An incapacitated captain? Smoke in the cockpit? A lightning strike? Why did we suddenly lose cabin pressure? Were we completely out of danger? Was the crew withholding important information so we would not panic? There were still too many unanswered questions hanging in the air, pun unintended. The oxygen masks were still hanging from the ceiling, dangling in front of us symbolically, like the noose around our neck, a testimony to what we had just been through, and a reminder that we were still perhaps not totally out of it. The crew seemed to be smiling again. Perhaps fake and plastic or trying to hide how petrified and shaken they, too, felt inside. Whatever it might be, they were smiling again.

At that reduced altitude of 10,000-odd feet, the rest of the trip was uneventful, much to my relief. The airplane never soared or regained its altitude after that, but we managed to fly back to Oslo and land successfully. As promised, the captain made an announcement immediately after landing about the technical problem, first in Norwegian, and then in English. In the airline world, this was probably a good problem to have at cruising altitude. Everyone was listening intently, in stunned silence. In a measured tone that probably suited the Oracle from the Matrix, the captain ended with "We practice this on simulators hundreds of times. Today was our test in real life. Thank you for your cooperation." Phew! She said that she would be happy to answer any questions.

While disembarking, I looked around and thought to myself "These are people I am not meant to share an obituary with." A deathly silence still hung in the air. The passengers assembled their cabin bags and queued up mechanically, perhaps emotionally exhausted and still trying to make sense of everything that just had happened. Maybe it was cultural. Maybe people here do not talk to strangers. However, I could not stop myself. I knew I had to talk to someone. Anyone. I started talking to two men behind me, and soon, their emotions started pouring out. Both of them were avid travelers like me. However, neither one of them had ever experienced anything like this before.

As I was going down the stairs, I debated about whether or not to ask our captain any questions. Part of me felt that ignorance is bliss, and I was just happy to be alive. However, the engineer in me got the better of me. If I did not ask now, I would never know. I motioned to her, and asked her what had gone wrong. She calmly told me that one of the pressure valves had probably been leaking from the beginning and been overlooked, perhaps inadvertently. As soon as the cabin pressure dropped below a certain threshold, the oxygen masks automatically dropped and the emergency procedures kicked in. They had to reduce altitude fast, in very little time. If we had not lost altitude quickly enough, hypoxia or oxygen-depletion could have started a slew of health issues, not to mention compromising the ability of the captain to make sound decisions. The Helios Airways Flight 522 had experienced just the same before it eventually crashed.

Having lived in the United States for more than a decade now, a thank you reflexively slipped out of my mouth. In the United States, this phrase has been abused to the extent of practically losing its meaning. On that day though, the "Thank you" I offered her meant a lot more than a mere "Thank you for the information." She was my hero that day, the person who had saved us from a life-threatening disaster of enormous proportions. She had made sure I lived to tell the story.

Back in Oslo, there was another flight getting ready to take us to Tromso. After what had happened mid-air not too long before, one would think most of us had lost interest in flying, at least for awhile. Surprisingly, most of us were ready to hop on another plane and get to Tromso. After all, it is all statistics, right? The odds of dying in an airplane are lower than the odds of dying in a car. And what are the odds of two back-to-back flights having technical problems of the same magnitude? On the brighter side, the airline promised all of us free meals and drinks. We were not dead, and now we were going to get a free meal, too? Given how expensive food is in Norway, a free meal is probably a close second to life itself. As they say in this part of the world, "Takk." Or, thanks.

This time, Miss Smudgy Eyeliner asked me if I would like to sit with her. It was not a full flight and the seats between us were empty anyway. On this flight, we did not stop talking for a minute. It was perhaps a subconscious effort to keep our minds off the things that could possibly go wrong, or not notice the tight knot that involuntarily formed in our stomachs every time the ride got bumpy. This time, we landed safely in Tromso. Right before landing, we exchanged contact information, seeing if we could meet again in Oslo. I doubted it though. She lives north of the Arctic Circle where there is no sun for 3-4 months every year and plowing through 18 feet of snow is considered normal. I cannot even handle the winters of Middle America, mild winters compared to the extreme temperatures she lives in. However, like the Argentinean hippie artist or the Brazilian fellow traveler I met in South America, we will share a very deep, personal connection for the rest of our lives. Two strangers, bound by having shared a potentially catastrophic fate, a coin-toss, a few worried gazes, smeared mascara, a "calm-down" hand gesture, and an hour and a half of sharing life stories!

The Tromso airport was buzzing with routine activity. We picked our bags from the carousel and dispersed into the crowd, becoming another one of those 7 billion humans crawling on this earth, bound to carry memories of those ten-minutes of flying experience with us for the rest of our lives. As I sit in my hostel bed contemplating how to spend the rest of the day, there are so many things, people, to be thankful about. So many things have gone right in my life. More than that, I feel like thanking my failures today. The things that have gone wrong have taught me much more than the things that have gone right. My failures have, slowly but surely, chipped away at my fear of death. My life today is immeasurably different than what I had thought it would be ten, or even five years ago. The girl told me later that she was crying, thinking she was too young to die. All I can remember of those ten minutes is an unusual craving for some basic information and a long wait to see whether I was truly going to die that day.

I had to recover quickly from my freaky flight incident in Norway. Given my packed European itinerary, there was no time to take a break and relax. Rainy Tromso provided the perfect backdrop for recovery. From the minute I landed to the minute I left, it was rain, rain, and more rain. Forget about the midnight sun, there was no sun at all. Writing this journal and reconnecting with friends and family helped a bit. So did the conversation with some locals at the only bar that was open at night. They all said that, even though they had never experienced loss of cabin pressure and oxygen masks, air turbulence is an everyday thing in this part of the world. No big deal. Plus, there is nothing that a few repeats of the albums *Dark side of the Moon* and *Animals* cannot fix. Time to shake it off!

So what are you waiting for? Make your bucket list and start working on it. Most of you will not do anything about experiencing things from your bucket list but, one day, death might just look you in the eye when you least expect it. Mostly because we keep wishing death away in our make-believe worlds.

GETTING READY TO FLY

2

2. USA: SWITCHING OFF THE INNER ALARM

April 1, 2012
Louisville, USA

Other than reading Ralph Potts's *Vagabonding*, a major preparatory step for my yearlong sojourn involved switching off the dreaded symbol of the corporate world, my Monday-to-Friday morning alarm. The realization that I should do that came to me when I woke up to the alarm in my Louisville apartment a few mornings before the trip started, only to realize that I had left corporate America behind, at least for the next year. Instead of whining and moaning in protest before dragging myself out of bed, I would now wake up to my internal alarm, when I felt fully rested. Now that is a novel concept!

When the line "Alarm is set for so many hours from now" disappeared from my smartphone, the realization did not sink in until four days later. It took some getting used to. Like Phil Connors in *Groundhog Day*, I kept waking up at the same time. Getting rid of an alarm was an important first step in weaning myself off the 9-to-5 opium that had kept me going in the past. Actually, step zero was saying good-bye to my job, although not out of any hatred of the daily grind. For most of the past few years, I had awakened every day excited about going to work and learning something new. However, it was time to move on. My job reminded me of the Tolstoy quote from *Anna Karenina*: "Happy families are all alike; every unhappy family is unhappy in its own way." In the context of a job, your circumstances might be unique and your reason for being unhappy might be legitimate. Does it really matter? The trick, I guess, is moving on at the right time. For the middle-class Indian psyche, quitting a well-paying job is never easy. A one-year, round-the-world trip is not even in the realm of possibilities. Moreover, at my age, being gainfully employed and single is virtually unheard of. Even people from my graduating class who thought marriage wasn't for them are now married. So, quitting my job and deciding to travel for a year was sheer lunacy. No girl wants to marry a guy who doesn't have a job and is planning to travel for a year! Naturally, my diminishing arranged marriage prospects were weighing on a lot of people's minds...except mine.

Anyway, back to *Vagabonding*, the book. As I leafed through this quick and easy read, it almost felt as if the author was secretly speaking my mind. It is unlikely that I will ever adopt long-term travel as a lifestyle, but all the changes in my life over the past decade or so have been pushing me toward a one-year, round-the-world trip. I am not sure how much my academic degrees have contributed to my understanding of the world around me. However, I knew that the upcoming trip would certainly be all about education. At the very least, I hoped to walk away with a degree in human nature.

One of the surprising aspects of the book is the quotes taken from *Upanishads* and *Dhammapada*. These ancient texts, whose origins can be traced back to India, extol the virtues of studying new cultures and developing a deeper understanding of the human condition by way of traveling. Unfortunately, for many Indians living in or outside India, such long-term travel lives in fantasy-land or lunacy-land. It points to the huge gap between the richness of ancient Indian thought and most of the prevailing interpretations of it. That, in turn, probably explains the apathy toward subjects like history and humanities in the Indian educational system. I will leave that discussion for another day.

I wonder why the idea of long-term travel belongs to fantasy-land for so many Indians. Money and health could be two legitimate reasons. What else? If you sit down and run the numbers, a round-the-world trip on a shoestring budget is not that difficult. At roughly $100 a day, I was actually doing it lavishly. There are backpackers out there who do it for as little as $20-$30 per day. Of course, the budget depends heavily on what parts of the world you choose to travel in. For $20-30 a day, Italy in the middle of summer is a bad choice. Australia or New Zealand? Worse. Scandinavia? The worst! South America or Africa? Heaven. South East Asia? Seventh heaven! Sites like Couchsurfing help you find local hosts who will let you stay for free. The number of countries you visit and your style of traveling matter a lot as well. My ambitious plan had more than 35 countries in it. Such a plan practically rules out hitchhiking and taking your time to go from one point to the next. If you choose relatively cheaper countries and do one country a month, you can complete a yearlong trip for less than your yearly payments for your car or home. However, these are just the how's and where's. With some research, you can sort them out in a month or two. Like everything else in your life, all you really need is the burning desire to make it happen. You can figure out most of the details once you hit the road.

There is another problem, perhaps even bigger than the absence of the burning desire. It is the ego. I guess it is true that everyone, from custodians and security personnel, all the way up to the CEOs and managing directors, are important to ensure the smooth functioning of any organization. However, somewhere along the way, we all start feeling we are the most important cog in the wheel. Our ego also builds the sweet illusion in our head that our family and friends will fall apart if we disappear from their lives. It makes us think that we are more important to our surroundings than we truly are. I can safely say that, regardless of what you think of yourself, your skills are utterly replaceable. To give a travel spin to an old Marathi adage, people will mourn your disappearance for a week or two and move on. So, what is stopping you from quitting everything, moving on, and embarking on your dream trip?

Bidding my job good-bye – check.
Financial planning – check.
Tetanus/Yellow fever/Hepatitis shots – check.
Getting rid of my worldly possessions – check.
Deciding what to take in one small, 70-liter backpack – check.
Saying good-bye to friends – this box will always remain unchecked.

*　　　　　*　　　　　*

15

April 7, 2012
Louisville, USA

With my lease expiring, it was time to walk out of my empty apartment. It took me a long time to convince myself that if I had not used something or looked at a document in the past five years, I am never going to need it. I eventually overcame my emotional attachment to all of my college notebooks and homework assignments that have had no utility in my daily life for the past few years.

However, there is more to my story. After having spent most of my life thinking that I would never live by myself, I have managed to do just that in this city tucked away in the northeasterly fringes of Kentucky. It was not an easy transition to make, but this individualistic country can give you more than a helping hand when it comes to that. Soon, you start "owning" the place you live in. Before moving to Louisville, I always had someone to share the house with, in Baltimore, Champaign, and in Pune. You move in, and things are already set up. The furniture is there, the heating, the electricity, and the internet is working. You move out, and you leave roommates behind. The Louisville experience was different. A couple of years earlier, I had moved into an empty house and now, I was leaving behind an empty house. It is perhaps not so much about the things that I accumulated while I was here. When I moved to Louisville, I knew that it was not where I was going to settle down, or live long-term. Therefore, I never really had anything memorable to become attached to. After all, attachment to things comes from the memories we have of them. Things done sitting on that beanbag or things said lying on that bed, getting used to that door that would never shut fully, or that damned door lever that would jam every now and then. Some of them were experiences shared with friends or family, but most of them were mine. Although I never really owned this place, it was my little corner of the world. In the past, moving out was always followed by moving in somewhere. This time, I was moving out, into the whole wide world. For the next year or so, I would not have my own place to call home. Even after the trip ends, I did not know where my next home is going to be.

Talking about packing, I am also taking with me an invaluable treasure of personal and professional experiences that have helped me grow as a person. The solitude of my first few months here taught me how to write. The friends I made and relationships I built over the years taught me not only how to survive, but also how to thrive in an unknown city in which people from my ethnic background were hard to find. After spending six years of my life on American university campuses, I finally got a taste of the non-urban heartland of the country that is Middle America. It is here that I built a certain degree of respect for the American Constitution. I still have not read the Federalist Papers, but sitting here it is easy to see the lure of the constitution. It puts a tremendous amount of faith in its citizenry and gives its constituents incredible freedom in choosing what kind of life they want to live. The Indian Constitution is famous for being the longest constitution in the world that enumerates all the roles and responsibilities of the government. The American Constitution, on the other hand, is probably the shortest in the world and lists the aspects of human life the government cannot get involved in. It puts a premium on the decentralization of power. Imagine a world in which people making political and economic decisions about local communities are the ones who will have to deal with their consequences. So refreshing, right? It is not rocket science. Tax breaks and government support for start-ups might make sense in the Bay Area, where the support structure – R&D infrastructure, top schools, investors willing to take risks, abundance of talent, and the good weather to attract more – are already in place. Who is going to go to Nebraska to start a company just to benefit from tax breaks? But I had to get out of the heavily liberal-leaning world of American academia and spend a few years in the so-called "red state" or "fly-by country" to get the real import of the conservative ethos of America.

Sure, the American Constitution probably has its flaws. Those that have not been corrected yet will be corrected in due time. There are other philosophical aspects, too, that challenge the basic assumptions underlying the American Constitution. These include, for example, the degree to which humans behave rationally and whether the establishment of a republic instead of a democracy has captured all human idiosyncrasies. However, given natural human instincts, it seems astonishing that the framers, with such a vast swath of land and all its resources at their disposal, chose a path of such humility when putting forth the guiding principles for running the country.

Alas! Four years in Louisville also showed me that that dream seems to be coming apart at the seams. Some wounds seem to be self-inflicted, while others are forces of nature not under their control. A couple of decades of unchallenged financial and military supremacy have bred complacency. Delayed gratification is a thing of the past. In a country where nobody wants to pay taxes, everyone wants at least a small portion of the pie – free education, free medical care, subsidized housing, and the ability to rack up huge credit card debts without having a plan to pay them down. The paradoxes in Middle America are a dime a dozen. Just like the academic campuses.

Then there are forces of globalization. In this age of ever-shortening news cycles, the country-cycle seems to be shortening even more rapidly. How long will America's dominance last? What about China, the country next in line? The founding fathers were probably right in terms of building a nation that can stand on its own feet. However, what is the recipe for success when you are constantly running three-legged races...and changing partners every other day? It is a hyper-connected world now. We are all in it together!

Nonetheless, the education continues. As a staunch conservative, growing up in a country in which scarcity and government overreach were a way of life, I took a liberal turn when I switched to being a minority and noticed an abundance of pretty much everything in this country. This town has made me free now: politically, for the foreseeable future; personally, for at least a year.

Leaving the empty nest behind and flying away. As I prepared to do that, I was awash with a sense of excitement and curiosity. Where would I be, and what would I be doing after my yearlong trip ended? I did not really have the answer to that then, but I thought of a few realistic and other surreal possibilities.

I might move to India, find a job that pays the bills and provides some intellectual stimulation, and get married.

I might come across a non-profit organization that does commendable work in some remote corner of the world, and move there for the next few years to help.

18

Maybe I will become a successful travel writer and keep traveling beyond one year, maybe for the rest of my life.

Visit some monastery and decide to become a monk.

I could see myself visiting a commune, getting hooked onto some recreational "stuff" and singing Bob Marley tunes for a living.

I might meet an exotic girl somewhere on a South East Asian island or in South America and just decide to settle down there.

I might come back to realize that the 9-to-5 grind is just too hard to get back into, and decide to pick up a tour guide or hostel manager's job in Africa or Australia instead.

I might meet some entrepreneurs on the road and end up starting the next billion-Dollar company.

I might pull an *Into the Wild* or *The Grizzly Man*. Walking in the footsteps of Cheryl Strayed and hiking the Pacific Crest Trail does not sound bad, either.

Who knows, maybe I could go through a horrible kidnapping experience and decide not to backpack ever again.

After all, life is full of such incredible possibilities, and given my record as an adventure-seeker and a traveler, all of the bizarre options are on the table.

*   *   *

April 27, 2012
New Haven, USA

In less than 24 hours, I will be leaving the United States to start my yearlong trip. I will be back here for sure, because my round-the-world ticket says so. As I wrap things up, I am getting introspective, trying to wrap my head around all those moments that have defined my life in the United States over the past decade or so. The other day, I heard on the radio that what happens in your twenties can truly help you break out of the shell that has surrounded you since your childhood. Perhaps it is because our twenties is the time when many people face the real world for the first time. It hasn't been long since I stepped out of my twenties, but I can already say that my experiences in that decade of my life challenged my views about pretty much everything, changing me as a person. That judgmental guy who used to measure a person's success based on his academic qualifications and the nature of his job is history. America has taught me to respect every kind of job that contributes to society in some way, shape or form. When I meet new people now, I no longer ask "What did you study?" or "What do you do?" I prefer asking, "So, what's your story?" Most of the people still respond with their academic degrees and the nature of their work. Every now and then, there are those who talk about the trials and tribulations, triumphs and tragedies, or moments of ecstasy and agony that have defined their lives. Those are the ones I look out for, people with a story to tell. I think we all have a story hidden within us. Sadly, in this fast-paced, hyper-connected world we live in, most of us never have the time to take a deep breath, reflect back on our lives, and make a mental note of the moments that have made us who we are today. Here are some of the most memorable moments of my American decade, in no particular order:

Moving to the United States.
My earliest adult memory of the United States is landing at the O'Hare International Airport in Chicago on a balmy summer evening, after a 26-hour flight from Mumbai via London. My brother was waiting for me, and once my jumbo-sized suitcases and I were settled comfortably in his brand new sedan, we hit the freeway. With orderly traffic, road signs clearly written in white on green background, and the utter absence of traffic lights, straying dogs or cattle, litter, and other such distractions, the distinction between where I grew up and where I was headed became stark in less than 15 minutes. As we raced along I-94 northward to get to my uncle's home in Milwaukee, I wondered, much to my amusement now, if I would ever understand the interstate freeway system in the United States.

Losing my grandparents, and being unable to say goodbye.
I grew up in a home with my grandparents living with us. They were an integral part of my childhood, my upbringing. Living thousands of miles away, this was the first time I had felt so helpless, wanting to be physically there to bid them goodbye, but unable to do so at such short notice. A webcam good-bye just does not do it.

Getting drunk for the first time.
In India, I never went beyond two drinks as a college student. I was financially dependent on my parents, and squandering money on alcohol filled me with guilt. The guilt left me soon after I started earning my stipend as a graduate student. I grew up in a part of the world where heating your house is unheard of. If there are holes in the ground, they have to be part of the drainage system. After getting drunk for the first time in my life, and making a mess in the bathroom, all I could think of was cleaning it by trying to drain it all through the heating system. A very bad idea in retrospect.

Attending my first American wedding.
My lab mate from graduate school was getting married. In most parts of India, weddings are auspicious occasions, with no alcohol, and no fish or meat. This time, the wedding started with a pre-wedding-ceremony drink at eleven in the morning. After a couple of hours of wedding ceremonies, we promptly got back to post-wedding drinking. Needless to say, by ten at night I had stopped making any sense. My friends dutifully informed me the next day that I would start a sentence and not complete it, bursting into hysterical bouts of laughter in between. To make matters worse, another childhood friend was visiting from out of town and wanted to catch up that night. Driving 20 miles, in that condition, to meet a friend of mine was not a good idea. I was planning to pick my friend up and drive 50 miles more to party with another friend. Fortunately, reason and my sober friend prevailed to stop the train wreck after the first 20 miles. Being under 25, single and male means the highest auto insurance bracket. Insurance companies are pretty smart that way!

Traveling extensively in the United States.
The travel bug hit me hard and fast, and I was fortunate to be

able to cover more than forty of the fifty states within a span of twelve years. It is hard to pick favorites, but some of my fondest memories are marveling at the mystic view of the Golden Gate Bridge and the charming mountains around it in San Francisco. Or walking down Bourbon Street in New Orleans, sipping a Hurricane and listening to the soothing tunes of jazz oozing out of every bar. Or enjoying the Freedom Trail in Boston and admiring the marketing skills of a country that has a meager two hundred years of "history." Or hiking in and out of the Grand Canyon and camping on the banks of the river at the bottom. Or climbing up the continental divide and looking down on the glaciers in Glacier National Park. Or watching a breathtaking sunset in Bryce Canyon on a clear September evening and soaking in the heavenly breeze, perfect temperatures, and blueness of the Pacific Ocean near San Diego. Then, there was the epic, 10,000-odd mile 9-week road trip with my family, that took us from West Lafayette, Indiana, all the way up to Niagara Falls, Boston, down to Tampa, back to West Lafayette and then down to New Orleans, west through Texas and Arizona to San Diego, up to San Francisco, back to Las Vegas, the national parks in Utah, up through the Rockies to enter the Dakotas, and, after a brief pit-stop in Milwaukee, back to good old West Lafayette, where my brother was wrapping up his graduate degree.

And then, the big South American adventure happened.
Traveling extensively in the United States for 8 years had created a hunger in me now to go explore the world outside it. Fortunately (for me) or unfortunately (for my parents), the American spirit of adventure and the never-say-die attitude had won over my middle-class Indian sensibilities. Once I finished graduate school, I decided to take a break from my routine life to ride a motorcycle, solo, for 5,000 miles from Cuzco in Peru to Cordoba in Argentina and back. My list of adventures during that South American trip could fill an entire book, which is precisely what I did. I knew I would end up writing something longish before hitting thirty. It was supposed to be a PhD dissertation, but ended up being a memoir. Who cares?

Deciding to quit my PhD after more than four years of hard work.
I distinctly remember the day my graduate adviser and I decided

things were not working out quite as planned. This was the first "reality" moment in my career, easily one of the darkest days of my life. It taught me that science can be pretty unforgiving at times, and effort doesn't necessarily ensure a reward. As one of my dissertation advisers pointed out, succinctly but rather rudely, "The only place where you get reward for effort is Heaven." In the academic world of the lowly Terra Firma, publications are the only currency people trade in.

Attending the plenary session of a neuroscience conference in New Orleans.

I vividly remember watching a video of a Parkinson's patient being treated by sticking an electrode in his brain, and stimulating it with a battery-powered, pacemaker kind of device. That was when I started to get passionate about pursuing neuroscience. My career in neuroscience also gave me an opportunity to interact with a few Nobel laureates, like Paul Lauterber, who invented the biomedical applications of MRIs, and Eric Kandel, who established the basic building blocks of memory formation in the brain. It was awe-inspiring, yet demystifying to know that we are all made of the same flesh and blood.

Holding my niece's hand for the first time.

The entire family had gathered at my brother's place in Connecticut for Memorial Day, eagerly waiting for my niece to show up. My brother's in-laws had traveled all the way from India, a couple of cousins had come from Boston and Peoria, and I had flown in from Louisville. But my darling niece took her own sweet time. She waited until we all went home, and showed up two days later. I flew back again three days after her arrival in this world. It is not as if I had not seen 2-3 day old babies before. However, I distinctly remember her, all pink and perfect and bundled up, a sight of beauty. Perhaps it was special because she is family. Watching her grow and reach new milestones over the years has been just that...a miracle to me.

Living in this city of vices in Middle America.

The erstwhile capital of gambling, liquor, and tobacco, Louisville has granted me solitude, taught me how to write, and given me my first best friend, who is a girl. A Venezuelan, no less! I was always skeptical of the notion of a guy and a girl being close friends, but this girl has proved me wrong.

Falling in love, and losing it all at very short notice.
The day I saw her for the first time and the day I was fully intoxicated and listening to *Huzoor is kadar bhi na* (an Urdu song) with my friends. Staring into nothingness outside the window, tears started flowing even when I did not want them to. Maybe I did. That moment taught me how to cry as an adult. It was messy, but it was a cathartic experience.

This time next week, I will be in Tahrir Square in Egypt, the start of a brand-new chapter in my life at the very place of rebirth of an ancient civilization.

3. GERMANY: BRIEFLY IN FRANKFURT

April 28, 2012
Frankfurt, Germany

My year-long journey started with a trip from New York to Egypt, with a quick three-day stopover in the financial capital of Germany. I wanted to catch up with some old friends before starting my solo trip. What came as a bonus were some great German Brot (bread), passion fruit ice cream, and bratwurst (sausages). In the minimalist culinary culture of Germany, one should be happy with that.

Frankfurt is an interesting city, a spectacle of contrasts. Newer buildings in perfect rectangles mingle with the old world European architecture, telling the onlooker which buildings had survived the war. Right under the blue Euro sign, surrounded by glittering yellow stars, the Occupy movement is desperately trying to keep its flame burning. The Great Recession that hit the United States in 2009 and spread like wildfire all over the world, wreaked havoc in all sections of the society. Politicians lost their jobs. Thousands of high-flying investment bankers and hedge-fund managers on Wall Street were unceremoniously laid off overnight. Start-ups were unable to find the risk capital to fuel their innovative ideas. Dwindling tax revenues led to massive cutbacks in academic research budgets, leading to retrenchment and massive increases in fees on college campuses. But the hardest hit were the blue collar workers; not just because of job losses, but also due to the huge budget cuts in welfare programs, unemployment benefits, and healthcare for the underprivileged. When they heard the obscure "too big to fail" term gaining instant popularity and found out that the big banks and multi-national corporations were being financially bailed out at taxpayers' expense, they were furious. The system was – and, in spite of diligent efforts by various stakeholders, still remains – blatantly rigged. It is a classic case of "If I owe you a million Dollars, it is my problem, but if I owe you a billion Dollars, it is your problem."

The indigent and unemployed, who are lowest on the food chain, descended on Wall Street to "Occupy" it. Through social media, the brand and method of protest quickly spread to other financial centers around the world. Frankfurt and the larger Eurozone have one more problem, though. Unlike the United States, countries that have accepted the common Euro currency are not exactly "United." Widely varying work ethics and social contracts across European countries have put an enormous amount of strain not just on the European economies, but also on the common Euro currency. Watching the clean-shaven bankers in their Armani suits walk past the ragtag army of protesters wearing worn-out clothes and staying in makeshift tents is a jarring sight. With the Euro and the Occupy movements both struggling for survival, it is hard to say whether anyone has an upper hand. Oh well! It is just another day at work.

As we were walking down the sidewalk, John, my friend, pointed at one of the palm-sized tiles made of metal inserted in the sidewalk in front of one of the apartment buildings. It had four names written on it, with numbers indicating the year in which those Jewish people were taken away from that building to a concentration camp. Perhaps this is the Germans' personal Nuremberg; their way of moving on and ensuring that the past does not repeat itself.

On the other hand, when walking on one of the many old bridges across the Main river, I noticed hundreds of locks hanging around the railings, with names of couples inscribed on them. Apparently, lovers bring locks with their names or initials inscribed on them, hang them by the railings, and throw the keys into the river to signify an eternal bond. Starry-eyed optimism, a stone's throw away from steely-eyed determination.

MIDDLE
EASTERN
TURMOIL

3

4. EGYPT: FIRST IMPRESSIONS

May 2, 2012
Cairo, Egypt

The flight to Cairo was on time and immigration was smooth. Two back-to-back flights on time are quite unheard of in my part of the world. My Egyptian refugee friend in Louisville had warned me against taking public transportation, but I went against his advice and took public transportation from the airport to the city center. I think there is a certain allure to using public transportation. It tells you how ordinary people commute. It integrates you into a place, albeit ephemerally, and distinguishes you from the average tourist. And it was fascinating.

With no experience in recognizing Arabic numerals, I had looked up the number of the bus going to the city center when leaving Frankfurt. It was bus number 356, but the number 356 looked like a bunch of squiggles. As the bus approached the stop, I asked in English whether it was going to Tahrir Square. The bus driver did not understand my question, but just said no. I asked a bystander why the bus was not moving. The bystander asked me, instead, where I wanted to go. I said Tahrir Square, and he guided me to another bus. He gave me clear instructions. He said that I should take the bus to the Ramses Railway Station, the main railway station in the city, and take the metro from there to Tahrir Square.

Now, Ramsi's Café of the World happened to be one of my favorite restaurants back in Louisville, Kentucky. It served the best grilled sandwiches stuffed with dried tomatoes and hummus. Naturally, the name intrigued me and I decided to follow my bystander's advice. Other than taking the taxi, which I had decided not to do, there were no options at that point anyway. I was definitely taking the bus.

I eventually got on a big red bus with white lines. With an hour to kill, I started chatting it up with the guy sitting next to me. A young lad in his late twenties with curly black hair, sharp features and a warm smile, he happened to be an urban planning engineer who had briefly visited India once, a couple of years ago. This is it, I thought, my ticket to public transport bliss. It had earned me my first friend in Egypt. Okay, maybe not a friend, but a co-passenger-acquaintance. We continued to talk for the next hour, about everything from the bonhomie between India's first Prime Minister Nehru and Egypt's second president Nasser that had led to the Non-Aligned Movement in the 1960s to the current political turmoil in Egypt.

My friend decided to get off at the Ramses Station with me, escorted me to the metro station, bought me a metro ticket, and refused to accept money when I offered it to him. He even accompanied me to the platform to make sure I boarded the train going in the right direction. While waiting for the train, we continued to chat about the ongoing revolution in Egypt as a part of the Arab Spring and the upcoming presidential elections in Egypt. He told me that he was planning to vote for former head of International Atomic Energy Agency's (IAEA) head El Baradai's new political party. I asked him what the name of the party was. Guess what? It was called "Dastoor."

Excited, I told him that we have the same word in Hindi.

"It means the system of ruling people." he said.

"Constitution?" I asked him.

"Yes, something like that." he said.

Funny, after having heard the word a million times since childhood, in Hindi cinema and Urdu shayaris or poetry, I finally got to learn the meaning of the word from a stranger on the Cairo metro. By spending three Egyptian pounds instead of fifty for the taxi, I actually managed to add something to my Hindi vocabulary. It also briefly rekindled my love for Eastern or old-world languages. Some of the words in these languages have no good translations in English. The closest translation of "Dastoor" in

English might be "Constitution," but like a lot of Hindi, Urdu and Sanskrit words, there is something more to its meaning that English cannot capture. It is like "Dharma" in Sanskrit or Hindi. The Western world tends to translate it into "Religion," but anyone who has studied Sanskrit or Hindi will tell you that the meaning of "Dharma" goes well beyond a set of rules or tenets to live by. When my Egyptian friend said that the concept of "Dastoor" was similar to the constitution, but not quite, I knew what he was talking about. It was good to be back in the old world.

My friend disappeared into the crowd without exchanging any contact information. One more guardian angel experience for this itinerant atheist.

Meanwhile, a few hours before I took the metro to Tahrir Square and walked to the hostel nearby, eleven people had died and a hundred odd had been injured in protests less than a mile away from my hostel.

Sometimes ignorance is bliss. Or perhaps, fortune favors the stupid.

*   *   *

This urban sprawl of Cairo instantly reminded me of Mumbai. Having flown in and out of Mumbai a thousand times now, it has subconsciously become my frame of reference for all other cities. If you change all the signs in Cairo to Hindi or English, and swap the mosques for temples, you will be in Mumbai. There are old parts of the city, with small alleys, dusty roads, creaky buildings, narrow footpaths with storefronts encroaching on them, drying laundry hanging from the balconies, and people wearing traditional clothes effortlessly mixing with those wearing jeans and t-shirts. With sprawling shopping malls, high-rise buildings, and other telltale signs of urbanization that make every developing city look somewhat identical, it is these distinct sights that make a city stand out.

Then there are the suburbs. Mostly cuboidal, concrete structures of varying heights breathing down each other's necks, terraces crowded with satellite dishes serving Western culture on a platter in every living room, complex webs of cables running from one building to another, and gigantic bridges or flyovers rising out of nowhere and with no aesthetic value.

Sure, there are swanky neighborhoods with fancy malls and movie theaters frequented by the young and restless. But what reminded me of Mumbai the most is the commingling of the new and the old. A modern-looking store with a glass door selling fancy lingerie right next to a dingy store selling spices or a run-down street-side food stall that hasn't been renovated for decades. You can choose how you want to spice up your life.

And then, there is the traffic. Traffic police are deployed at the traffic lights to ensure that people are obeying the lights. Talk about redundancy! Even with the cops next to the lights, cars start inching toward the middle of the intersection when the light is still red. After sunset, all the traffic lights switch to flashing yellow. On Fridays, there are flashing yellow lights all day long, with cops still monitoring people. What, exactly, are they trying to monitor? To top it all off, one cop starts chatting with another cop instead of regulating traffic, unnecessarily holding up traffic on one end. A few cars honk at the cop, reminding him of his duty. The cop collectively screams at all the cars, moves out of the way, and lets them go. I love chaotic traffic! On a busy evening, when looking from one of the balconies up top, it almost seemed like a Rubic's Cube. They all seemed to be moving around in a square, nobody really getting anywhere. I'm sure when Nehru visited Egypt to kick-start the Non-Aligned Movement, he must have felt that Egypt was a natural ally. I wonder what the urban planning engineer I met in the bus thinks about Mumbai. If he is trying to use Mumbai as a model for urban planning in Cairo, he doesn't have to do much.

However, the real treat in this land is its history. The first pyramid. The red pyramid. The bent pyramid. The tallest pyramid. The Sphinx. They are all around Cairo. Then, when you go south along the Nile and reach the city of Aaswan, wake up at three in the morning, cram yourself into an overcrowded van and go further south, near the Sudanese border, the story of the restoration of the gigantic Abu Simbel temple by UNESCO is awe-inspiring. According to the history I learned at the visitor center, the Egyptians built a dam on the river not too far from the original location of the Abu Simbel temple, without giving much thought to the possibility of the backwaters drowning this ancient marvel of architecture. When they realized that Abu Simbel's days were numbered, the UNESCO stepped in and literally cut the entire temple into small pieces, moved them to higher ground, and put them back together. It sounds like kids playing with Lego blocks, but the most astonishing aspect of the restoration is the care taken to preserve not just the look and feel of it, but also the original east-west orientation of the temple. The astronomers of ancient Egypt had designed one of the temples in such a way that the rays of the rising sun would first hit the Sanctum Santorum on the days of the summer solstice and the winter solstice. Guess what? That is still true.

Halfway between Cairo and Aaswan, in the city of Luxor, they have the Valley of the Kings, Valley of the Queens, the famous Tut Ankh Amen mummy, Karnak temple, Luxor temple and countless other smaller historic wonders in and around the city. After constructing five or six pyramids, Egyptians apparently realized that building such humongous monuments for dead kings is not practical. So they created the Valley of the Kings near Luxor. The queens got their Valley of the Queens as well. Tens or maybe even more than a hundred kings are buried in the Valley of the Kings and the locals say that the excavation and search for more tombs is an ongoing process. If you are not overwhelmed by what has already been discovered and restored, I guess there is much more to come.

Back in Cairo, a visit to the national museum near Tahrir Square was no different. The four to five-thousand-year-old mummies are a treat to watch. You cannot touch them, but you are looking at them from just a foot or so away. You can see their facial features; hair, teeth, and sometimes, even their manicured nails. They say that the kings and the queens, at least, used to have manicured nails. And it is easy to see it. But just like the birds, cattle and snakes in the hieroglyphics of Abu Simbel temple, they do not say a word either. The huge statues, the boats they were given to use in their afterlives, all the other toiletries, pots and pans, the artifacts found in Tut Ankh Amen's den. All of it is standing there in studied silence, testimony to an incredibly rich culture, overwhelming us by the minute. With all this history, it makes you wonder whether the world should just declare the entire country of Egypt a gigantic museum, settle all the political differences, and bring peace back to this ancient land. We are now entering John Lennon's *Imagine* land.

Back to reality. When I was done with Cairo, Aaswan and Luxor, I didn't even bother going anywhere else. The library in

Alexandria, one of the Seven Wonders of the Ancient World, was on my list. But when the locals started saying that Alexandria is more of a touristy beach town for Europeans than a must-see destination for history buffs, I dropped the idea. The Red Sea resort town of Sharm-al-Sheikh was another option. It is quite popular among the backpackers who want to learn scuba diving on the cheap. I have kept scuba diving for Thailand, which is supposed to happen sometime in November or December. There was no need to cram another city into my two week stay in Egypt because these three cities were enough to convince me that there is no dearth of cultural history in this land. I used to get excited seeing tiny hieroglyphic paintings in some random cave or hidden under the rocks in some national parks in the United States. In Egypt, you have chapter after chapter written in hieroglyphics. Abu Simbel temple has the entire story of Lord Ramses the Second's exploits in a war and his coronation as one of the Gods; all in hieroglyphics!

All in all, Egypt is just badass. It took me less than two weeks to come to that highly scientific conclusion. No matter how many times you watch all the history on television or hear about it from other people, you have to see it for yourself to believe it. Nothing can prepare you for the grandeur of it all. The size and scale of these historic monuments are just impossible to convey in words or pictures. Standing in front of all the painted walls in the Abu Simbel temple, you are looking at those depictions of kings and screaming inside, "Say something, damn it! Don't speak in that cryptic language of birds, cows, snakes, and squiggly lines." But those stoic faces never say a word, leaving us at the mercy of the tour guides. They try their best to explain it, but unless you enroll in a PhD in Egyptian Pharaonic History, I guess there is no way to decipher all those hieroglyphics.

In addition to all this incredible and perplexing history, another experience that has stayed with me is cruising down the Nile on a fancy ship. You can do it from Luxor to Aaswan or the other way round. It doesn't matter much. And if you are a daredevil, willing to brave some political aftermath of a revolution, you can get half-price tickets as well. Listening to Fuzon's rendition of *Raaga Khamaaj, Yeh Houslaah* from the Hindi movie *Dor*, and Miles Davis's *My Funny Valentine* as the desert scenes from Aaswan to Luxor passed by was a mesmerizing experience. Maybe it was the sense of despair or longing in the songs that resonated with the seemingly endless desert. It was still the season of political revolution in Egypt, and only a handful of tourists were on board; most of them minding their own business. The occasional sights of small port towns and people busy with their everyday lives along the riverbanks – women washing clothes, men crossing the river on little rafts, kids bathing to escape the 35-40 degrees Celsius sun – kept me mildly interested in what was coming next. However, it was the kind of scenery that you will not regret if you miss it because the songs have taken you on a nostalgic trip to a distant past. The slow pace of the cruise liner, monotony of the muddy river, and the barren landscape served as the perfect canvas to reminisce about my colorful past. I might have sold off my material belongings and left the American shores, but my mind had not fully embraced the uncertainty and excitement about the year ahead of me.

The isolation from the political chaos surrounding us, and my reflective mood, were a welcome break from the hectic sight-seeing in the scorching sun. Once you are able to expand your mind's horizons, it is all puzzling, at least on two counts. Every time you visit an ancient culture, its fall and the current state of disarray of the country makes you wonder how it all came down. But as an Indian, the more puzzling part was trying to understand how the Egyptians could have completely disowned this part of their history. Indians take everything in. The country's symbol comes from King Ashoka. Muslim ruler Akbar and his lieutenant Birbal's stories are taught to all Indian kids. Taj Mahal, built by another Muslim ruler, is our own. Kids read Arabian Nights and Alibaba and the 40 Thieves. All the British-Indian history is also our own. But in Egypt, other than some symbols used on the currency notes, people have left the ancient culture behind and wholeheartedly embraced Islam. Out of curiosity, I asked one of the tour guides who had studied some Egyptian history what her favorite historic period was. She immediately said that it was the pharaonic period. I told her that it seemed ironic that nobody in today's Egypt follows the ancient religions or traditions. Other than nodding her head in agreement, she didn't say much.

As I wrapped up my Egypt tour, a couple of thoughts crossed my mind. What is it about half-human, half-non-human mythical creatures? Almost all the ancient cultures have conjured up images of these hybrid entities, even though evolutionary biologists are yet to find any evidence of such species. At some level, the remarkable similarity of human imagination across cultures is astonishing!

And then, what are we leaving behind for 7000 AD?

5. LEBANON: THREE-POINT TURN IN BEIRUT

May 11, 2012
Beirut, Lebanon

The Cairo-Beirut flight was a near-miss. Continuing the legacy of my air-travel luck, my e-ticket got tagged as suspected fraud. The burly lady at the check-in counter, with her perfectly manicured red nails and a deadpan expression, asked me for the credit card I had used to book the flight. As luck would have it, this was one of the few flights I had booked before leaving the United States and I was not carrying the particular card I had used to book this flight.

My admission that the credit card was in the United States, and my earnest plea to board the flight only gained me her "Good luck with that, dude!" disapproving look. Mr. Murphy's spirit must have been hovering somewhere close, for my attempt to guess the last four digits of the card was only 50% correct, in terms of the digits, and not necessarily their accurate placement. This made her even more suspicious.

The first ray of hope in this impending crisis came when she picked up the phone. After exchanging concerned, cryptic one-liners with her boss, she informed me that I would have to access my account online and show her my entire credit card number, all sixteen digits in their correct positions. A man in a navy blue suit appeared from nowhere. I guess this was the boss she had spoken to. The man took me to a hotspot nearby. Lo and behold! The hotspot wasn't working. Less than thirty minutes to depart, and I was already beginning to feel my heart race. A Samaritan from Barcelona volunteered to help with his 3G phone. However, my bank would not let me access the account from an unknown device. Twenty-six minutes prior to departure, the hotspot finally started working under some mysterious conditions. I quickly punched in my password, careful not to make a mistake this time. Finally, I was able to show them the numbers, 15 minutes prior to departure. They quickly printed and shoved the boarding pass in my hand, and rushed me through the nightmarish immigration and security lines. Zipping through the chaotic crowds with the maximum horsepower I could muster, I finally made it to the gate. Last person to board the flight, 10 minutes before departure. I did a mental victory dance the moment I stepped into the airplane. Phew! One of these days, I will have to write another book called "100 ways to screw up your air travel."

After 10 days of the Egyptian heat, the cool Mediterranean breeze at the Beirut airport came as a big relief. Maybe the adjective "balmy" was coined here in Beirut. Given the Egyptian weather, I felt pity for all the workers who must have built those ginormous monuments in the sweltering heat. No wonder Moses wanted out. If I had had the option, I would have signed up for water-splitting instead of moving those gigantic boulders around to build shrines and carve hieroglyphic chapters. As an added bonus, I would have asked the world to throw in "the chosen ones" tag.

Beirut turned out to be an incredibly beautiful capital city. My hostel was in a fancy neighborhood called Gemmayzeh, right in the city center. That evening, I took a long, leisurely walk around downtown and the waterfront. Downtown Beirut has the most charming shopping district I have ever seen, and this comes from a person who hates shopping. For me, doing groceries is shopping. And shopping is an unwanted effort. Although I have been to enough shopping districts now, in New York, Los Angeles, San Francisco, Chicago, Tokyo, Paris, London, Zurich, and Munich, I loved the one in Beirut the best! The shopping district of this coastal city is the right mixture of the east and the west, the new and the old. The buildings might look clean and new, but the architecture is decidedly Middle Eastern. Unlike the American or European shopping districts, which are dominated by Western fashion brands, the Gucci, Ralph Lauren, and Prada outlets in

Beirut fight for a space with stores packed with colorful sarongs, salwar-kameezes, and occasional sarees from the eastern world. The Parisian-style cobblestone roads and soft street lights blend seamlessly with the people on the streets greeting you in the harsh Arabic tones. There is enough to soak in even if you are not a shopaholic.

The 3-4 mile stretch of waterfront I walked along was equally impressive. In the three hours I spent lazing around on the Mediterranean coast, I saw the latest models of at least five Ferraris, 15-20 Porsches, and countless BMWs and Mercs. Women were toe-to-toe with men in texting while driving, driving aggressively, and yelling at the other drivers, doing everything with admirable finesse at the same time. Families out on picnics were smoking hookah together. The women happened to be some of the most beautiful I have seen anywhere around the world. Young women flaunted their curves in tank tops and shorts. And middle-aged women tried to be like them.

Tall apartment complexes facing the ocean in various stages of completion dotted the entire shoreline. Giant yellow cranes flexed their monstrous arms. With the construction boom, the skyline looked less like downtown and more like cranetown.

Up until the 1970s, before the civil war between the Christians and Muslims in Lebanon broke out, Beirut was a favorite stomping ground for European tourists because, as the common refrain goes, it is the only city in the world in which you can go from sunbathing, on a soft, sandy beach, to skiing up in the mountains, in just a couple of hours. In those days, when my dad was studying medicine in the United States, he visited this charming city and still raves about it. So much so, that when I decided to start this yearlong trip, he insisted that I visit Beirut. It used to be known as the "Paris of the Middle East" because of its French architectural influence and the lively cultural atmosphere. With the hilly landscape, it looked more like a mix of Paris and San Francisco to me. But not quite. Beirut is Beirut! The breathtaking waterfront, at least, is all decked out and ready to impress anyone who is willing to check it out. It probably came before Paris and San Francisco, anyway.

By the second day, I happened to be so in love with this city that I just wanted to walk around and take it all in. I looked up some landmarks on the map and started heading in that direction.

Some of the landmarks had a heavy security presence, and some were completely cordoned off. After crossing the heavily fortified UN compound and heading south of the city center, there was a palpable change in the landscape. The fancy coffee shops and restaurants with international cuisine were replaced by local fare. The streets of a central bazaar smelt like a concoction of vinegar and rotten vegetables. The buildings were dusty, old, and some were badly in need of restoration. As I found out later, this neighborhood had a mix of Lebanese citizens and Palestinian refugees. But even with all its imperfections, I was in love with this city. I could walk around for hours and not feel tired.

By the third day, a couple of my Lebanese acquaintances had become friends. When I started my 365-day trip, I was worried about the possibility that my early enthusiasm to see the world might start waning after the first couple of months. To keep myself engaged, I had planned to interview one person in each country and ask the same set of questions to people from around the world. The questions were related to the socio-economic conditions in each country and my Jordanian friend back in the United States had put me in touch with some of her politically active friends in Lebanon. After meeting them on my second day in Beirut and interviewing one of them, we all became friends. After all, what are the chances of a Lebanese person bumping into an Indian backpacker traveling around the world? When our lengthy chat about India and Lebanon turned to history, one of the Lebanese guys suggested I should visit the town of Baalbek, which is an interesting combination of two-thousand-year-old Roman ruins and a modern-day Hezbollah stronghold, located in the Beqaa valley about 55 miles from Beirut. My Lebanese friends told me that they would arrange for a tour guide to the Roman ruins for me. It was a no brainer.

As I was finishing the free breakfast at the hostel, I met two girls. One of them was an American graduate student doing her PhD in street art in Beirut and another one was a Spanish economics major starting out as a stock trader in Switzerland. After the quick introductions, I found out they were headed to a Palestinian refugee camp to help the refugees with some paint jobs. I thought they were planning to paint homes or temporary shelters of poor refugees. Although I am nowhere near being a good painter, how complicated would it be to paint walls? Plus, the idea of visiting a refugee camp had piqued my interest. How often do you get a chance to visit one? Baalbek could wait. As long as I promised not to take any pictures inside the refugee camp, they were ready to let me tag along. It ended up being one of the strangest days of my trip.

Unlike me, the girls had spent a few weeks in Beirut and were well-versed in the language, the people, and the transportation system. We got into one of the private taxis crisscrossing the chaotic traffic of Beirut and reached the entrance of Burj-al-Barajna, one of the earliest Palestinian refugee camps, established in the heart of Beirut in 1948. At the camp entrance, I was given a crash course on what we were going to do there. The Spanish girl talked to a couple of guys who came to greet us and the guys pulled out the rough sketch of the drawing we were supposed to paint. It showed three guns on the backdrop of a Palestinian flag and a map. It looked like I would be advocating violence to resolve this crisis. All of a sudden, I had a queasy feeling, no longer so sure about spending the entire day there. But I decided to play along. A short, well-built American youngster showed up from somewhere, along with his local ally. As the girls started up the ladder to start painting, I asked one of the refugees about the current mood and political situation in the country. After giving me some vague answers about Palestinian President, Mahmoud Abbas, the good work his finance minister, Salam Fayyad, was doing in the West Bank, and the declining popularity of Hamas in Gaza, he shrugged his shoulders and said another armed uprising was inevitable. As an outsider who had looked at the centuries-old Israel-Palestine conflict through the narrow window of Indian and American media, I was optimistic about the prospects for peace. Yasser Arafat, the corrupt Palestinian leader, was gone. Mahmoud Abbas, the new president of the Palestinian Liberation Authority (PLA), had appointed Western-educated Salam Fayyad as the finance minister to focus on economic development. My naïve mind was hoping to see sprouting of some hope about a non-violent, prosperous future. The nonchalance with which he talked about the inevitability of the next armed conflict was a rude awakening for me.

I went up the ladder, but started looking for excuses not to draw or paint anything. I struck up a conversation with one of the Palestinian students on the painting team of about seven or eight youngsters. An energetic, well-groomed guy, he was finishing his last year of a bachelor's of business management. It sounded like an academic degree that would help him get a well-paying job. If he seemed to be headed toward a secure future, why was he feeling the need to incite violence? He described how their own leaders and heads of NGOs had failed them and that, with 60% unemployment and other restrictions in the refugee camp, he would have no real work opportunities after graduation. Resistance was the only message that would unite all Palestinians, which is why he was painting three guns on that wall across the street from a mosque. I wasn't sure how far or how effectively the message was being propagated. In a nearby coffee shop, middle-aged men, most of whom seemed unemployed, were making a beeline to check out the scene. None of them felt like asking the main actors about the purpose of painting the mural, or contributing their bit. My guess is they were there just to admire the two white girls. Maybe that's just me! As I reluctantly drew half a line of one of the guns, the American guy abruptly asked us to take a lunch break. He insisted that we go to a nearby KFC. KFC in the middle of Beirut? I could not help but be amused.

Over lunch, the American suddenly started to narrate his side of the story. This ex-army youngster in his mid-twenties had been deployed in the Middle East for a couple of years before he quit the army and decided to contribute to peace in this region through non-violent means. He had visited this refugee camp for the first time about a month before with his message of non-violence. Apparently, he had trusted a handful of refugees at the camp to work with him to change the entrenched mindsets of the locals and grow his movement of peaceful conflict resolution. After his first month in the camp, the initial bonhomie seemed to have given way to hostility. When he arrived, they put him up in a tiny room for free. Now the landlady was demanding an exorbitant amount of rent. The American guy had arranged – or was arranging – funds from some American NGO for infrastructure development, but the locals had started advancing their own, narrow interests. After listening to his tirade for 15-20 minutes, it sounded like the locals were taking him for a ride and we just seemed like a few pawns in the local political game.

We tried to calm him down and told him that building trust and initiating a change in this part of the world takes a long time and a lot of patience. Maybe it was just one of the false starts before he found success. The young guy was still fuming that he was putting his meagre savings and prospects of a peaceful life back home on the line, was willing to trust the local people, but all the locals were interested in was advancing their own agendas. So young and so idealistic!

In the middle of all this, the American girl studying street art in Beirut noticed the ex-army guy's worn-out passport hanging out of his back pocket. She got very concerned, and asked him to put it in a safe place. Here was a guy who had, at some point, put his life on the line for some abstract, man-made notion of a nation-state. Perhaps an extension of some evolutionary concept of one's community, but abstract, nonetheless. And here was an innocent girl asking him to take care of his passport. People who wear their hearts on their sleeves do not care about mundane issues like passports. After her two failed attempts, I reminded her that he was an army guy. Taking good care of his passport did not figure in his list of priorities.

After lunch, we decided that instead of leaving the camp abruptly, we would spend another half an hour or so, help out with painting the guns on the wall, and leave the camp. But the Spanish girl seemed intent on finishing what she had started. And I did not know my way back home. I had to wait for the girls to finish. About an hour later, the American guy changed his tack and said that the local political game was tilting his way. He still wasn't sure whether he should support painting guns, but by then, the Spanish girl was even more enthused about doing so. In the middle of all this confusion, there was a death in the neighborhood and the body of the deceased, middle-aged man was being brought to the mosque. One by one, the women in his family came for the final visit and were dragged away, crying and wailing. The final rites were performed, and were then followed by a funeral procession. We were asked to stop working and sit down in silence. The American graduate student was somewhat surprised with how a death in the neighborhood was being mourned publicly, out in the open. It was a stark contrast to how funerals are held in the United States. The Spanish girl was overwhelmed to the point of crying. And I was left wondering whether she was aware of the irony in crying at the sight of a stranger's death, while painting guns on the wall.

By that time, I had decided to be a bystander, and not actively paint anything. I helped them draw the outline of their desired homeland and started looking around. If there was one word to describe the scene, it was "neglect." Makeshift, concrete structures, the sky filled with a mesh of cables, narrow lanes littered with potholes and trash, kids playing hopscotch on the streets, with mopeds whizzing by and narrowly missing them, an occasional fancy convertible passing by and blowing dust on the bystanders. How and why was that convertible owner living in that neighborhood? The only comforting thing in this bizarre situation was the generosity of the locals toward us. Other than our lunch at KFC, for which we had stepped out of the refugee camp, they refused to let us pay for food or drinks throughout the day. A steady supply of falafel sandwiches, hummus, pita breads, and soft drinks continued throughout the day.

After coming back to the hostel, the Spanish girl went away to video-chat with her boyfriend, the idealist American ex-army guy advocating non-violence hit the local bars in search of pretty girls, the American graduate student started video-chatting with her best friend from back home, and I started looking for accommodation for the next day in Petra. Later, as I lay on my bunk bed, I realized that Beirut didn't seem like the paradise it had been on the first day. The historic baggage and daily contradictions of life in this part of the world could leave you clueless, even depressed. I have to say, though, that if you are a tourist, this city is still worth visiting, at least for the gorgeous waterfront and the best shopping district in the world!

*   *   *

It's Raining People!

May 13, 2012
Beirut, Lebanon

Besides experiencing weather extremes over the last three-four weeks, I also met a lot of new people in Egypt, Lebanon, Jordan, and Israel. Not just random people; random people with mind-numbing perspectives. At long last, Egypt has seen political turmoil. And Lebanon? Well, they have been in a state of perpetual turmoil, political and social. After spending two weeks talking to strangers in these two countries, I was not surprised to feel at a loss for words!

I remember meeting a writer in his mid-thirties living in Cairo who had been at Tahrir Square during the revolution that had happened a year earlier. He showed me half a dozen bullet marks on his sleeve, and let me feel one bullet that's still sitting underneath the skin on one of his arms. Small, perhaps non-lethal, but metal bullets nevertheless! Or shards, maybe. When they hit you, you do not know what kind they are. He told me how things hadn't changed much in the last year or so. But he was still hopeful. I told him that building democratic institutions is a multi-generational project and asked him whether Egyptian youth were patient enough to plough through it all, so that their grandchildren might enjoy the fruits of a real democracy. We discussed democratic experiments in Greece, the USA, Russia, Serbia, India, and Pakistan. I told him that getting to be a functioning democracy is a coin-toss. He thought that, with the power of the Internet and global free flow of information, the time to build democratic institutions could be shortened. But it is about changing people's psyches. Making them feel that they can't just blame the regime anymore. Making it known that they are responsible and empowered to make change happen. He was hopeful, and I wished him luck.

On my last day there, a divorced mother in her mid-thirties, a film director from Cairo, took me out to a couple of bars in town. While hanging out with her friends, she told me about her marriage, and how her ex-husband could not handle the fact that she was strong, independent, with a mind of her own. She didn't seem to have the desire to marry again. However, she felt like being a role-model as a mother, trying to sacrifice as much as she could out of sheer unconditional love for her child. While discussing the revolution, she gave me her personal account of events that gave me goose bumps. She had been there from Day 1, and nobody had expected the regime to fall. It started as a humble attempt to make a statement against the regime, but had suddenly turned into an uprising. In chilling details, she described the day she lost her fear of death and how it had kept her going throughout the revolution. Not sure though how it squared up with her desire to be there for her child. That's the magical world of the mind!

Then, I met a business major in Lebanon who had gone from

working in the industry to the humanitarian assistance (industry) before moving to activism for democracy. Some other country in the region had issued an arrest warrant against him for attempting to spread democracy. When he heard the news, he was in a different country. He immediately rushed back home and had been lying low for a while. Among other things, he told me how the Lebanese democracy works. To end the civil war, the political parties had decided to divide the entire country into something called a confessional system, where half the seats in the parliament are meant for Christians, and the other half for Muslims. You have to go back to your hometown to vote. If you were born in a constituency that sends a Christian to the parliament, there is no Muslim to vote for. And vice versa. Talk about institutionalizing discrimination. Just like the Indian reservation/affirmative action system, it was decided to review this arrangement and phase it out over time. Good luck with that! He was the first one I had met who admitted that it is a fucked-up system.

I met a graphic designer in Lebanon who was describing life in Beirut during the bombings a few years before. They used to patiently wait for the weekly day of bombings. Once the evening/night raid was done, they would go out and enjoy for 3-4 days. Then, they would hunker down again for a few days. He also talked about how Hezbollah ran the show in Lebanon and how the Lebanese would indulge in trading anything. Expired medicines, expired milk, expired ice cream. There is a price for anything and everything here...except for hope, perhaps. There seems to be a chronic shortage of that commodity.

Another business major working for a multinational corporation talked about how his small town of mostly Christians was bombed by the Syrians. He told me about his friend's innocent mother's death. His feelings toward the ongoing Syrian uprising ranged from indifference to a sense of "You deserve it." None of these Lebanese expected anything to change vis-a-vis Israel, and were not bothered by it.

I talked to a Palestinian refugee in his early twenties who was studying in a college in the refugee camp to become a business major. His grandfather had lost his house in 1948, and he had been born and raised in the refugee camp. His options after graduating college? Practically none. As a refugee, with no country to call home, he had no citizenship. He got a card from Lebanon saying that he was a refugee. He could not buy land, afford a Lebanese college education, or be legally employed in Lebanon. He could not leave the country, either. Even other Arab countries do not let Palestinian refugees in. His only realistic option was finding a job in the refugee camp, a place with an unemployment rate of 60%. Could he start a business? Nothing moved in his refugee camp without the blessings of the faction that controlled the camp. And he didn't agree with the faction's philosophy either. He told me about how the Palestinian political parties and NGOs spent only 10% of the money they got in donations from around the world and pocketed the rest. The head of one of the NGOs active in his camp lived in a castle in a rich neighborhood and sent his children to a $20,000 a year school. Hezbollah talked about resistance, but didn't have time to improve conditions in his camp. So they lived in squalor. If that were not enough, he was a "1948 refugee." His grandfather's home was not even on the negotiating table. His best hope was some form of right to return in the negotiated settlement. Does anyone in his camp think that that's around the corner? Nope! But when your own political parties are not helping you, all you can do is pin your hopes on an elusive settlement with Israel. "How about peaceful means to oppose Israeli policies?" was my naive question. He said that he had been at the border last year for peaceful protests. However, they were welcomed with sewage water and firing.

"Another armed uprising is inevitable," some other Palestinian refugee shrugged off his shoulders nonchalantly. Would he take part in it? "Of course," he said reflexively.

It all reminded me of a big hieroglyphic slate in the Egyptian museum in Cairo. In that 1200 BC slate, in the last few lines, it said "Israelites are crushed." Apparently, that is the first mention of Israel in Egyptian history. Looks like these guys have been at it for a while now.

6. ISRAEL: NO COUNTRY FOR LIBERTARIANS

May 20, 2012
Tel Aviv, Israel

Jordan didn't give me any opportunity to go off script. I flew from Beirut to Amman, caught a bus straight to Petra, and told the hostel reception lady that I would like to spend a couple of hours in Petra before heading back to the capital city of Amman. She smiled knowingly, asking me "How big do you think Petra is?" Obviously, I had no idea. Like an ignorant American, I had shown up without doing my homework. When she asked me whether I could walk 25 kilometers in two hours, I knew where that conversation was going. Petra is huge. Petra is hot. Petra is dry. And Petra is grand. More than a thousand years ago, it was one of the top trading outposts in the Middle East. Members of the local Bedouin tribe used to cross the desert on camels and travel thousands of miles to the east, all the way to India and China, to buy spices, porcelain ware, medicinal herbs and spices, and sell them to the European merchants in Petra. It is an abandoned town in the middle of a desert now, but the Jordanians, with a generous helping hand from UNESCO, have done a great job of preserving this important piece of glorious human history.

You walk through a deep gorge for two kilometers before you get to the main entrance of Petra, also known as the treasury. An imposing red-rock building with a two-storied façade, this is where the people of Petra used to store their money and weapons, and the goods they used to trade. Then come the caves the Bedouins used to live in, followed by the main street lined with ruins of temples and storefronts, leading to the central square. In the old days, this main street and the central square were the site of all the trade in Petra. Above the central square, after climbing some seven to eight hundred steps in the unbearable desert heat, there is a big monastery. They say that the elderly members of the community used to spend their last few years here in solitude, but for us hapless tourists, not used to the scorching heat, evading a heat stroke while scrambling up and down the stairs would be the first step toward attaining nirvana!

They say that in ancient times, Moses passed through this same gorge at the entrance of Petra. I wonder if he was into splitting rocks, too. More than Moses, it was the huge convoys of Bedouins' camels and horses that used to pass through this city, bringing the east and the west together. According to the sound and light show in the night, it was great to find out that India has always been on the Jordanians' minds. Back then, India was known for its spices and fragrances. Today, it is known for its Bollywood culture. European fragrances may have taken over the world, but every Jordanian knows Amitabh Bachchan. Some of them know Dharmendra and Shahrukh Khan, too. However, in this part of the world – Egypt, Lebanon, and Jordan – Amitabh Bachchan, or the Big B, rules the roost. In the Egypt of the seventies and the eighties, they aired a Bollywood movie every Friday on state television. I do not know whether or how Bollywood contributes to portraying the image of India in foreign countries, but as much as I hate all those candy-floss romances and no-shades-of-grey, good versus evil Bollywood movies, they seem to help Indian tourists a lot. A big hug to Bollywood for ensuring that I wasn't getting ripped off as badly as the Westerners.

Petra is rich in history. Greek, Roman, Persian, Byzantine, all the empires conquered this place and have left their mark on it. In addition to the temples, there are some impressive engineering feats like dams built for water storage and canals constructed to divert flash floods away from the deep gorge. However, a powerful earthquake in the 6th century finally took this city down. Today, the trading hub has moved to Amman. I have been told that there is nothing touristy about Amman. Other than a couple of not-so-impressive Roman-era ruins, there is not much else to see or do in Amman. Luckily, my short stay in Amman turned into a serendipitous opportunity to renew some of my old friendships. A couple of my friends from college were in town for business. Another Pakistani friend joined us from Dubai. My college friends could not take a day off, but a day trip to the Dead Sea with the Pakistani friend was great. Floating on water without any effort happened to be quite a strange and thrilling experience. Your body does it effortlessly, but your brain refuses to believe it. I also learned firsthand what a bad idea it was to shave in the morning. A cut on the skin, even a minor one that generally does not hurt, is going to burn like hell in the Dead Sea water. And don't expect to stay in the water too long. The water is so salty that, within a few minutes of entering the sea, you get a layer of salt on your entire body. You start feeling it right away, almost as if you are bathing in oil. As the salt dries, it starts stretching your skin. In the Middle East sun, this leaves you with a painful burning sensation. Despite burning skin and salty layers, though, this is definitely one of those things you should try in your lifetime. Or before the Dead Sea dies. According to one of the locals, the main feeder of the Dead Sea, the Jordan River, has dried out completely. Because of that, the water level in the sea is going down by 80-100 cm every year. Your time starts now!

I also ended up going to my only Jordanian friend's engagement party. The food, the dancing, the drinking, the venue were things I could keep raving about. I was told that my friend did not invite her whole family. They invited only eighty of the closest family members! Except for the drinking bit, it felt like an Indian engagement party. With the beautiful Jordanian women decked up from head to toe and most of the men in suits and ties, my humble jeans and t-shirt were clearly out of place. For once, though, I had an excuse to be underdressed. I have shown up at important graduate school interviews in jeans and sneakers. I have been the cause of a bouncer not letting a group of my ten-fifteen friends into an upscale lounge in DC because I was the only one not wearing shoes. And not being clean-shaven is a recurring theme in my life. However, for this engagement, I had a badass excuse of being on a round-the-world trip. Even though I was not really dressed like the best man, by the end of the night, I had a couple of tipsy aunts fighting over whose house I should visit before leaving

Jordan and whose daughter I should get hitched to. What a memorable experience it was.

*   *   *

As brief as my stay in Israel was, it was interesting. Spending a couple of hours walking around the narrow alleys of old Jerusalem was a lot of fun. In India, Ramjanmabhoomi (the alleged birthplace of Lord Rama) and Babri Masjid (a mosque built for Babur, one of the Mughal rulers of India) sharing the same site in the town of Ayodhya is a cause of significant religious strife. Some of the 800-900 million Hindus are angry about it. Old Jerusalem reminded me of Ayodhya. In the Al-Aqsa mosque complex, Jews, Muslims, and Christians have been fighting amongst themselves for ages over who did what and when. Here is the Al-Aqsa mosque, allegedly built by destroying the synagogue there. And there is the path that Jesus took on his way to his crucifixion. As an atheist born into a Hindu family, standing in front of the mosque built on the ruins of a synagogue, and a stone's throw away from Jesus's path to crucifixion, I felt like I was covering a lot of religious ground. I felt like singing

"I'm every prophet...
It's all in me...
Any faith you're following, baby...
I can feel it naturally!"

To me, the most interesting thing is that the Quran recognizes Moses and Jesus as prophets. They are just not as important as Muhammad. So if followers of Moses are the chosen ones, does that make Muslims the chosen-chosen-chosen ones, too? Where does that leave the poor Hindus? And the poorer atheists?

The religious identity crisis was no match for the experience of getting in and out of Israel. Israel was not originally on my list. However, the cheapest flight out of the whole region – Egypt, Lebanon, Jordan, and Israel – to Greece was from Tel Aviv. So I decided to cross over into Israel for a day. Overland. The Allenby Bridge, or the King Hussein Bridge, connects Jordan with Israel. It was also the shortest route from Amman to Jerusalem. I had heard about the multiple wars and innumerable smaller skirmishes Israel and Lebanon had had over the past few decades. I knew that these two countries were sworn enemies and were constantly at each other's throats. None of that could have prepared me for the hostile reception I would experience after the Israeli immigration authorities noticed a Lebanese visa stamped on my passport. Here is an assortment of questions I had to answer to get in and out of Israel.

My name. My father's name. His father's name. The meaning of my name. The meaning of my last name. My religion. An extempore speech on Hinduism. Is it like Buddhism?

And then, why did I visit Lebanon? The immigration officer had already concluded for me that there was nothing to do there. *Thank you, officer, for being my tour guide.* How long was I in Lebanon? Who did I meet? Where did I go in Lebanon? Why did I go to Egypt despite the political problems there?

Further along, why was I spending just one day in Israel after I had spent five days in Jordan? Apparently, there is much to see and do in Israel. *Thanks, again, for being my tour guide.*

Why was I visiting the holy sites in Jerusalem despite being Hindu? Why did I quit my job? Why was I traveling for one year? Where did I get the money? How much money did I have in my bank account?

These questions do not even include the special treatment I received when I was flying out of Tel Aviv. Two hours of thorough searching of my body and my baggage. Within the first 15-20 minutes, I had established a good rapport with the special immigration officer assigned to me. When he noticed the bottle of chyawanprash in my bag, he made me open it and eat it in front of him. When I told him that it could cure his acid reflux, he immediately noted it on a piece of paper, and told me that the Elf Hostel in Prague was great and that I should check out the heavy metal music scene in Germany. When asked, I gave him my review of the quality of the backpack (amazing!). He told me about his desire to take a year off and travel to Eastern Europe and Central Asia. But none of this friendly small talk stopped him from doing his job of frisking and screening me for potential threats. Everything inside my backpack was removed and tested for traces of explosives. I was taken to a special room and frisked, or pretty much molested, by American standards. I wasn't allowed to take my backpack with me as carry-on luggage. I had to check it, but I could not check it at the airline counter. It had to go through a special elevator. Phew! Perhaps the only question they did not ask me, or could not ask me was, "Why do you want to enter Israel when you are male, single, brown-skinned, young, jobless, and have a Lebanese stamp on your passport?"

Unlike a conscientious objector, I didn't object to any of this, and I kept my side of the bargain by cooperating and being honest. I realized that if I had had an Israeli stamp on my passport, the Lebanese wouldn't have even let me in. There is also no dearth of admiration, in my mind, for what the Israelis have built in this incredibly inhospitable climate. In the middle of a desert, they have built a democratic country with world class infrastructure, agriculture, a high-tech economy that has earned it the "start-up nation" tag, and a national defense and intelligence establishment that is arguably the best in the world. In spite of all of these achievements, don't the Israelis yearn for a life free from suspicion, threats, and massive national security budgets? When are the Israeli and Arab politicians going to find that extra bit of courage to solve their centuries-old problems and end the seemingly endless bloodshed on both sides and, along with it, the long hours wasted at immigration checkpoints?

Had I refused to cooperate or answer their questions, I'm pretty sure the Israelis would have politely kicked me out of the country or put me under detention. You need to enter Israel. Israel doesn't need you. And when loyalties shift every few miles and life is constantly under threat, liberty and freedom take a backseat. I'm sure Ron Paul and his Austrian gurus advocating libertarian political philosophy wouldn't go too far here.

7. TURKEY: "IYI MISIN?"
"- EVET."
"TAMAAM, TAMAAM, TAMAAM."

June 25, 2012
Safranbolu, Turkey

I had first visited Turkey in 2010, and Cappadocia was the only reason I decided to visit Turkey again. One of my former colleagues from graduate school lives in Ankara, the capital city of Turkey now, and I decided to visit him before heading to Cappadocia.

After reaching Istanbul and taking an overnight bus to Ankara, I was in conversation with the mustachioed gentleman at the metro ticket window, trying to figure out the process of buying a train ticket. I had just withdrawn some Turkish Lira and didn't have the exact change to buy a ticket. From out of nowhere, a Turkish gentleman appeared and told the ticket seller that he would take care of my metro ride. The ticket seller said "Tamaam" and the gentleman pulled me out of the ticket line. I had no idea what it meant. I did not even ask the Turkish Samaritan for help, and neither did he wait for my SOS. He looked like a daily commuter and, like a Mumbai local train regular, had a wad of metro tickets in his pocket. He just came from behind me, offered me a metro ticket, and refused my offer to pay him. This has happened to me so many times now. In fact, my journey started with a gentleman buying me a ticket in metro and teaching me the word "Dastoor". I wonder how many backpackers bump into kind locals paying for their metro tickets.

As we started the metro ride, we started making small talk. He told me that he is a veterinarian. I introduced myself as Indian, but he did not understand it. As I realized later, this is really my first country, and perhaps the only one, where people do not refer to India as India. You have to say Hindistan or Hindustan. And that is almost always followed by the "Are you Muslim?" question.

When I told him about my work in the field of Alzheimer's disease and the time I have spent in the United States, he was quick to inform me that he has no desire to visit America. He then went on an unprovoked rant about American hegemony and imperialism. On his way out, he concluded with "They are all blood-suckers!" Coming from a Turkish guy, this is a little more than just ironic. Wasn't it just a few hundred years ago that the Turkish Empire was one of the biggest empires in the world? It would be stupid to paint all the Turks as descendants of brutal rulers, but they have their share of skeletons in the closet, too. The Armenian genocide, anyone? Oh well! It's hard to imagine a world without a superpower, or superpowers at different timescales in the history of human civilization. Yet hating superpowers happens to be the favorite worldwide pastime for many.

Aside from such occasional America-bashing, though, the Turks generally seemed to be a gregarious bunch. I realized that they take a tremendous amount of pride in their history and their current place in the world. Atatürk, the founder of the modern Republic of Turkey, wanted this country to adopt Western mores. With the disappearance of black burqas and white robes and the widespread acceptance of the Western dress code, the façade has certainly changed. However, their cultural DNA is definitely Eastern.

My colleague turned out to have a pretty busy psychiatry practice at the best and most prestigious hospital in Turkey. Even with the packed professional schedules of himself and his wife, and the full-time responsibility of raising two middle-school aged girls, they turned out to be very gracious hosts and took some time off to catch up with this long-lost backpacker bumming around with no real agenda. What followed was hours of grilling meat, drinking beer, and late-night conversations in spite of it being a weeknight. In Eastern cultures, we do not wait for Friday and Saturday nights on Western calendars to tell us when to hang out with friends. We hang out when friends show up.

When the conversation moved from professional to personal, I was pleasantly surprised to discover how far back in time the cultural ties between Turkey and Hindustan stretch. Just like the ancient Silk Road, which was used to trade goods between China and Europe, the Turkish people coined the term "Baharat Road," originating in India and carrying spices to Africa and Europe. In fact, spices are called "Baharat" in Turkish. I wondered whether this term had anything to do with Bharat, the real name of India.

The conversation then moved to traditional music. Oddly enough, the Turks play a Shehenai-type instrument at weddings, just like the Indians do. I found out that Turkish classical music is every bit as complicated as Hindustani classical music. Vocal music doesn't just come from the diaphragm, but from the highly-trained vocal cords. The beats and cycles are more complicated than those in Western music, but not as complicated as those in Hindustani classical music. However, all that is well-compensated for when it comes to Turkish musical notes. There are nine subtle semi-notes between the Western C and D, which is nothing short of mind-boggling. I am sure that it would take a highly trained ear to know whether or not the singer is hitting the right semi-note.

After all of this cultural education, my friend lent me his second car to drive down to Cappadocia for a few days. Driving in Turkey turned out to be an experience in itself. The huge highway projects underway meant that one had to face oncoming traffic in sections where construction was going on. The construction crews put on red cones to divide the road, but the Turks still drove through these red cones in a zigzag fashion to overtake other vehicles. At 90-100km/h, you are overtaking vehicles and dodging cars and cones at the same time, enjoying your personal F1 race. Cheap thrills! After entering a town or a city, waiting in the rightmost lane at a traffic signal and then suddenly cutting through all the lanes to take a left turn at your whim and fancy is acceptable; expected, even. The GPS is as unreliable as in any other country. On my way back to Ankara, it asked me to jump over dividers to take left turns. In the name of the fastest route, it diverted me and took me on a dirt road straight into the fields. Damn you, GPS! If you are going to make my car cut through lush green fields full of knee-length grass, the least you can do is show some courtesy and ask me if I am driving a car, truck, or a tractor.

But beyond all that, this culture has a human touch, quite literally. If you are sitting in the navigator's seat, the driver would casually touch your leg when explaining something or drawing your attention to something. When you ask for directions in a busy market, the local dude would jokingly ask for five Lira and then nonchalantly put his hand on your shoulder, while giving you directions. In Safranbolu, when I asked a vendor for a good place to watch the Euro cup match, he grabbed my arm and dragged me to his cousin's hole-in-the-wall tea stall just a couple of blocks away, where a group of friends were watching the match together on a small, old TV, literally shoved into a hole in the wall. Soda and Turkish tea were on the house!

However, the human touch vanished as soon as I reached my next destination; the Scandinavian countries. The Scandinavians seem to have it all! They are blessed with lots of natural beauty. Mountains, lakes, fjords, islands; you name it! Additionally, what these countries have managed to achieve in terms of social development is truly astonishing. After centuries of Viking brutality and the more recent history of abject poverty, these countries have built societies as close to perfect as possible. With pastel colors, I should add. Whoever coined the term "pastel" would be proud of the Scandinavians for perfecting the color schemes. More importantly, these countries are topping charts in all human development indices. In Sweden, the push for gender equality forced the royal family to accept daughters as heirs to the throne. The crown prince had to give up his right to succeed to his older sister, the first-born in the family. Treating women as equals is an article of faith here.

In Norway, even after discovering huge oil reserves, the politicians have demonstrated an astonishing degree of restraint and sense of responsibility to invest in social welfare and save some of the spoils for future generations. The contrast with Middle Eastern oil-based monarchies is jarring.

For their sizes, the Scandinavian countries have huge humanitarian assistance programs going on all across the world. These countries take in a large number of refugees, too, which makes their cities pretty multi-cultural. They are definitely not as homogenous as I had expected. Of course, the diversity is nowhere near what you would see in London or New York, but it's noticeable enough.

In spite of all these strides in socio-economic development, a certain air of detachment is palpable in the Scandinavian air. Maybe the harsh weather here makes people shy or reluctant to interact with others. Maybe it's because of their governments' striving for human well-being, both within and beyond their borders, that they don't feel the urge to show any warmth toward others. Maybe they have outsourced humanity to their governments. But compared to the Turks, Scandinavians seem a little shy and distant. After walking in a park in Oslo and talking to some strangers, I managed to make some good Norwegian friends. After a couple of hours of conversation, even they confessed they had been suspicious of me when I first started talking to them. At first glance, they thought I was a salesman, trying to sell them something. It was pretty much the same after the near-death experience on the Norwegian flight from Oslo to Tromso. If I hadn't started a conversation while disembarking, my co-passengers would have probably walked away without sharing their thoughts about the entire episode.

In the hotel lobby in Tromso, I was sitting with a somber face, staring at the drizzle and listening to Roger Waters, all by myself...

"All you touch, and all you see, is all your life will ever be."

If I had been in some smoky, hookah-filled café in Turkey, surrounded by people sipping Turkish tea and playing backgammon, I could imagine someone putting his arm around my shoulder and the conversation going:

"Iyi misin?"

"- Evet."

"Tamaam, tamaam, tamaam!"

EXPLORING EUROPE

4

8. GREECE: A GREEK TRAGEDY

June 1, 2012
Athens, Greece

Greece was fabulous, but not in the way I had expected it to be.
This land of Socrates, Aristotle, Galileo, Archimedes, Euclid,
Pythagoras, and, most importantly, the birthplace of democracy,
has always had a special place in my mind. Anyone interested in
geometry, physics, and neuroscience is bound to have some
romantic notions about Greece, but those notions were shattered
within hours of reaching Athens. The rich history of this land is
limited to a few scattered sites in this modern European capital.
Acropolis, temple of Zeus, and the Agora cover most of it. At the
Agora, you can walk the same steps Socrates walked before he was
sentenced, but it's just a small mound. You can't feel the gravity of
the place. The temple of Nike, the goddess of victory, is fully
restored, but the Parthenon is in the middle of a multi-year
restoration. And most of the statues are confined to the museum
walls. The museum in the Agora has some interesting relics of early
Greek democracy. A pseudo-random jury selection apparatus, the
tokens voters used to ostracize politicians; it's amazing to see how
advanced this direct democracy was. But instead of decorating
showcases of museums, all of these items should be outside. Here
is where so and so did this, that is the hall where the jury for
Socrates was selected by that contraption, and that is where so and
so wrote that. Unfortunately, that's not the case. As one of my
fellow travelers told me, a lot of the historic sites were destroyed

during renaissance, when artists tore down several old buildings and used the remains for all kinds of other artistic endeavors.

But the Greek food made up for all that disappointment. The Kalamata olives tasted different here, because these guys don't need any preservatives for them to reach their dinner tables. Spinach pies are great, and so are the green peppers stuffed with rice and all the big slabs of sweet things they eat. The two-Euro pork sandwich was my staple, though. Tight budgets don't bother you much in Germany, but they hurt a lot when you have so much good food around you.

Except for the Arkadi monastery, where a group of Cretans decided to blow themselves up instead of surrendering to the Ottomans, the island of Crete is decidedly average. The damaged skulls of the monks who blew themselves up are neatly arranged on a shelf, an eerie sight you generally don't associate with monasteries. But as I have learned during my brief stay in Greece, Cretans have always been known as great fighters and a fiercely independent bunch. The Nazis allegedly attacked the island, thinking that they would capture it in a day. It took them five days! And Santorini? There is a reason it is one of the top tourist destinations in the world. Black and red sandy beaches in the south create an interesting contrast to the all-white, eye-squinting (I just made that word up) town of Oia in the north. And so do a bunch of rag-tag backpackers to all the honeymooners on the island.

But no matter how hard I looked, there was no sign of the impending collapse of the Greek economy. Sure, there was uncut grass along the metro tracks and an occasional dumpster that was overflowing. The rest of the country seemed to be running fine. There weren't any strikes or violent protests, public transportation seemed to be running fine, the parliament building in Athens had no one shouting or yelling in front of it, and everything was open for business. I had read that even when they have protests, they are generally well-targeted (toward the appropriate institutions). Maybe I had skipped those institutions, but the bankruptcy seemed to be hidden in the Greek hearts and minds. For these pioneers of democracy, Goldman Sachs bundled up their bad debt, the American rating agencies gave them sterling ratings, the Germans welcomed them with open arms and exported all kinds of German goods and, after the financial collapse, the Chinese were waiting in the wings to buy anything and everything in a fire-sale. They would buy up all the natural resources, ports and such, and send a bunch of Chinese people to manage it all. It was hard to escape the sense of irony when talking to the Greeks here. One foreign country mismanaged its money, another exported all kinds of goods to it, and the third was waiting to send a few of its billion plus citizens to take over the country. In this globalized world, if politicians don't take care of their own constituents, outsiders will have their cake and eat it, too. Things haven't changed much from Greek times, after all. Politicians are the same, and so are the imperial instincts of creditor countries.

The best part of my stay in Greece, though, was trying to figure out Greek words. As an engineer, before I visited Greece, phi had to be some angle. Rho had to be density. Chi couldn't live by itself. It had to be squared and had to be related to statistics. Delta had to connote some minor difference in measurements. In this country, it's a full-fledged language. All these guys are part of the alphabet the Greeks use every day. A fellow backpacker told me that he couldn't figure out anything in this country. It was how I'd felt when I was in the Middle East. There was no way to figure out the alphabet. But when he said that, I told him I could figure things out here...sort of. At long last, I could figure out a real-world application of all the nonsense I had crammed into my brain during my undergraduate days as an engineering student.

*　　　　　　*　　　　　　*

The March of the Ants

June 3, 2012
Crete, Greece

The Samaria gorge hike on the island of Crete turned out to be a bit of a downer. It is a good 15km hike, but it is all downhill. Sure, it was good practice for climbing Kilimanjaro, which was coming up in a couple of months, but after getting up at five in the morning and rushing to catch a bus, I was expecting better scenery. I finished the hike by two in the afternoon and reached the port from which I was supposed to catch a ferry back to the hostel in Heraklion, only to find out that I had three and a half hours to kill before the next ferry. Tick…tock…tick…tock.

The beach in front of me was an option. After the Middle East leg, my skin had burnt multiple times over. I did not want to go through another round of flaking. I found a spot in the shade and looked around. I hadn't brought a book with me because I was expecting a strenuous hike. There was no internet. Most of the people I could see were sunbathing on the beach. How could I kill three and a half hours now?

I was not really hungry, but I pulled out the pack of peanuts from my backpack and started munching on them. I moved on to one of the four cereal bars I had been carrying from the start of the trip. It was not one of those chewy bars. It was one of the ones that invariably spit crumbs on the floor as soon as you open the wrapper. This time, it spit four. Three in a cluster, and one to the side. Rolling...three...two...one...action!

A wandering ant stumbled upon the crumb that was a couple feet away from the cluster of three. It spent a few seconds at the crumb, almost as if making sure it was a legitimate catch, and started probing it from all sides. After it was done probing, it decided to drag it along instead of picking it up in its jaw. Not for too long, though. Within a few seconds, another friend from the same family showed up. Then, another one. And another. And one more. As soon as there were five, the second one left the scene, made a couple of rounds around the moving crumb, and joined the group again. By the time it came back, I could see a big recon team on its way.

The cluster of three crumbs was more than a foot away from "ground zero" right between my two legs. I was curious about how the ants were ever going to get there? For the next ten minutes or so, most of the recon team focused on the area around ground zero. After 10-15 minutes, one brave soul managed to venture out toward the cluster. As soon as it was halfway between ground zero and the cluster, I found myself rooting for it. It made 3/4th of a circle, clockwise, around the cluster and went back in the direction of ground zero. *Damn it! How did you miss this treasure trove? It's right there!* Oh well, these guys may never find it.

Another five minutes passed. Nobody came back to that area. Did it go back and tell others that there was no action in the direction of the big cluster? But wait, there was another brave soul heading in the direction of the cluster! *This one's gotta find it.* It seemed to be following the general route the earlier ant had followed, but not quite. For some reason, it went around the cluster in a tighter circle, still clockwise. *C'mon now! All you have to do is take a right turn instead of going back.* For a brief moment, it seemed to take half a step inward, but like a pump-fake, decided to go back to ground zero. *Man, these guys are just clueless. Wandering around and just wasting their time!*

But I looked around ground zero and they were wasting their time on the other side of ground zero, too. *Let's go, ladies. Keep trying. Sooner or later, you are gonna find the Holy Grail.*

After another five minutes or so, one of them went straight for my right shoe. It did not seem to be following the footsteps of its predecessors. But hey, what the hell do I know about ants! For a second, I thought about blocking its way and guiding it in the right direction, but I did not want my vibrations to scare the ant away. Plus, my shoes were new and the soles were spiky enough that they might feel more like a series of tunnels to the ant.

It went into one of the tunnels formed by my sole for a few seconds and barged out, straight toward the cluster. *Let's go! Let's go!* It was like the home stretch of the Kentucky Derby now. *Just keep going straight. Don't screw this up now!* Sure enough, it missed the first one. The second one. It was about to miss the third one, too, when it finally made a left turn and bumped into the third one. *Phew! Finally! Now go check around and find those other two bits before you start moving this one away.*

But nope! It had other plans. It didn't even bother to go around the crumb it had bumped into to gauge how big or small it was. It was almost as if it already knew the significance of its discovery. After feeling it out from one side, it ran straight back, brought a few of its friends, and then moved on to find the other two crumbs.

Before its friends could pick up the first bit and start taking it back, they managed to find the other two bits. Awesome! But wait, there was an even bigger recon team coming from behind. Hold on, guys! *You are wasting your time now. There is nothing more to find. Go spend your time somewhere else, for God's sake!* Of course, no entienden lenguas de los humanos!

Wait! It was not over yet. The first group seemed to be going in the wrong direction. They were taking the crumb away from their home. For a moment, they resembled a bunch of drunk people, stumbling around, trying to move a big boulder. Oh no, stupid humans! The ants cleverly turned the bit around so that it was easier to navigate a bump in the road.

All three crumbs were on the move before I knew it. After they were well on their way, a few members of the recon team were glued to the site of the crumb in the middle. Did it leave a sugary residue behind? I was not sure, but as the ants were doing their clean up (or whatever they were doing), the recon team looked like it carpet-bombed the whole area. This recon team was much bigger than the one assigned to ground zero.

The whole drama ended a few minutes later, as the recon swarm made its way back empty-handed. All in a day's play, I guess. As I thought about it, in hindsight, this was an incredibly efficient operation. Given their cognitive abilities (rather, my imagination of their abilities), it was astonishing that they discovered the cluster in their third attempt in that direction. As a search operation, with virtually no chance of finding anything, this looked like one of the most efficient ways of finding food. Even the recon teams for ground zero and the cluster of three seemed to be proportional to the size of the "catch."

I'm not an entomologist, but someone needs to make an ants' version of *March of the Penguins*. I'm sure the entomologists know enough about how ants search for food, and instead of getting Morgan Freeman to narrate it I would use Samuel L. Jackson. The nasty *Pulp Fiction* or *Snakes on the Plane* SLJ. These poor, hard-working ants don't need philosophy; they need personality. A little bit of attitude. I am already imagining the conversation between the one who found the first of the three crumbs and the others, when it went back to recruit more volunteers. Maybe the first ant it bumped into was Denzel Washington.

SLJ - "There are some motherf***** crumbs on the motherf***** porch!!!"

DW - "N**** what?"

SLJ - "I didn't know there was s*** piled up all the way to yo ears, b****! There are some m-o-t-h-e-r-f-*-*-*-*-*-*   c-r-u-m-b-s o-n t-h-e   m-o-t-h-e-r-f-*-*-*-*-*   p-o-r-c-h!!!"

DW - "Bull****! I've been followin' yo ass fo two months now. The last three times I listened to yo sorry ass, we didn't get s***. It was f***** Splenda all three times. You know damn well that shit's got no suga in it. Ima give you one last chance now. If there ain't no s*** on the porch this time, it's yo ass! Look into my eyes...it's you and me, baby!"

SLJ - "If those dumass humans keep eatin' that Splenda s***, that ain't my fault. But this is the real s***, man! So, get yo lazy ass up and follow me."

DW - "Awight, awight! It better be the real deal."

And then, when it was all done, Denzel puts a hand on Jackson's shoulder and says "Muh n****! I knew you would come thru. But you gotta learn how to tell Splenda from the real deal, man. Yo ass is way too old fo' that s***."

SLJ - "Awight, awight! Ima work on that motherf*****."

DW - "Fo sho, n****."

I don't know about you, but I'd pay to see that documentary. Or docudrama.

As I looked around, my thoughts slowly drifted back to Egypt. I thought about the tour guide in Luxor having reminded me that at least one of the tombs in the valley of the Egyptian kings has not been discovered yet. In a way, people looking for fossils and historic sites have the same problem. Those archeologists need to talk to these ants! Or the people who study ants. They can tell them about efficient searching algorithms.

I checked the clock. I had managed to kill just one hour. Two more to go.

Tick...tock...tick...tock...tick...tock.

Should I throw a few more crumbs on the porch? I felt like feeding these hard-working ants some more crumbs, but I could almost hear Samuel L. Jackson going "Who the f*** is that human motherf*****? Why can these motherf***** humans not throw all the motherf***** crumbs in one go?"

Now that's a real catch-22!

*   *   *

June 5, 2012
Athens, Greece

As I came back to Athens and started preparing for my long overland journey to Bulgaria, my mind was still trying to process the situation in Greece amid the ongoing economic crisis. Here is some food for thought:

What do you call politicians who enable undeserving people to buy homes?

And what do you call politicians who pay bureaucrats 14 months' worth of salary for working 12 months?

What do you call people who rack up thousands of Dollars in credit card debt without any plan to pay it off?

And what do you call people who take 6-8 week paid vacations per year after working 30-hour weeks?

What do you call agencies that give AAA ratings to junk assets?

And what do you call agencies that help people find ways to avoid paying taxes?

What do you call "well-connected" business houses that don't pay any taxes?

And what do you call "well-connected" business houses that don't pay any taxes?

The former is called American and the latter, Greek. Greece is a has-been superpower and America is the reigning superpower. So, America is more equal than Greece.

9. BULGARIA: RECOVERING FROM AN IRON HANGOVER

June 6, 2012
Sofia, Bulgaria

After looking at the map of Bulgaria, I realized it made sense to spend three or four days in Skopje, and another three or four days in Sofia before heading to Turkey. Obviously, that was not meant to be. As I got to Thessaloniki, the Greek border town city, from Athens, I realized that the last bus to Skopje had already left, but there was a bus to Sofia later in the night. Tough luck, Skopje! I booked a hostel in Sofia online and got a bus ticket to Sofia. An evening stroll along the Thessaloniki waterfront seemed like a good break before jumping onto the midnight bus to Sofia.

The city of Sofia has nothing to do with the hot and sultry Sofia Vergara. It is actually named after Sofia, the Roman (or Greek maybe!) goddess of fortune. No, I think it's Roman. When you are in this part of the world, it is hard to keep your mythologies straight.

All the passengers were woken up around three in the morning for immigration. We were in Sofia by five in the morning. The hostel website had told me it was just a 20-minute walk from the bus station. It was a bit chilly, but with my backpack, I knew it wouldn't be too long before I started sweating. The only problem was that there was nobody on the streets at that ungodly, or ungoddessly, hour. The bus driver wasn't much help. Neither was the half-asleep person at the information desk. Taxi drivers wouldn't tell me how to get there because I wasn't using their services. And there was no way to figure out the half-Greek, half-Cyrillic script of Bulgaria. Take your backpack and start walking!

I saw a couple of liquor stores open on the way, but they weren't of much help either. Three blocks before my destination, I finally noticed a middle-aged lady crossing the street. When traveling, middle-aged ladies are my kind of demographic for asking all sorts of questions. They are the most non-threatening bunch. I'm sure most of them are moms and they are generally pretty eager to help out lost kids like us. This one was different. With a half-full coffee cup in one hand and a cigarette in the other, she figured out that I was looking for something. As she approached me, I asked her where Hostel Mostel was. "Hostel? Hostel?" she asked me a couple of times, pretending to not fully understand what I was asking. I thought it would be useful to pull out my tablet and show her the map. As soon as I started taking my backpack off, she put her arm in my arm and started saying "You, me, hotel?" Clearly, she was looking for something totally different. I looked around to see if I could find someone else on the street, but it was totally deserted. The couple of taxi drivers who passed by weren't in the mood to stop. After insisting on "Hostel Mostel" for ten minutes in louder and louder tones, I had to yell at her to let me go. After at least an hour of walking around on deserted streets, getting in and out of wrong lanes, and struggling to identify landmarks shown on my map, I finally reached the doorstep of the hostel.

This bad first impression grew a little worse as I stepped out for breakfast. Like a lot of Indian towns and villages, this city is dominated by small stores and kiosks. Supermarkets are hard to find. As I stepped in and out of a few stores searching for milk, all of the store-owners seemed as if they were still recovering from the "iron-hangover." Scarcity wasn't the problem. The stores were full of all kinds of things, but the store owners seemed incredibly robotic. In most of the countries, when people notice you are a traveler, most of them try to understand you and help you out. That wasn't the case here. In three different stores, I faced middle-aged stone faces with no interest in helping me find milk. In the fourth store, I bought something resembling a milk carton. The store owner nodded when I asked her whether it was milk. Sure enough, it turned out to be buttermilk. Typically, there is nodding of heads and an exchange of smiles when you manage to cross the language barrier. It's just the pure joy of being able to communicate with another human being. In these stores, though, they didn't seem to have any interest in selling their goods or communicating with others. Like that donkey Benjamin in Animal Farm, the only thing they seemed to say through their cold eyes was "I've lived a long life and experienced a lot." Given the recent history of this country, that was probably true. And then, every third man walking on the streets looked like he belonged to the Russian mafia. Either tall, or burly, or both. Wearing jeans, dark tee-shirt, black leather jacket, a balding head, and scowling at someone on the phone. Smiling faces were hard to find. Oh well!

After a breakfast of a half-liter of buttermilk and biscuits, it was time to catch up on some much-needed sleep. The 36-hour journey from Athens to Sofia and the early morning search for the hostel had worn me out. The city tour and the monastery tour had to wait. The next day, the city tour guide told us that this is a pretty old city, dating back to Roman times. This was one of the main cities along the way from Rome to Constantinople. That history, though, is all buried underground and is in the process of being excavated. Add to that the ongoing construction of an underground metro, and the city looked like a dug-up hodge-podge of new and old. Not necessarily a pretty one, though. The more recent history of how the Bulgarian king saved thousands of Jews from being sent to the concentration camps (Schindler style), and the turmoil during Soviet times, is slightly more intriguing, but not quite.

The all-Bulgarian lunch I had after the walking tour was definitely interesting. Not knowing how cheap restaurants here are, I walked into a fancy-looking restaurant. With a courtyard for outside seating, I thought the prices and quantities there would be similar to those in the Greek restaurants catering to tourists from all around the world. But the salad, meatballs, and entree I ordered were three meals. It was all incredibly delicious and just for twelve Dollars. What they call meatballs here are round only in two dimensions, not the third. They are flat and pretty big. They are actually regular-sized meat patties. Finishing it up and skipping dinner were the only option.

The Rila monastery tour was much better than the city of Sofia.

71

One of the patron saints of the Greek Orthodox Church decided to seek God by going to the beautiful Bulgarian mountains surrounding Sofia and leading an ascetic life. The colorful monastery, nestled in the lush-green hills, seemed like a good place to sit back and contemplate the meaning of life.

On my way there, I finally found out that Sofia is not the best city to visit in Bulgaria. Plovdiv and a couple other cities are much better in terms of natural beauty. By then, it was too late. I had already booked a hostel in Bucharest. After coming back to Hostel Mostel, I decided to check out the city tour guide's live jazz recommendation. The bar was more like a modern lounge, but that was one of the rare nights when they didn't have a jazz band. Instead, they had one of the well-known Bulgarian bands playing Beatles music all night long. Not bad at all! Gone were the stoic faces of all the store-owners. In this bar, everyone was high on Beatles. People from all age groups were singing and dancing along to the mellow, lovey-dovey tunes. Maybe it had something to do with the $3 scotch-on-the-rocks. Yep, you read it right. Chives Regal, no less. With my low budget, the trip had been mostly alcohol-free, but Eastern Europe made it hard not to indulge!

The last four songs were *Let It Be*, *Imagine*, *Hey Jude* and *All You Need Is Love*. I guess there is no better way to end a Beatles night. But when the whole bar stood up and started swaying to *Imagine*, it made me wonder "Didn't they try *Imagine no possessions* in this part of the world? Human jealousy, hunger for power, and greed prevails, right?" Even decades after John Lennon's death, the hangover remains. Amazing how powerful music can be!

10. ROMANIA: 20:30? 20:40? OR 00:30 TO BUCHAREST?

June 7, 2012
Bucharest, Romania

Bucharest was a last-minute addition to the itinerary. On the map, it looked a little out of the way, but Skopje's loss was Bucharest's gain. Plus, I had seen a few Romanian movies like *12:08 East of Bucharest*, *California Dreamin'*, and *Death of Mr. Lazarescu*. These (mostly quirky) movies from the Romanian movie-renaissance era had piqued my curiosity about the country. This was my opportunity.

After doing ferries and buses in Greece, I really wanted to take the train, so I could lie down when traveling. The Bulgarian train website said the train to Bucharest was at 20:40. In this part of the world, the military style 24-hour clock is more common than the AM/PM business. When I reached the station at 20:35, the lady at the ticket booth refused to sell me the train ticket.

"The train is not here," she said.

"Well, I just want to buy one ticket. If it's not here yet, can I buy one ticket? Is the train full?" I asked.

"No, the train is gone."

"Wait, isn't the train at 20:40?"

"No, it was at 20:30."

Oh, well! Train travel was not meant to be. At least we shared a funny lost-in-translation moment. I walked over to the bus station nearby and found out the bus to Bucharest was leaving at 00:30. I had another 3-4 hours to kill. The French Open was on TV when I left the hostel. It made sense to go back and watch the matches instead of killing 4 hours at the bus stop. Pick up your backpack and start walking back! Every time I feel like walking is a pain in the butt, I think of Kilimanjaro now. It made the 1-1.5km walk back to the hostel much more bearable.

After another middle-of-the-night border crossing ritual on both sides, I made it to Bucharest with all my cramped up limbs and back still intact. The middle-aged prostitute in Sofia was replaced by another unsavory character in the wee hours of Bucharest. This tall, young Romanian, wearing a polo t-shirt and something that was halfway between cargo-shorts and capri pants, approached us three backpackers as soon as we got off the bus. With his spiky, gel-soaked hair, socks, and Crocs, he looked pretty goofy but the "Security" badge around his neck fooled me for a second. "Where are you from?" he asked. As soon as I said India, he said "Oh, Raj Kapoor. Awaara." That was impressive. Most of the Indians younger than me won't even get that Bollywood reference. As he followed me to the information booth and tried to force himself into a conversation as the translator, it was easy to tell he was a first-class bullshitter. When we started looking for a taxi to go from the bus stop to the central train station, he tried to scare us by saying that some combination of mafia and gypsies would kill us! As we finally found a taxi on our own, however, I noticed out the corner of my eye that he had quietly taken off the security badge around his neck. As we reached the train station safely, I learned that 1) Crocs and socks seemed to be acceptable professional footwear in Romania, 2) Bollywood references didn't always save you from getting ripped off, and 3) neither mafia nor gypsies run the taxi/public transport system in Bucharest.

At the hostel, I met up with two Danish girls and decided to tag along with them for sight-seeing. First stop, the gigantic monstrosity a.k.a. the Parliamentary Palace built during the Ceauşescu era. The building manages to evoke all kinds of emotions in you. At first sight, you are overwhelmed with its size. This is the second largest administrative building in the world, after the Pentagon. As the guide pointed out, the Pentagon is a military building, which makes this monstrosity the largest civilian administrative building in the world. From the outside, it is squarely square. Ceauşescu, the cold war era communist dictator of Romania, wanted to build something larger and grander in Bucharest than the Champs-Élysées. Larger it is, but grander? I'm not so sure. It lacks the beauty and aesthetics of the Champs-Élysées.

As you step inside, it manages to redeem some of its glory, just based on the sheer scale of everything. The guide said that almost everything used to build this monstrosity was made, mined, or manufactured in Romania. And everything – cement, steel, marble, crystals for the chandeliers, rugs, wood – was either in hundreds of thousands or millions of tons. After the first few statistics, it wouldn't have mattered if the guide had said 5 million tons instead of 1 million tons of such-and-such. It was all staggering. Some parts of the building looked beautiful, too. Some chandeliers, the big wooden doors with intricate carvings, grand hallways with red carpets; not bad at all!

The guide even told the story about how the BBC car show *Top Gear* was given special permission to race expensive sports cars in the basement parking lot of the building. Yeah, you can race cars in the basement of this building! It reminded me of a distinguished Indian friend of mine who once decided to go to the Pentagon parking lot to practice his driving skills before going for his driving test. And this was after 9/11! Not surprisingly, he got pulled over immediately and given a citation. The comparison with the Pentagon and the mention of the parking lot just made me think of my esteemed friend. I'm sure he is the only person to date, the only brown person, I should add, who thought practicing his driving skills in the Pentagon parking lot just after 9/11 was a good idea! I thought about interrupting the guide and saying, "Hey, I have a better one," but the crowd probably wouldn't have found it too amusing.

Anyway, my friend's antics are beside the point. The trip to this monument to Ceauşescu's ego lasted about 90 minutes. In those 90 minutes, we managed to see barely 5% of the building. The palace is that big. Even after having all the federal offices, the senate, the congress, the President's office in it, and then renting out parts of it for all kinds of conferences, they use only 30-40% of the building. The price tag? Someone calculated in 2001 that it took them around $12 billion Euros to build it. Man, you could bail out a country or two with that kind of money. Ask all the Greeks to move in and buy their whole land!

During the tour, the guide also gave us some nuggets about the Cold War era. I had learned about the mystery surrounding the Romanian revolution through *12:08 East of Bucharest*, but Ceauşescu was a big hole in my understanding of the Cold War history. It was interesting to learn how this megalomaniac was playing a double game with Russia and the West, how the Secretariat (the Romanian version of Stasi) spied on its own citizens and kept files on everyone, how the defection of his chief spy to the West destroyed his reputation, and how his attempts to pay back all external debt, combined with the money spent on this monstrosity, ended up starving the whole country. Apparently, by 1990, Romania had paid off all its external debt, but that was after the revolution had taken Ceauşescu's life and millions of Romanians had been forced into extreme poverty and starvation. In a lot of ways, Romanians are still trying to recover from that shock.

Sovereign debt is a tricky thing, isn't it? How much is too much? And how little is too little? Money, after all, is a man-made concept. Its intrinsic value is based on some intangibles, like trust and people's confidence in certain institutions. Wall Street said "Oh, we know what we are doing." American rating agencies said "Oh, we know what we are doing." All the banks in Iceland said "OK, we trust you. Here is all our money." One fine day, Lehman Brothers said "My bad" and poof! There went the entire banking system of Iceland. As one of my former next-door-neighbors used to say, "The best retirement plan is to own a decent-sized ranch to grow crops and raise some cattle".

Back to Bucharest. Other than this monstrosity, I found the city to be pretty charming. The two main thoroughfares are lined with buildings from all different eras, which make for an interesting collage. The city is not that old; the earliest records suggest it was established between the 1200s and 1400s. A baby compared to the other big European cities. But the old part of the city is beautiful, with a lively night-life, and so is Victory Boulevard. There are ruins of the courthouse of some fellow named Vlad, who used to terrorize the attacking Ottoman armies with his cruel torturing methods. They say Dracula's character is based on this guy. With no knowledge of Dracula, his legend, or his myriad movies, it was hard for me to contribute to that discussion. Next time someone talks about Dracula, I'll have something to contribute! And then, there are all kinds of churches tucked away behind the big buildings from all those different eras. I was told that communist-era officials had wanted to make people forget all religions other than the state religion. To make people forget Christianity, they built a lot of buildings around the churches, so they would be hidden from public view. What it does now is create a certain sense of mystery about all the churches.

All in all, I liked Bucharest, definitely better than Sofia. The locals hate the gigantic palace built by Ceauşescu, and understandably so. Other than one man's ego-trip, it's hard to justify its existence. But isn't that true of the pyramids in Egypt, too? The Pharaohs made thousands of people toil in the desert heat for decades to build something gigantic, so they could enjoy a happy (and hypothetical) after-life. Turbulent times and immense sacrifice were shoved down people's throats creating an icon of human imagination. All you can do is hope that, a century or two later, the Romanians will embrace the building as a part of their own history.

11. GERMANY: ONE HISTORY COCKTAIL, PLEASE!

July 1, 2012
Berlin, Germany

I'm in the European heartland now, learning and experiencing things faster than I can process them. Amsterdam, one of the busiest ports in the world, is where the concept of insurance, investment through stocks, and yes, the East India Company started. The British East India Company, one of the erstwhile rulers of India before the British royalty took over, was modeled on this Dutch East India Company. Then you have Bruges, a tiny city in Belgium, which used to be a bustling trading port until a flood came along and deposited massive amounts of silt, effectively pushing it inland. Bruges had to wait for Napoleon to come along to recover its lost charm. After conquering the city, he dug several canals, reconnected it to the ocean, and rebuilt the entire city. Some Europeans say that it feels like an artificial city, like Disneyland. As a fly-by tourist, I still think it's really pretty. All these stories, the intertwined legacies; it makes you feel like you could put all those history books in a mixer and drink it, once and for all, so that you know it all!

It's Berlin that takes the cake, though. Hands down! The amount of social, political, economic, and intellectual turmoil this city has seen is just staggering. Sure, there are other cities, like Istanbul and Delhi that have a rich past, but what makes Berlin so intriguing is the short period of time in which all the churning took place. Even if you spent a year walking around and exploring every nook and cranny of this city, I'm sure there would still be something new, something more to explore. When you are at the epicenter of two of the most destructive wars in the history of mankind, it has to be that way.

This is not the prettiest of European cities. You have the central district, with some imposing buildings, but 90% of the city was destroyed by the end of the Second World War. When hundreds of thousands are starving and without shelter, architecture is the last thing to worry about. To add to the uninspiring, square landscape, the reunification seems to have unleashed the graffiti artists, too, making this a graffiti city. Once you start walking around with your tour guide, all these square buildings come alive. The Berlin wall was standing here just a couple of decades ago. How did anyone think that locking up the entire city of West Berlin would actually work? The guide tells you that during the 11-month blockade and the Berlin airlift, there was a military plane landing in West Berlin every 60 seconds. For 11 months in a row? Just to save democracy in West Berlin? Wow!

Checkpoint Charlie is all jazzed up and touristy, just a stone's throw away from the Stasi museum. The Stasi network, the most extensive spy network the world has ever seen, had one spy for every 6.5 people! You probably need some kind of spy tax to run a country like that. The ghost metro stations and the Frederickstrasse station served as the gateways to West Berlin. And in spite of all this, you can meet old East Berliners who would say that life was better before the wall came down. Apparently, East Berlin never had those empty grocery store shelves or the long lines for food that had come to symbolize communism and life in the Soviet Union. They didn't have all the freedoms, but they had the basics. It's all very intriguing and perplexing at the same time.

But it's the Nazi history that is just unnerving. Our Third Reich tour guide, Sam, deserves special mention for his efforts. A PhD student of history, studying 18th century political satire, he was passionate enough about his job to recreate some of the important events. Even more interesting were the moral and ethical dilemmas we discussed as a group.

Sam spent a lot of time explaining the socio-economic crises that led to the war; the First World War, the punishing treaty of

Versailles, establishment of the Weimar republic, two cycles of hyperinflation in the 1920s, and then posed the counter-factual "If it weren't for Hitler, would we still have had the war?" In his opinion, yes, we would still have had it. Hitler was just a gifted orator who managed to ruthlessly exploit people's anger and despair. After thinking about it for a while, you say, "Yeah, that's probably true." Before you can finish that thought, you are standing on top of the underground bunker in which Hitler killed himself, symbolically stomping your feet all over him.

The tour takes you to the imposing Soviet War Memorial and you learn that they lost some 25-30 million soldiers in the war. This is one of the highest numbers of casualties in the Second World War. No matter how you feel about Soviet ideology and the atrocities they committed themselves, standing in front of the memorial is a humbling experience. After a moment of reflection, it makes you wonder...such an enormous human cost to end fascist atrocities, only to usher in an era of communist atrocities. It is all very disorienting.

It is easy to draw some modern-day parallels to these dilemmas, though none as destructive or brutal. Egypt's Mubarak ruled his own people with an iron fist, but kept the peace with Israel. Gaddafi gave up nuclear weapons so that others would let him do whatever he wanted with the Libyans. Obama's policies brought up similar moral dilemmas. He passed an executive order banning torture of captured "enemy combatants," yet he also drew up lists of terrorists he wanted to kill with drone strikes. It's a pain in the butt to handle captured terrorists, so why not just kill them, without due process, with an unmanned plane?

You then stand in front of the destroyed propaganda ministry building and learn about Goebbels's sickeningly successful campaign of posing the Jewish question and your mind goes numb. You look up to the Nazi Air Ministry Building, the Detlev-Rohwedder-Haus, one of the few surviving buildings from the war, and wonder how Goering managed to nearly take over all of Europe.

The killer, of course, is the site of the destroyed SS headquarters, the Topography of Terror. In a weird twist of fate, the Berlin wall shielded this site from the eyes of West Berlin during the cold war. Communist ideology hid the epicenter of fascist crimes with a wall. Standing in front of the ruins, the guide tells you about the systematic campaign to eliminate an entire race. When the discussion moves to Himmler and Auschwitz, he says "The camp was designed to solve the Jewish question by way of extermination. At the height of the war, it was running 24/7 and killing 175,000 people a month."

No matter how many times you've learned it from your history books, you hear those words in front of the SS headquarters and a chill goes down your spine. 175,000 a month? All the clouds of moral dilemma clear away and your mind says "Somebody please tell me this is not true."

Next stop, Auschwitz.

12. WATCH YOUR STEP, PLEASE!

July 4, 2012
Auschwitz, Poland

The day started on an ominous note. It was supposed to be almost 40 degrees Celsius in Kraków, with very high levels of humidity. The ten minute walk from the hostel to the bus stop was enough to make me feel like ripping my shirt off. The hour-long bus journey turned out to be a drag, too. But all of these so called first-world problems disappeared at the first sight of "Arbeit Macht Frei", the biggest lie in the world.

Barbed wires, one- or two-storied red brick buildings, square chimneys, 15-20 foot tall perimeter walls, and the periodic watch towers stand as mute witnesses to one of the worst tragedies humans have ever seen. The dehumanizers and the dehumanized are long gone, leaving behind inanimate objects to tell this horrible, heart-wrenching story.

I had expected this to be an emotionally charged day. I was actually dreading the thought of some tour guide like Berlin's Sam recreating the horrors of the holocaust for us, but this guide turned out to be one of the worst so far. From the first word to the last, the middle-aged Polish lady refused to put any emotion into her speeches. After the first ten minutes though, I wasn't sure whether I wanted anyone to do that for me.

The first part of the tour, which lasts for more than an hour, is actually not the worst part (it is all relative, really). The oldest part of the camp, Auschwitz - I, used to be Polish military barracks that were converted into a camp. Since liberation, this part now hosts the museum with some of the most depressing artifacts. It has hundreds of pictures of the victims; doctors, lawyers, welders, teachers, carpenters, blacksmiths, miners. It has the execution wall where thousands were killed with a gunshot to their heads. It also houses the first gas chamber, where Zyclon B was tested for the first time on Russian POWs. There were thousands of unpaired shoes of children who were killed. Two tons of hair, cut right before the victims were exterminated, was to be used like wool to make thermal and insulation products. Clothes belonging to little girls and hundreds of suitcases victims had brought to Auschwitz, hoping for a better life. It reminded me of a quote from *Up in the Air*. George Clooney's character asks the audience what they would pack if all they could take with them was just one suitcase. Not in a philosophical way, but in a very depressing way. Needless to say, all of this is just a fraction of all the evidence. As I was walking through the grim museum – a series of rooms filled with chambers, each chamber giving you a glimpse of the deepest stains on humanity through spotless glass windowpanes – I learned that there is a state of mind that goes beyond our ability to feel any emotion. It is beyond comprehension and it is an opportunity to learn what mind-numbing truly means. Your mind wants to deny this reality and escape from it, but the surrounding barbed wire holds it down. It is as if all humanity is sitting in those dark-brown watch towers, watching how we humans confront the worst of our own past.

But this is just a precursor to the real shocker; Birkanau or Auschwitz - II. After the decision was made to exterminate Jews, POWs, Jehovah's witnesses, blacks, homosexuals, and anyone and everyone who opposed Nazi rule, Birkanau was specially designed to be an efficient killing machine. The iconic train station, barracks full of bunk beds, and the now destroyed gas chambers and incinerators. The barren landscape, 37-38 degrees Celsius temperatures, and the high humidity were making our bodies cry. As we stepped into one of the barracks, the trapped heat suddenly made us feel like we had stepped into an oven. But when the guide informed us that the victims had to sleep here in winters with no sheets and one layer of clothing even when temperatures were below -20 degrees Celsius, my heart sank again for the umpteenth time and went into a deep freeze.

In a mere four hours, they wrapped up the tour; a brief history of the killing of more than a million people. But it gives you food for thought that will last you for the rest of your life; the most fundamental of which is the nature of evil. Berlin's Sam would argue that nobody is inherently evil and that atrocities can almost always be traced back to socio-economic factors. I don't necessarily agree with it. In my world of statistics, there are outliers on both sides. People like Hitler who, perhaps because of the way his brain worked, lacked empathy for a large group of people. And people like Gandhi, who famously addressed Hitler as "Dear friend" before pleading with him to abandon his campaign of pogrom. It's a thought provoking argument, nonetheless. Human rights, after all, have a very short history. Just a few centuries ago, in Roman times, treatment far worse than this was considered acceptable (on a much smaller scale though). Even today, stoning and cutting off of hands as punishment are morally accepted in some societies. Although we seem to be moving toward more humane societies, some of the most advanced nations haven't abolished the death penalty even today.

I happen to be against the death penalty, but when is the killing of a human being justified? Can it be justified? Even Hindu scriptures famously justify killing in the name of "dharma," or a just cause. When I was in Norway, I got into a discussion with some locals about Breivik, the Norwegian terrorist who killed 77 people in the infamous 2011 attack. According to Norway's laws, if he is proven to be mentally unstable, he will live in a hospital under full state surveillance. If he is proven to be mentally stable, he will live in a jail for the rest of his life. The price tag to keep him in a hospital or a prison is estimated to be about $5000/day. Who is picking up the tab? It is the Norwegian taxpayers, some of whom are victims and their relatives. Given all the oil resources Norway enjoys, it is easy to argue that they can afford to pick up the tab. But what if Breivik were a Somalian, shooting innocent and starving people waiting in line to get food aid? Would it make sense for the bankrupt Somalian state to save Breivik for $5000/day for the sake of the anti-death-penalty principle? Or save 5000 starving children with $1/day? I am, admittedly, ambivalent about such hypotheticals and at peace with my ambivalence, but I would like to know what a staunch anti-death-penalty activist thinks about it. And if killing a human being can be justified, are we back to socio-economic factors as the genesis of evil?

These thoughts are obviously tangential to the evil you are confronted with at Auschwitz, but even this tragedy of unprecedented proportions brings up issues of its own. The punishing treaty of Versailles led to the first cycle of hyperinflation in Germany. Introduction of a new German currency corrected it, only for the Americans to invest heavily in Germany in the early-to-mid- 1920s, then ask for their money back during the Great Depression. The second cycle of hyperinflation, combined with a wave of xenophobia and the rise of fascism, pushed humanity to the Second World War. Even in Auschwitz, the healthier inmates were the ones lying to those entering the gas chambers, telling them they were just entering the bathrooms to get a shower. If I had a gun to my forehead, I would probably lie, too, but that is beside the point. It is easy to blame everything on the Nazis. The more difficult lesson to learn is that we are all in it together.

In Auschwitz - I, the guide was telling us "Watch your step, please" every time we were leaving a room. With all those clothes, shoes, utensils, and suitcases on display, this announcement sounded facetious. Watch your step? Really? It was borderline insulting to all the victims who died here...and those who survived. Or maybe it's just me. Sometimes, the litigious Western culture, and the Western sensibility it has spawned seem hopelessly out of place. Back in the hostel, as I was taking a shower, getting ready to board my train to Prague, I felt that maybe it is a message to all humanity.

We humans are notoriously bad at learning from history. For someone like me, who staunchly believes in evolution, our animalistic tendencies probably force us to develop a strong sense of cultural and social identity, and even to kill in the name of preserving such identities. For those of you who have seen the famous battle between the heads of two monkey tribes, it is easy to understand that if we are also animals, on a different evolutionary branch, war-mongering instincts are natural. Sure, as Steven Pinker seems to argue in his book, *The Better Angels of Our Nature*, we seem to be moving toward a less savage world. With our large prefrontal cortex, our enhanced ability to feel empathy, and other mental faculties at our disposal, maybe it's not too surprising that we can go beyond the narrow definitions of "my society" and recognize the value of not destroying other cultures, but instead, learning from them. We have even developed means and weapons to minimize collateral damage. In this co-dependent globalized world, countries can ill-afford the human toll. In today's complex world, wars seem to be moving away from conventional conflict to the realm of currency manipulation and cyber warfare. That is the good news.

But the world is becoming so strange that traditionally "good" economic behavior, such as that of the Swiss, gets punished in today's economic collapse. They have to announce their appetite for unlimited capital controls just to keep their economy competitive amid a global economic meltdown. Can you predict the reason for the next big war? And the means with which it will be fought? Even in these paradoxical, confusing times, the bottom line remains. In the face of adversity, it doesn't take us humans too long to fall back on our prejudices and cultural identities.

As we usher in tomorrow's complicated and globalized world, full of unintended consequences, I think it is important for everyone to visit Auschwitz. Before using tomorrow's tools to fight tomorrow's wars, I hope the lady at Auschwitz will appear in your dreams, urging you to "Watch your step, please." After all, at the end of the First World War, I'm sure nobody thought we humans would be stupid enough to have another one and, more importantly, have the holocaust. As the Argentinians would say, "Nunca mas", or never again.

13. CZECH REPUBLIC: WEIRDLY BEAUTIFUL & BEAUTIFULLY WEIRD

July 7, 2012
Prague, Czech Republic

Weirdly beautiful and beautifully weird. In one sentence, that's Prague for you. After visiting Auschwitz, things can only get better, and there is no better way to make things better than to visit Prague. It is eccentric, eclectic, weird; it is the anti-Paris. Paris is all about its beige-and-grey architecture, its gardens, its cafes, French wine, the Eiffel Tower, wide-open waterfront, and Champs-Élysées. Prague is anything but that. For starters, it has a lot more hills than the flat Paris; something I would love for every city to have. Paris is a city of flat-top buildings; Prague is the city of spires. Parisian coffee and a glass of Bordeaux are replaced by beer and a glass of absinthe in Prague. The beer here is so cheap it will convert even a non-beer-fan like me in a matter of days. Unlike Paris, there is virtually no theme to the architecture of Prague. Parisian architecture makes it charming; the eclectic mix of architectural styles in Prague makes it mysterious. The 3-4 storied buildings are just enough to hide what's around the corner. And whatever is around the corner will always surprise you and draw you to the next corner. If there is one thing the two cities have in common, it is that they are both cities in which you can wander around aimlessly for hours and still not get bored.

Some of Prague's weirdness might be for historic reasons. Paris has always been the epicenter of everything French. Prague, on the other hand, has been all things to all people. And all things to all countries. In the past one hundred years, the name and character of the country to which Prague has belonged have changed at least nine times! They tried the Austro-Hungarian Empire, a couple of monarchies, communism, and Czechoslovakia, to finally settle on Czech Republic. And this is all reflected very well in the architecture of this city. But a lot of it comes from self-inflicted wounds. Or, as I would like to call it, self-inflicted beauty. The main gothic cathedral in the old town square has two spires of identical design, but one is larger than the other. The famous astronomical clock in the old town square is also the largest cuckoo clock, putting on an elaborate musical show every hour. If that is not enough, they also have a Hebrew clock in the Jewish quarter that runs counter-clockwise!

Then there is the church with a human hand hanging from one of the walls. According to legend, a thief tried to steal something from the priest's wife a few hundred years ago. The town decided to cut his hand off, carefully embalm it, and hang it from the church wall to deter others from stealing. You can see the hand, in all its glory, hanging by a chain. There are lots of other churches all around the city, but since 90% of the country is atheist, the trustees of the churches weren't sure what to do with all those churches, so a lot of them have been converted into bars, clubs, hotels, and restaurants.

Then there is the Prague castle. The palace of Versailles, just outside Paris, is considered a fine example of French architecture. The Prague castle, on the other hand, has buildings with all types of architecture. Due to budgetary problems, it took a thousand years to complete this castle. Instead of sticking to one style, they decided to build buildings with the prevailing styles over those thousand years. The main cathedral in the castle was intended to be gothic, but they ran out of money and had to halt construction halfway through. When they finally got the money to finish it, the architect decided it would be okay to throw a baroque spire into the middle of a bunch of gothic spires.

The story behind the bone church, in the neighboring town of Kutna Hora, is equally weird. A few hundred years ago, a priest brought some holy soil from Jerusalem to Kutna Hora to bury prominent members of society. Before he knew it, everyone was burying their dead in the holy soil. For a few decades after it was full, the graveyard was an abandoned piece of land. One fine day, someone decided to build a church and started digging around. Even after discovering all the human bones, he decided to go ahead with the construction of the church. What do you do with all those bones? He decided to decorate the entire church with all those bones. What do you get? A church with a human-bone chandelier, a few showcases artfully decorated with human bones, the cross surrounded by a bunch of bones, and a huge plaque made out of, once again, human bones.

Back in Prague, rain played a bit of a spoilsport when it came to nightlife. On each of the three nights I had in Prague, it started raining just as we were all getting ready to go out. Even on the day of the Italy-Spain Euro cup football final, when there were hundreds of people out in the old town square enjoying the match on the gigantic screens, it started pouring halfway through the second half. By that time, though, the Spaniards had effectively sealed the deal. The only thing we missed was the humiliation part.

Bad weather notwithstanding, this city keeps wowing you for as long as you can walk. It keeps challenging your sense of continuity, drawing you in until you completely fall in love with it. If you have to choose three European cities to visit, I think you should pick Paris, Berlin, and Prague. It's that good! The Czech people, though, seemed a little bit cold. It was pretty difficult to talk to the local people. At first, I thought it was due to the language barrier, but I found out on my third day there that it is mostly because of the country's communist past. Like a lot of other Eastern-bloc countries, espionage was rampant in the communist-era Czech Republic. The people here haven't recovered from all the mistrust yet. On that same third day, though, as I was about to write off Czech people as being too cold for comfort, I hopped onto a train to visit Kutna Hora and sat next to an absolute stunner. Or a "tenner," in guy-speak. For the first half hour or so, she was mostly playing defense. Pretty normal girl stuff. But during the next half hour she managed to change my perception of Czech people.

Mysterious Prague is not just mysterious anymore. It's intriguing, too!

14. AUSTRIA: SO, YOU THINK YOU CAN BACKPACK?

July 14, 2012
Vienna, Austria

After navigating the mysterious world of Prague, it was time to enjoy the idyllic world of Vienna. Apparently, Vienna has been consistently ranked in the top five cities in the world when it comes to standard of living and people's happiness. But on my way to Viennese heaven, I managed to pull a hip muscle. In hindsight, it was probably a blessing in disguise, because Vienna doesn't offer much to backpackers. It is actually a nice European city. Mozart used to play music here regularly. He wouldn't choose a bad city to call his home, but it seems like you need a lot of money to enjoy the true treasures of Vienna. Things like watching ballets and operas in the grand opera house, going to a classical music concert, visiting the art gallery to watch the Gustav Klimt collection, or watching a Shakespearean play; this town is all about highbrow entertainment.

But you can trust backpackers to find avenues of cheap entertainment. There was a free open-air film-festival. Unfortunately, the theme of the festival was musicals and biographies of famous ballet dancers; still highbrow for a group of travelers. Next on the list? A tram party! Once a year, the public transport authorities convert one tram into a club and keep it running around town all night long. Strobe lights, dance music, cute Austrian girls selling beer and rum-and-cokes, and a jam-packed tram. Sold! I've been in Europe for a few weeks now and the music scene here is totally different than the one in the United States. You have the occasional hip-hop or R&B song, but the scene is dominated by a hardy mix of techno, house, trance, and Latin American music.

The quick Salzburg stopover was ruined by bad weather. It wasn't as if I was dying to do the Sound of Music tour, but it would've been nice if it hadn't been raining all the time. The only thing the weather allowed me to enjoy was the Werfen ice caves. Tucked away high up in the Alps, these caves get virtually no sunshine throughout the year. The sub-zero temperatures inside the dark caves have created gigantic stalactites and stalagmites out of ice. The 50-to-100 foot ice domes and all the other weird ice formations are a treat to see, but it's unfortunate that photography is prohibited in the caves.

From the frigid temperatures of the ice caves, the next stop was the town of Split in Croatia, where temperatures were nearly 40 degrees Celsius, with lots of humidity. Still nursing my pulled hip muscle, it was difficult to enjoy it all, but if you are looking for a not-so-expensive European destination with lots of natural beauty, this is the spot. And then, a group of British girls asked me to join them for dinner, making things even warmer. They were all students, studying art, history, philosophy, and film-making. When the topic turned to blogging and making documentaries, one of the girls said her dad was in the movie industry. When I probed around a bit more, she told me he is an actor and generally plays the quirky, elderly British guy in movies. Who was this guy? Maybe he played some minor roles here and there, but I needed to know more.

"Have you seen *Mama Mia*?"

"- Nope."

"Have you seen *Pride and Prejudice*?"

"- Nope."

"Have you seen *The King's Speech*?"

"- Of course! Wait, he is your dad?" I asked incredulously.

"Yes, but let's not talk about it."

I asked two of her friends whether that was true. Not because I thought she was lying, but because you don't expect to bump into such people when backpacking. Two thumbs up for being so grounded! If you are reading this, you know who you are.

Out of sheer curiosity, I got back to the hostel and searched online to check whether he has a daughter. I couldn't find anything and left it at that. In any case, walking around with a limp hampered my ability to go out hiking, but it made me think about all the not-so-sexy aspects of these long-term backpacking trips. Obviously, there are lots of different ways of doing such trips. Some decide to work along the way; earning money and then spending it in the country they are staying in. Some take it easy and decide to cover just a handful of countries in one year, learning a lot about a few countries. No matter how you try to do it, it forces you to make some lifestyle adjustments. My ambitious plan of hitting 30-odd countries in one year was no different. A shoe-string budget didn't make it any easier.

As I was finishing up three months of my trip, I thought I would jot down a few fun-facts, not-so-fun facts, tips, tricks, warnings, and other random perils of being on the road all the time.

Long-term backpacking

Long-term backpacking is the ultimate non-marathon marathon. I've seen some of my former roommates run marathons. It takes extreme amounts of physical discipline to prepare for and actually finish a marathon. Sure, you need a lot of fiscal discipline if you are backpacking on a low budget, but any semblance of a physical routine goes out the window on Day 1. You still have to keep going.

To visit Abu Simbel from Aswan, the tour leaves at 4 AM, which means you have to get up at 3:30 AM. The cheapest ferry from Santorini to Crete is at 3 AM. So just stay up all night and get to the docks at 2:30 AM. The flight from Tel Aviv to Athens is at 7 AM, but everyone warns you that you need to get to the airport by 4 AM to jump through all the airport security hoops. The airport is outside the city and there is no public transportation at 3 AM. You don't want to pay $40 for the 3 AM taxi, so take the last train and reach the airport at 1 AM. Sleep at the airport for 2-3 hours and submit yourself to intense interrogation when you are half-asleep.

Soaps

All soaps are equal, but some soaps are less equal than others.

When you are traveling with five T-shirts, you can't afford to put that smelly one in your backpack. Everything else will start smelling before you know it. Plus, you can't bank on finding laundry services in every hostel. Welcome to washing your clothes every day. It's not a big deal, really. It just adds some annoying 10-15 minutes to your bathing ritual. You realize that when you start washing your clothes every day, it doesn't take too long for the skin on your fingers to start peeling off. But that's a minor issue. The bigger problem is that you start running out of soap all the time. Instead of running to the grocery store every week, you decide that the liquid hand soap in the hostels is a legitimate substitute for detergent. Pretty soon, you end up in a hostel that doesn't refill the empty liquid soap dispensers. And your shower gel is just enough for one shower. So shampoo becomes a legitimate substitute for detergent. One fine day, you reach the island of Hvar and climb up a couple of kilometers in sweltering heat to find a hostel. You unpack and realize that you have run out of shower gel and shampoo. You are too tired to go all the way down the hill just to get some soap. You just want to take a quick shower and take a nap before your brain can start working again. On such days, liquid hand soap is a legitimate substitute for shampoo and shower gel. Then the big day arrives. You end up in a hostel that doesn't have a kitchen. You walk into the bathroom and start washing your clothes before taking a shower. You pour the liquid soap and start rinsing the clothes, but they smell a bit funny. You check the soap dispenser and realize that you have used dish-washing liquid to wash your clothes. Since the hostel doesn't have a kitchen, they have kept the dish-washing liquid in the bathroom for people who still want to wash some utensils. Damn it! Some soaps are definitely less equal than others.

The back and the stomach

Your back and stomach are ticking time bombs. And so is the rest of your body. You will most likely never see pictures of the dorm rooms I stayed in because you don't want to know what kind of mattresses I slept on every day. It's fine if it's a bad mattress. Your back gets used to it after awhile. But when you sleep on mattresses that are bad, worse, worse, bad, worst, worst, worse, all in one week, your back starts screaming. You have to incorporate a solid 10-15 minute stretching session into your daily routine.

The kind of food you eat doesn't keep your stomach happy, either. If you want to stay reasonably healthy and escape the cycle of diarrhea and constipation, you have to constantly remind yourself to eat enough veggies, fruits, meat, and bread. When you walk into a grocery store, the aisles are not full of food items anymore. All you see on the shelves are protein, fiber, vitamins, carbs, and anti-oxidants. Even then, if you are like me and have a penchant for eating street food, there is no way to escape the occasional bout of diarrhea. As my granddad used to say, starve yourself for one day and you will be back to normal.

Your back and stomach are the most vulnerable, but other parts of your body are not too far behind. Your hips are not used to running when you have a 10-12 kg backpack strapped to your back. When you try to do that to catch European trains that are almost always on time, they give up. It's not rocket science. When you are running with your backpack, the backpack builds its own momentum. When you stop to board the train, your body stops, but the backpack keeps going; taking your upper body for a ride. When that happens, that hip muscle you didn't even know you had starts protesting. Some of this running is self-inflicted. If you hadn't spent those extra 5 minutes on the toilet seat reading on your smartphone why Federer is the greatest of all time for the millionth time, you wouldn't have had to run to catch the train. But then you remind yourself that it's Federer we are talking about. If he can stay fit and at the top of such a demanding sport for such a long time, you should be able to take care of such minor niggles. A not-so-fit, yet fitting tribute to a champion!

But some of these sprints are unavoidable. You go to the Eagle's Nest, just outside of Salzburg, to see Hitler's summer guest house up in the Alps. It's supposed to have some of the most breath-taking views of the Alps. The thick cloud cover reduces your visibility to less than 10 feet, ruining your trip. On top of that, they come back 30-40 minutes late. Instead of having an hour to catch your train, now you have just 20 minutes. Run, Forrest, run!

Smoking

People around the world smoke...like chimneys. In countries like Egypt, smoking bans in public places are either non-existent or not enforced. When you get into a taxi, the driver rolls up all the windows, blasts the AC, lights a cigarette, and offers you one. You look outside at the bumper-to-bumper Cairo traffic and all the noxious fumes surrounding the car. What kind of poison do you want to breathe? It's a tough choice! Even in so-called first world countries like Italy and France, where smoking bans in public places are strictly enforced, smoking hasn't lost its charm. It is socially well-accepted. Having spent the last decade or so in the United States, I was a bit fussy for the first few days about my clothes smelling like smoke. But it didn't take me too long to realize that in a lot of these countries, everyone smells like smoke. You just have to get used to it.

A sense of direction

Develop a sense of direction and a sense of timing. When you are walking out of a train station in a new city every third day, it is exhausting to stare at new maps all the time. Developing a sense of direction by looking at your own shadow helps a lot. So does developing a sense of timing. If you are an American, the first step is to get a feel for the kilometer-to-mile conversion. Everywhere else in the world, the kilometer system is fairly well-entrenched. It is very common to hear people say "Go 600 meters and take a left." And more often than not, those 600 meters will be on a winding road. Developing a sense of how long it takes you to walk 600 meters, with or without the backpack, will go a long way.

Money

Money matters. It matters a lot when you are trying to survive on a $100/day budget. On top of that, currency keeps changing every few days and you have to constantly calculate how much a carton of milk or a liter of orange juice is in US Dollars. To make things worse, countries like Norway have currency units that are cheaper than the US Dollar, but are some of the most expensive countries in the world. When you withdraw money from a Norwegian ATM, you feel like you are the richest man in the world, but even a basic dinner is 150 NKR. Before you know it, you are making another run to the ATM! *Why didn't I think about it when I was withdrawing money the first time around?*

Body language

Learn body language. It is more useful than any other language in the world, when it comes to round-the-world trips. As exhausting as it is, you get used to keeping your guard up at all times. What helps you the most in avoiding catastrophes is understanding body language. When people notice that you look Indian, they start saying all kinds of things like Namaste, Gandhi, Raj Kapoor, Amitabh Bacchhan, Shahrukh Khan, Kareena Kapoor, Delhi, Mumbai, Taj Mahal, Sholay, Chicken Tikka Masala, Ramayan, Mahabharata; you name it! You want to believe that the guy means well, but your brain has to be tuned to the non-verbal cues at all times to make sure you don't end up on the streets with no money and no luggage.

Walking and waiting

Get ready to walk a lot and wait a lot. I have already mentioned walking a few times. Even with the great European public transport systems, sight-seeing requires you to walk a lot. Approximately four to five kilometers a day. If you don't want to waste your precious money on taxis, add some more walking to the mix. Then there is waiting. Train delays are rare, but not unheard of in Europe. And sometimes, you try to wrap up the tour early because it is unbearably hot. You have already checked out of your hostel and you are carrying your luggage with you. You have six hours to kill. What do you do? Hit the train station, find a shade, and wait. These are the times when hobbies like reading and writing come to your rescue. You also thank Pink Floyd a lot for composing inordinately long songs and creating concept albums. *Echoes*...25 minutes. *Dogs*...17 minutes. *Division Bell*...a solid hour and a half. Is it time to board yet?

Complaining

Most importantly, stop complaining, mostly because there is no one to complain to. It would be nice if, instead of half the people in your dorm sleeping at 4 AM and half of them waking up at 6 AM, everyone went to sleep at 11 PM and woke up at 7 AM. It would be nice if someone gave you a back massage. It would be nice if you didn't have to walk five kilometers in 40 degrees Celsius and 80% humidity to get to your hostel. It would be nice if someone washed your clothes after you'd spent the entire day hiking around Cappadocia in the dry desert heat. It would be nice if it didn't rain in those fifteen minutes when you are desperately running to catch your train, holding your butt with your left hand because that pulled muscle is hurting a lot. It would be nice if you could just not worry about money and enjoy a sumptuous dinner, overlooking the white buildings and blue domes of Santorini. It would be nice if the Bulgarian grocery store owner understood the word "milk" and didn't sell you buttermilk instead.

But then, the Bulgarian immigration guy wakes you up at 2 AM when you are desperately trying to catch up on sleep in a cramped minibus going from Thessaloniki to Sofia. He takes your passport away and comes back after half an hour to hand it back to you. Half asleep, you flip the pages of your passport to see how the Bulgarian stamp looks and what it says. With every flipped page, you can feel your travel ego getting a boost. But when you get to the page with the Bulgarian stamp, your mind goes back to the Palestinian refugee camp. For a moment, the helpless face of the 21-year old refugee who cannot even get a passport flashes in front of your eyes. You close your passport, slip it back into your front pocket, and go back to sleep with a word of thankfulness and a sense of contentment.

15. ITALY: IN THE DIVIDED STATES OF ITALY

July 21, 2012
Sperlonga, Italy

In the divided states of Italy, do as the tourists do. There is so much to do and so much to see in this country that I am declaring Italy a new continent, at least for tourism and travel writing purposes. Plus, there are so many tourists here that if you just tag along with one of these groups, you will end up seeing the whole country. Even after a mere two weeks in this country, and sticking just to the main attractions, it's hard to believe that these damn tourists have left any parts of Italy unexplored. There are so many of them, even tourists get annoyed with other tourists. But the real problem is that this country has something for everyone. It is difficult to describe all things Italian in one chapter, but let's give it a shot.

Venice, not Virginia, is for lovers. Oddly enough, I had one of the most unlikely reunions in Venice. Nothing romantic, really, but interesting, for sure. From the day I decided to do a round-the-world trip, lots of friends and family members had promised me that they would meet me here and hang out with me there. For one reason or another, their plans had not materialized. One fine day in Croatia, I got an email from the crazy Brazilian guy I had traveled with in South America on a motorcycle four years before. When I started this trip, I emailed him and told him I would visit Brazil sometime in 2013, but never heard back from him...until I reached Croatia. The dude was finishing up some summer course in London. We decided to meet again in Venice. Not a very romantic story, but a decent one for Venice, I guess.

So, Venice was a blur! On a liquid diet of local Chianti, priced at 2 Euros a bottle, it was fun to catch up with "el otro loco" or the other crazy guy. All of a sudden, the gondola ride wasn't necessary to enjoy Venice. Just walking around town and seeing how this guy talked to the entire world and got himself in and out of trouble was wholesome, free entertainment.

This shouldn't take anything away from the city, though. Sure, this mosquito-infested city is smelly at times. But what do you expect from a city floating on water and sinking a few millimeters a year? Once you get over the smell, the itch, and the fact that the city is burning a hole through your pocket, there are way too many reasons to fall in love with this city. If you think Prague is mysterious and makes you lose your sense of direction quickly, try walking around Venice. You will get lost even with a map in your hand. And here we were, two guys who don't believe in maps. On one of our nights in Venice, we heard that there was a free music concert somewhere on the island. By the time we got there, the concert was over, but the crowd there didn't disappoint us. I bumped into two Italian students learning Hindi! Having spent the last decade or so in the United States, I discovered that talking in proper Hindi was really difficult for me. I couldn't even sprinkle a bunch of English words in the middle. Their first language was Italian. It was a timely reminder of how bad my Hindi had become (Disclaimer: I'm working under the assumption that Mumbai Hindi is good Hindi). After just an hour's worth of conversation, I was mentally exhausted!

But my Brazilian amigo was not done partying yet. We decided to part ways because I was thinking about calling it a night. I was fairly confident of my sense of direction and thought that I'd be back in my bed in half an hour. After an hour of crossing all kinds of bridges and bumping into a dozen or so dead ends, I ended up in the same square I started in. These canals will make you think you know where the hell you are going. Not true! After wasting that one hour, I was thinking about starting in the same direction and forcing myself to take "wrong" turns in order to find my hostel. But miraculously enough, I bumped into my amigo and some of the new friends he had made. After another couple hours of revelry, we finally managed to stumble our way back home.

For the millions of tourists who actually follow maps, Venice has Piazza del San Marco, the central market, the art gallery, and gondola rides. For me, the most charming part of the city was getting lost in those canals and walking around aimlessly (well, not quite) at 2 o'clock in the morning. Every once in awhile, we turned a corner and saw a homeless person sitting in a corner or a drunk guy peeing in a dark alley. I felt like telling the peeing guy "Dude, the canal is right there!" In Venice, though, I was willing to give him the benefit of doubt. He probably tried his best to find the canal, but gave up after awhile. Such unpleasant surprises, though, are no match for the dimly lit facade of some small, not-so-touristy church, or the sight of the middle-of-the-night ferry you can see at a distance, but cannot get to, whizzing by through the Grand Canal. In Venice, you don't walk around to get anywhere. You just walk around to fall in love with the city.

The lack of sleep in Venice kept haunting me even after I reached Florence. The map told me to head east to find my hostel, but it took me a good half hour of walking west to realize I was heading in the wrong direction. It wasn't too bad, after all, because I managed to bump into Santa Maria Novella without reading or hearing anything about it. When you change cities twice a week, there is no way you can read up on every city you are planning to visit. Even the train station here is called "Firenze S.M.N." hinting that S.M.N. might be a big deal. But all I could care about was ensuring that Firenze is Florence. S.M.N.? Who cares? Care you will, when you accidentally bump into Santa Maria Novella. Even in the 35 degrees Celsius heat with my backpack on, I just couldn't stop staring at this marvel for a solid 10-15 minutes. All the heat and the seemingly endless chatter of the throngs of tourists surrounding me dissipated instantly and I was left with pure bliss! Built in the 1400s or 1500s, this imposing church defines the city of Florence. It is considered the epitome of Italian architecture and the paintings and frescos inside are supposed to be some of the best renaissance era art in the world. Unfortunately, the line to get in was so long that I would have had to tolerate the heat and my backpack for at least a couple of hours to enter the church. The art could wait.

Go to the hostel, freshen up, hydrate yourself, and head to

Piazzale Michelangelo to view the sunset. Mamma Mia! As the city opens her arms to embrace her lover, the one who gives her such a beautiful glow every day, she also takes all those breathless tourists into her magnanimous embrace.

Italy wasn't all about beauty and grandeur, though. The tour next day demystified some of the Roman history for me. Two hours is hardly enough time to even scratch the surface of a two-thousand-year old empire, but for someone schooled in India, Roman history is like Martian geology or solid-state physics. Four to five thousand years of Indian history is so overwhelming that the Indian educational system has no time to waste on teaching kids Roman history. It was fun to finally learn how the Roman Empire, and the subsequent Byzantine Empire, weren't just monoliths. There was constant infighting among various provinces for gaining the upper hand. Among them, the Florentine and Sienese skirmishes are things of yore. Learning that Florence was a republic and Siena was more authoritarian, how the Florentines, after collecting taxes from the public, managed the construction of S.M.N. to be the most spectacular church, and how the church played an active role in all aspects of statecraft, helps you understand the complexities of Roman times. These age-old regional and cultural fissures have morphed into the modern-day political rivalry between the north and the south; making one wonder whether yesterday's Romans or today's Italians were ever a united country. However, the relentlessness with which I was being bombarded with historic monuments and endless throngs of tourists didn't allow me to think much about the divided states of Italy.

If Florentine renaissance art of Leonardo da Vinci and Michelangelo is not your cup of tea, the leaning tower of Pisa is just a stone's throw away. As if the tourists are going to go "This renaissance art is all fine, but Italy really needs one of those Seven Wonders of the World. Otherwise, there is no point in going to Italy." While on the topic of Florence, though, the best part of my short stay here was scoring an invitation to a barbecue hosted by a friend of an ex-colleague's ex-colleague. Yeah, bit of a stretch, but how could I turn down an invitation to enjoy home-cooked Tuscan food? In the world of backpacking, that would be a cardinal sin. Getting to the party venue, a summer home with a huge backyard in a small Tuscan village, was a bit tricky. The couple who had invited me to the party and graciously picked me up lost their way and politely switched to Italian to fight about who was right. The lady had an inkling, early on, that we had missed the turn, but the gentleman was confident that we were on the right track. When it became obvious that we had lost our way, he was reluctant to talk to the hosts on the phone and get the right directions. When it turned out that the lady was right, boy did he get an earful! Some things don't change...they are so basic they easily cross the language barrier.

That was just a fun prelude to the party. These men and women, in their late fifties and sixties, had been friends for more than 30 years and made it a point to get together on a regular basis. Most of them talked in Italian most of the time, while I maintained a laser sharp focus on my gluttony. This wasn't a structured 3-course or 7-course dinner party. It was a barbecue, with no rhyme or reason to it, and this eternally starved backpacker could not have cared less. The wine was flowing and so were all kinds of meats. And for the older, Italian friends, all kinds of animated hand gestures were in use. The wine made the language more lucid and the hand gestures more forceful. For a stranger, with a cursory understanding of Italian, just the site of such old friendships was worth cherishing. The details weren't that important anyway. Old friendships keep getting stronger by reminiscing about the same old and seemingly insignificant shared experiences.

As if all the history and culinary art are not enough, the earth has opened up a hole called Vesuvius in the middle of this country. A few hundred years ago, the ashes coming out of it famously asphyxiated people in Pompeii. A normal person would just take a quick, two-hour tour and move on. I had to take the audio guide and walk around the ancient town in the 35 degrees Celsius heat for seven hours. The map accompanying the audio guide told me there were some 80-odd places of interest in the city. I had to go to each of them and listen to what the audio guide had to say about each place. After point # 60 or so, even the audio guide gave up. Apparently, there was no more information to be absorbed. I was worried that if I punched in some number beyond 70, it would tell me "Dude, stop punching buttons and go back home." But it's hard to stop. To be honest, it was nothing like what I had expected. I had had some romantic notions of seeing lots of people frozen in the middle of their daily activities...in their homes, their shops, and on the streets. Other than a handful of asphyxiated people carefully preserved in glass enclosures, it is mostly a barren landscape of cobblestone roads and all kinds of houses, storefronts, and administrative buildings. The people "in action" I wanted to see are wisely preserved and tucked away in museums, but the careful preservation of the entire city paints a damn good picture of life in the Roman/post-Roman times. If you are a history buff and are going to Pompeii in the middle of summer, please carry a bottle or three of water with you. Consider yourself forewarned.

Things kept getting better as I hit the Amalfi coast. After blessing Italy with Venice, Florence, and Pompeii, did they really need to put such a beautiful coast in there? Maybe they should have put it in Moldova, so it would have become a major tourist destination overnight. But history and nature are both biased toward Italy. I have actually done coasts before. I have done a couple thousand kilometers on the west coast of South America and about a thousand kilometers from San Diego to San Francisco in the United States. Even then, picking up a two-wheeler and riding along the coast has not lost any of its charm. I wonder if it ever will. After teaming up with three other backpackers, I went from Sorrento to Amalfi on one of those mean machines. The wind ruffling my hair, tiny streams of water running through the corners of my eyes, and a sense of freedom in my head; everyone who loves riding motorcycles should do this trip. The Amalfi Mountains will blow your mind. The most enduring memory of my two weeks in Italy will always be floating in the warm waters of the Amalfi beach, looking up at the spires of the local churches on the backdrop of the tall mountains, and letting the world around me fade away...

And where do I even begin with Rome? It was everything I expected it to be...and then some. For the three days I was there, I heard a lot of people complain that it is a dirty city. The monuments are all dusty and a generous dose of cleansing wouldn't hurt. To me, though, that's part of the charm of the city. This IS an old city. The center of the Western world for more than a thousand years! It has all the famous monuments; the palaces, piazzas, cathedrals, the Colosseum, and all that. But what I liked the most about this city were the tiny reminders of Roman times scattered throughout. Every few hundred meters, you will see a few Roman columns. Or, on some nondescript street corner, you will notice a small water fountain; the water coming out of a lion's or fish's mouth. Someone decided to keep the Roman facade of some old building before converting the rest of the building into a modern structure. All this, even when huge swaths of the city remain underground and unexplored. One local ordinance here bans digging underground beyond a meter or so, even if it is your own backyard. Athens left me a bit high and dry because the ancient city is rarely visible, but these not-so-glamorous remnants, sprinkled among the big monuments in Rome, help you recreate the whole city in your mind.

And whatever your mind fails to recreate, the Vatican will recreate for you. The Vatican Museum and the Sistine Chapel were like the cherry on top of the sundae. This small area within the city of Rome is a country of its own; and deservedly so. Religious people have their own reasons to consider this place a separate country. Even for an atheist like me, though, the quality and quantity of historic relics this institution has amassed in its museum makes it rival national treasures all over the world. The Roman-era sculptures help you enrich your mental image of Rome. The paintings, frescos, ruins, and other artifacts of the Vatican museum, spanning all human civilizations, are just mind-boggling. In half a day, all you can do is just scratch the surface of this museum, figuratively speaking.

If you are not impressed by any of this, just wait until the sun goes down. It will be impossible for you not to fall in love with this city when they light up all the monuments and fountains in the night. Good luck trying to capture it with your camera.

Meeting "el otro loco" or my Brazilian friend, again in Rome meant we had to end our Italy reunion with a bang. A spontaneous, nonsensical decision to spend the last night on a beach in the nearby town of Sperlonga seemed a fitting end to the trip. On our way to Roma Termini, the central train station, we managed to recruit an American girl for the adventure. In the spirit of crazy begets crazy, this girl had an 8 AM flight out of Rome the next morning, but she decided to come to Sperlonga beach with us at 9 PM the previous night. Does the train go to Sperlonga directly? Nope. You have to get down at some random town called Fondi and take a 20-minute bus ride from there to get to the beach. Does the bus run all night long? Nope. Did she care to check it? Nope. Instead, she decided to trust us. God save her! How we managed to hitch a free ride from a local father-daughter pair, from Fondi to Sperlonga beach, and how the girl with us managed to catch her 8 AM flight out of Rome, are stories for another day. While the girl was boarding her flight, "el otro loco" was found sleeping on the Sperlonga beach with Zani's mask on his face and three layers of clothing on in 35 degrees Celsius weather.

You think life is measured by the moments that take your breath away? Nope. Life is measured by the moments that make you laugh out loud and go "Yeah, that was kinda stupid. Did I really do that?"

16. SPAIN: MI AMOR!

August 10, 2012
Sevilla, Spain

España, mi amor!

Where have you been? And why did I wait so long to meet you? After our two-week affair, I feel like living here forever. But I know that would not be good for me. I think it is time for me to move on, and since you are the type who believes silence is golden, I will say what I have to say and get the hell out of here.

After the old-world riches of Italy, the new-world riches of Monaco and Saint Tropez were a fun contrast. But these rich people are so cold and isolated that you can never really get a good handle on them. After a quick stopover in gritty, run-down Marseilles, I finally saw you for the first time when I reached Barcelona.

Man, was that a memorable experience! I had heard about your beauty through your music and language. Almost a decade ago, I was introduced to Buena Vista Social Club; my first Latin American band. Even though I didn't understand a word, there was something attractive about your language. People say that French sounds soft and polished. For me, Spanish has the oomph that French lacks. Visiting a bunch of Latin American countries only strengthened my desire to meet you someday. And hanging out with friends from Venezuela, Puerto Rico, Nicaragua, and Mexico, when I was living in Louisville, further built my anticipation for our first date. But nothing really prepared me for our torrid affair that started in Barcelona.

On one hand, you are a perfectionist. Gaudi, the son of the soil, has blessed you with some of the most astonishing and unique buildings. Seriously, who tries to create waves with concrete as the facade of a building? On the other hand, you embody out-and-out hedonism. Los Angeles is infamous for the cloud of smog hovering over it. If they check the air quality in Barcelona, I'm sure it will be all weed. Amsterdam has coffee shops. You have your streets! And that's just the start. Walking along the Barceloneta beach at night, I learned that weed is an appetizer in your world. They buy, sell, and consume pretty much all kinds of drugs here. Plus, it is on these beaches that you realize "Sex on the beach" is not just a cocktail served in bars and clubs.

And don't even get me started on the downright nasty side of you. In my first three days of meeting you, you tried to pick my pocket twice. This, after I had just finished an exhausting, three-month European trip, and was looking forward to relaxing a bit. I was thinking about letting my guard down, but when you tried to steal my money before I could even check into my hostel, I had to put my guard back up. By the way, what was that lying all about? You told me it would take me 30 minutes or so to get to the airport. It took me more than an hour! You knew my flight tickets were non-refundable. Why didn't you factor in the metro construction? Or were you just worried that if I went to Portugal, I would love her more than you?

They warned me about your split personality, too. The Catalan, who reluctantly, if at all, celebrated Spain's recent Euro cup victory, but consider Messi as the son of the soil. The Basque separatists in the north, who are still intent on using violent means to get their own country. And the southern Andalusian personality, which is the calmer, more sedate side of you. Even your history of relationships was a big red flag. You have a brutal history of plundering the wealth of South American countries and building monuments and museums from it. The wars with the Moors, or Muslims, coming from the south, are nothing to write home about. Forget the colonial history, even your recent past is made up of a fascist dictatorship and a bloody civil war long after the Nazis and Mussolini surrendered. It is hard to believe you were a dictatorship until the late 1970s!

In spite of all these warnings, I couldn't help falling in love with you. Walking along the crowded Las Ramblas, seeing the statue of Columbus - pointing to the west - imploring all of us to go explore and seek adventure, the plazas embodying the spirit of community, struggling artists putting up a flamenco show on the street-side in 35 degrees Celsius heat. And then, after a hectic day of sight-seeing, sitting on the beach, sipping your half-beer, half-lemonade combo, and listening to a bunch of hippies singing and dancing to *Chan Chan* and *El Cuarto de Tula*! Nothing like it! My body was relaxing with the beer, but I could see my mind tapping its feet and dancing in front of my eyes. It was that feeling of liveliness, the edgy groove of Barcelona that was so intoxicating!

Things didn't change much when I went to Valencia, the home of paella and sangria, and the laid-back, "mañana" or tomorrow attitude. If anything, they got better. With the mercury touching 40 degrees Celsius, it was easy to understand why people need siestas here. Afternoon naps have always been my thing. Even in corporate America, I always found ways to get my afternoon nap. But they have perfected that art here in Andalusia. Lunch time is 2 in the afternoon, dinner time is 10 at night, and you have no particular bedtime. How the hell do you operate? As a tourist, the bull-fighting ring, the old, gigantic entrances to the city, that used to serve as jails for noblemen, the river-bed converted into one mammoth garden, and the cathedrals sprinkled all over the city are all fun to visit. But people-watching here further strengthened my bond with you. In the morning time, there were old people gathering in plazas, wearing pants that were pulled all the way up to their chests. They probably didn't get the fashion memo, but you could see them sitting on the benches, remnants of their hair neatly combed, perhaps talking about politics or exchanging city gossip. Then there were middle-aged ladies, holding their mother's or father's hand and leading them through the crowded central market, making them feel like they are still a part of the society. In the middle of all this, I would see a mom casually saying "mierda" and spanking her adolescent son for dancing around the whole crowd, playing with his football. C'mon now, what do you expect when you take your son shopping and allow him to take his football with him? But it was all adorable in its own way. The kid just sprinted further away and joined the group of kids playing football in the next plaza. From one plaza to the next, the spectacle of life goes on.

If I were Spanish, I'd have adjusted my body clock to this seemingly never-ending celebration of life. But my body couldn't keep up with the daytime sightseeing and crazy nightlife. The flu that took me down for a few days in Valencia brought me back to my senses and made me reassess our relationship. Somewhere along the way, I even heard this song from Bebe called *Sinsentido*. The first time I heard it, even without fully understanding the song, I knew this would be the anthem of our encounter. It has a Dire Straits-esque feel to it. Perhaps it's Spain's answer to Mark Knopfler's *Romeo and Juliet*. As a friend of mine noted once, it never feels like Mark Knopfler is singing. He seems to be narrating some beautiful story with music sprinkled all over it. *Sinsentido* is no different. The meaning of the song, the voice capturing the emotions, the perfectly-timed silences; as I was heading south, from Valencia to Seville, the landscape that was getting more arid and brown by the minute made for a perfect background to this song. Her voice makes even the goofy lisp sound adorable! (I think I want to meet Bebe).

Don't get me wrong. Seville was great, too. The heat was even worse, but the celebration of life continued unabated there. To deal with the heat, you have invented tinto-de-verano here. I don't know how the world, especially the hot and dry parts of it, has not embraced this drink. It almost seems like a well-kept secret of Andalusia. And "mañana" here seems to switch to "de spues de mañana" or day after tomorrow. You go to a restaurant at 8 at night and it's empty. You sit at a table in a restaurant and nobody shows up for 15-20 minutes. You order paella and the waiter casually says "It'll take about 50 minutes." When the paella finally shows up, you see locals trickling in. Unlike the United States, there is no stark old-young divide here. An old gentleman on one table casually struck up a conversation with a young lady at the next table. Another couple on the third table joined in. As I was observing all this, I realized why the waiters here don't bother to show up for half an hour. You take the concept of "hanging out" very seriously here. And that makes me fall even more in love with you. When I was done with my dinner and pulled out a 100 Euro bill for a 12 Euro meal, the waiter didn't hesitate to give me the "You gotta be kidding me, dude!" look. Tourist or no tourist, you have to carry change, man! These are the kinds of small things I adore you for. On top of that, the post-dinner flamenco show told me, to my surprise, that a lot of the flamenco music and hand gestures are influenced by Indian dances. I had no idea there was any serious cultural exchange between Spain and India. This just added a new dimension to our relationship. You just can't stop seducing me, can you?

But as *Sinsentido* suggests, my body is a spent force now. I can't handle this anymore. It is time to collect the pieces and move on. A part of me says it would be great to move in with you and see whether we are a good match. But, as a democracy, you are pretty young and you are going through your first real mid-life crisis. When the rest of the world works its ass off and you live somewhere between "mañana" and "de spues de mañana," maybe it is not too surprising that you are experiencing a crisis of this magnitude. I'm sure it hurts your pride a lot, but that's how you learn. Plus, it looks like it's going to take you a while to recover from this crisis. It doesn't sound like a very smart idea to move in with you.

To quote my favorite Eagles song, "Maybe someday we will find...that it wasn't really wasted time." Even if it turns out that it was all wasted time, you will always have a special place in my heart. The Indian people, history, and culture are my emotional center of gravity. The American Constitution, jurisprudence, and entrepreneurship are my intellectual center of gravity. You are hard to pin down. Nonetheless, like that cheesy song *Sugar how you get so fly*, every time my thoughts drift back to you, I will feel like dancing to the tunes of your vitality.

Un beso, mi amor!

Yours Truly.

PS: Your women are so beautiful I wouldn't mind sending such letters to each one of them. But first, you gotta start wearing some clothes, girls! Or, maybe not. As a guy, I can't complain.

AFRICAN
TREASURES

5

17. MOROCCO: A BATTLE OF ATTRITION

August 20, 2012
Casablanca, Morocco

When hopping over from Spain to Morocco, you realize that this narrow strait called the Strait of Gibraltar stands between day and night. Developmentally, perhaps you go from day to night. In a lot of ways, it's like turning back the clock, but temperature-wise, which was my more immediate concern, it goes from night to day. Welcome to the desert kingdom of Morocco!

The battle of attrition I am referring to is somewhat related to the elements and the creatures, but is primarily a people thing. The battle started within an hour of landing at the port in Tangier in Morocco. To the disappointment of the three taxi drivers following me, I decided to walk the 2-3 kilometer stretch to the train station and got there a good two hours prior to the departure of the train to Marrakech. It was still Ramadan and the sun had just set, which meant all the employees were breaking bread. They were back to work within 15 minutes and the guy charged me 35 Euros for the ticket. I had enough Dirhams, but I also had some extra Euros in my pocket and didn't bother asking what the exchange rate was. The casual way in which he quoted the price in Euros led me to believe that paying in Euros was common practice here, but when I got the ticket, it said 350 Dirhams. Out of curiosity, I checked the exchange rate online. To my surprise, they had free wireless internet at the train station, which made it easy to cross-check. Sure enough, the exchange rate was 11 Dirhams for 1 Euro. In all likelihood, the railway employee pocketed the 35 Euros, put 350 Dirhams in the cash register, and exchanged the 35 Euros to make a few Dirhams on that transaction. In Europe, you get used to set prices. Even tipping is not a big part of European culture. You have to leave all that behind as soon as you cross over to Morocco. I can already hear the battle hymns! Rule of engagement # 1: Keep your Euros in your pocket.

The first thing I did in Marrakech the next day was book my 2-day, 1-night trip to the desert. It included some sight-seeing, a camel ride, and staying the night in a tent in the desert. I knew this was a bit of a tourist trap and it was not true camping in the wild, but, hey, I'm no expert on desert camping. I asked the hostel manager how much the tour was. He gave me a catalog full of pictures and the price list for various tour options. It said the one I wanted was 650 Dirhams. I was already on a mission to recover my losses on the train ticket, so I tried to get it down to 400, but we settled on 500 Dirhams. Not bad for a first salvo.

When booking the tour, he told me that everything was included. His promises did not hold up long, though. Our first real stop was a tiny, old Berber (the dominant tribe in Morocco) village in which movies like Lawrence of Arabia and Gladiator were shot. The local guide, dressed in the traditional Berber garb, explained the history and architectural style of the kasbahs. He then took us to an artist's shack, where the artist did a well-choreographed demonstration of how the centuries-old tradition of painting pictures on papers and then holding the papers on fire is still alive. They used a mixture of local tea, saffron, and sugar to paint a picture on a piece of white paper. Other than a tinge of orange on the outlines, it was hard to notice anything on the paper. The colors started emerging when he held the paper on fire and it started burning the sugar and tea in the mixture. It was all fascinating, but at the end of the tour, the guide demanded 10 Dirhams from each of us. When the Chinese girl in the group said she didn't have change, he coolly took 20 out of my hand and ordered me to get the 10 back from the girl. *What? We didn't even know each other. We were just random fellow travelers.*

It was not about money, really. It was about the principle. It was about the whole charade. And it was about the manner in which business was done here.

At lunch time, our group was ushered into an overpriced

restaurant with no other option in the vicinity. When we got there, we realized that lunch, of course, was not included. Oh well! The real battle started when we got on the camels. I was prepared for a bumpy ride, but after riding a camel for a good two-three hours, back and forth, I can confidently say that evolution is a myth. If humans have been riding camels for so many generations now, how come the camels haven't developed shock absorbers? If you are younger than, say, 25 or 30, you will probably be okay. If you are 30 to 40, unless you are in the top 25th percentile in terms of fitness, you will most likely spend 2-3 days recovering from back pain. And, if you have already crossed 40 and are not in the fittest 5th percentile, you will get off the camel with a couple of your vertebrae dislocated. This is all because when camels walk, sitting on them feels like spending an hour on that toy rodeo bull. Every time they take a step, a wave goes up your spine, pushing each vertebra back and forth. And when they start running, it is like jumping up and down on a bench, and landing butt first, with your legs in the air. (Statutory warning: do not try this at home!).

I survived the camel battle, only to enter a chamber of heat and scorpions. The tents in the desert trap all the heat during the day and take forever to cool down after sundown. Since it was the peak of summer, even nighttime temperatures were 35 degrees Celsius, with the temperature in the tent around 40 degrees. No matter how hard we tried, it was not possible to sleep in the tent. So we pulled our mattresses out into the open. The sky was a bit cloudy, but the clear patches of sky gave us a glimpse of how bright the sky would be on a clear night. Others were bummed out, but I've camped out enough not to be sad about one cloudy night. I was more interested in getting a good night's sleep.

As we closed our eyes, we heard the German guy in our group screaming and coming out from behind the neighboring tent. He was holding one of his toes tightly and just couldn't stop screaming. In a few minutes, he couldn't stand it anymore, and he laid down in the sand. His girlfriend, who had just lost her passport a couple of days ago, was trying to comfort him, but was clueless. As we found out later, it turned out to be a scorpion bite. What the hell do we know about scorpion bites? Are they lethal? How do you treat them? Do you just wait for the pain to subside? Even after half an hour, the intensity of his pain hadn't gone down. By then, everyone had a scared look on their faces. The camp managers wisely decided to take him to the nearest town which, luckily, was just 30 minutes or so away. And we were left to wonder whether sleeping outside was a wise decision. The scorpion bite episode had happened less than ten meters away. *What is better? Going in the tent and not sleeping at all? Or taking our chances sleeping outside?* A couple of girls decided to go inside and three of us decided to take our chances. We had solid 3-4 inch tall mattresses, after all. The scorpions would probably be too lazy to climb up the mattresses to bite us, right?

Even after fully covering ourselves with the sheets, it took us another half an hour or so to fall asleep. In the morning, it was good to look around and realize there had been no more bites. Even the German guy was back, after getting a few penicillin injections, and was feeling better. One more battle won. Phew! But wait! We were not done yet. At the end of our camel ride back, the local guide again demanded money. I offered him 10 Dirhams and he said "Oh, that's not enough. That's what you give kids here." *Tough luck, dude. No tip for you.*

On our way back to Marrakech, I decided to part ways with the group and stay in the sleepy town of Oaurzazate to relax and catch up on some writing. I realized that, for a change, I could actually afford a nice hotel room with air conditioning, television, and a bathroom of my own. Breakfast was included, too. The guy quoted 230 Dirhams a night and I managed to take it down to 180. Not bad!

When I woke up in the morning, the guy said there was no breakfast for me. Without telling me, he had conveniently taken out the breakfast. The reduced rate was not a discount, after all. I gave him a lot of grief for not telling me the day before that the discounted price excluded breakfast. After getting so much grief from me, he helped me find a charger that would charge my cell phone, and let me browse the internet for about two hours from his computer. In this small town, that counted for a lot. *Let's call this one a draw then.*

Even the weather here seemed to be in cahoots with the opposition. A 45 degrees Celsius day is considered a good day. The temperature has to cross 50 degrees for it to be a hot day. I was actually ok with 45 degrees and the dryness of the desert. That's the kind of climate I grew up in. I would take it over 40 degrees and 90% humidity any day. In the evening, when the temperatures were going down from 45 to 40 and there was a hint of a breeze, I decided to walk around and go to the plaza in the city center. All of a sudden, there was a huge storm. It started raining and I had to scramble for cover. That was not too bad, but because of the rain, it was suddenly humid and still a solid 35 degrees. The weather was probably saying "Gotcha!"

As if that were not enough, I sat down for dinner and one cat parked herself at my feet, meowing throughout my meal. I tried to ignore it for most of my meal. In the end, I looked at the leftover mix of bones and meat on my plate and said "What the hell!" That's exactly what the cat was waiting for. As soon as I threw a few pieces on the ground, six more cats came out of nowhere. *Holy shit! I gotta get out of here.*

Fez was no different. The city is actually more touristy than Marrakech and Oaurzazate. It is the religious and cultural capital of Morocco. The 4-hour walking tour here seemed a bit of a respite from the ongoing war. The guide seemed to really know what he was talking about and was not looking to extract money from us at every corner. He told us about the five pillars of Islam. Believing that Allah is the only God, praying five times a day, fasting from dawn to dusk during Ramadan, giving things away to charity (mostly money at the end of Ramadan), and going to Mecca at least once in your life. Even if you don't believe in God, fasting and charity are still appealing. Scientific data suggest that periodic starvation can actually prolong your life. And charity is, well, charity. Maybe there is life beyond the other pillars, especially when you compare the socio-economic development in the Islamic world with that in the non-Islamic world. After all, some 5-6 billion people seem to be doing fine without Islam in their lives. The atheist in me had already gone off on a tangent.

Obviously, I didn't want to broach that topic in the middle of a walking tour. The guide gave us lots of other interesting facts about Islamic customs and rituals. The doors in the town seemed to have been decorated with a female hand, the hand of Fatima, who was the prophet's favorite daughter. That symbol on the door is supposed to be a sign of good luck. The large entrance doors have two knobs, one used when the husband comes back home by himself, and the other used when he has company. If he has company, the wife needs to put on her veil before opening the door. Why do Moroccan women wear a veil that just covers their hair and not their faces? Women cover their hair because their hair is considered 50% of their beauty. Apparently, hiding 50% of your beauty is good enough in Morocco.

If a woman's husband dies, she has to wear white clothes for a little over four months, after which she can again wear normal clothes and can marry again. In the olden days, this white dress code was meant to be an easy way of ensuring that the woman wasn't pregnant with her deceased husband's child before remarrying.

There is a lot of interesting symbolism, too. The mosques in Morocco have three spheres on top, signifying the peaceful coexistence of Judaism, Christianity, and Islam; Islam being the topmost sphere. Green is the color of Islam, apparently because the pillows in heaven are green. And red is the second-most important color because it signifies sacrificing your blood in the name of religion. I asked him about the abundance of cats and near-total absence of dogs in all the Moroccan towns. According to him, dogs scare away Islamic angels. When the dogs are away, cats gotta play! In Morocco, you can't have a meal out in the open without cats harassing you for leftovers.

The tour left me with lots of questions on the logical front, but no clear answers. It all boils down to modernity, though. Symbolism and rituals in other religions are no less arbitrary than those in Islam. But as societies advance and our knowledge base expands, it makes sense to leave old dogmas behind. On the other hand, it was a bit embarrassing to have spent half of my life in the country that is home to the second-largest Muslim population in the world, after Indonesia, and be virtually illiterate when it comes to Islam. The tour was a much-needed correction in my life.

Meeting a guy who was half-Indian, half-Portuguese, born and brought up in Malaysia, and currently living in New Zealand, meant that we had to hang out! As soon as we chose a road-side food stall for dinner, the war of attrition was back on. We made the cardinal sin of not asking the price of the food we were ordering. When we were slapped with a 120 Dirham bill, for not a lot of food, we had just lost another skirmish. When we paid 200 for it, he gave us 80 back and nonchalantly picked 10 back up, saying "service charge" with a big smile on his face. This guy from New Zealand took that 10 back and said "No." So, it was not just me who was pissed off.

It got worse when I reached Casablanca. For all those who love the movie and have romantic notions about visiting this city, be prepared to be heavily disappointed. Yep, all the guide books are spot-on. Other than one big mosque, there is nothing worth seeing in this city. Even before getting to that mosque, the taxi driver taking me to my hostel charged me 30 instead of running his meter and charging me 15-16 Dirhams. Why? Because it was night time and the meter rates didn't apply at night. It also happened to be one of those rare occasions when I was not carrying a map from the train station to the hostel. *What the hell! You win!*

There was no respite, even after entering the mosque. You would think there would be a cease-fire in a place of worship, but when the mullah in the mosque noticed a tourist, he went straight for the jugular. He asked me if I wanted him to take my pictures. Unfortunately for him, he was talking to a guy who hates taking his own pictures. He tried another tack. He pretended as if there were a part of the mosque in which tourists are not allowed. He let me in that area and told me to take a few pictures and come back quickly, without lingering around. As soon as I came back, he asked for money. *What? Does Allah permit this kind of corruption? Is this how this guy serves his religion?* This time around, I flatly refused to pay. As soon as I refused to pay, he went from being the nicest person on earth to being the most combative on earth. *Good-bye, dude. It's not as if I'm gonna see you again in my life!*

Even when I was on my way out of Morocco, the taxi driver kept fighting the war. They had a set price of 250 Dirhams for a taxi to the Casablanca airport. The guy took me in and we stopped by a pizza joint on the way to pick up some food. When it started taking more than 5 minutes, I politely reminded him that I had a flight to catch. He hung out for another five minutes, got in the taxi, and started driving again. When I urged him to go faster, he didn't hesitate to say "If we have to go faster, it means it will be more than 250 Dirhams." I wanted to call his bullshit and get into a fight with him, but I tried my Indian roots. I told him that I'm not a European or an American tourist. I'm an Indian tourist and I am poor. So no extra money. He laughed embarrassingly and kept driving. When I got off at the airport, I gave him 300 Dirhams. As soon the money left my hand, I knew I had made a mistake. He pulled out a huge wad of money out of his pocket and had the gall to tell me that he didn't have change. I was about to dare him to hand me the wad of money, so I could check whether or not he had change, but I had a flight to catch. He pulled out some coins from his pocket, handed me 35 Dirhams and declared that the remaining 15 Dirhams were for his tea and snacks. *Screw it. I got a flight to catch. You win, man!*

As I was standing in the check-in line, I was wondering what had happened to me. I have rarely cared about money so much, especially considering the amount in question. Even after getting ripped off so many times in this country, I was still well below my budget. But it made me wonder: Where does this attitude come from? Why are tourists in Morocco viewed as wearing big Dollar-signs on their foreheads? Maybe it's because of the harsh conditions here. Desert life means it's a scramble for every penny, and tourists are the easiest targets. But things are not any different in India, a country with a history of abundance. Even the mullah asking for money in the mosque is no different than the big temples in India charging money for faster access to God. The only difference is that Indian temple trusts have institutionalized such behavior.

It can't be cultural, either, because it happens all over Asia, Africa, and Latin America. It probably boils down to a failure of institutions and resulting economic stagnation. All of a sudden, my train of thought was interrupted by the airline guy.

"Are you flying to Frankfurt?"

"Yes." Generally, this is a sign of trouble. I was about to say "Please don't tell me my flight has been canceled." But it turned out to be a pleasant surprise.

"Do you have any connecting flights?"

"I am flying to Tanzania, but I have a full day in Frankfurt."

"Sir, we are overbooked today and we are offering 400 Euros to volunteers willing to stay overnight and take tomorrow morning's flight. Hotel stay and transportation are included."

"I'll take it." I said without losing a breath. *Kha-ching!*

In my professional life, I've been offered such deals so many times I've lost count, but every time I was offered such a deal, I had a meeting to attend or work to go back to the next day. Not this time. More importantly, I didn't have a paycheck.

At long last, I had a big smile on my face. Morocco is a beautiful country with a lot to offer in terms of culture, history, and landscapes. The wide-open deserts, the canyons on the way to the desert of Zagora, the narrow alleys of Fez, the food and entertainment in Marrakech, the tanneries and textile mills, the dusty roads and the slow pace of life; it is all absolutely worth experiencing. For backpackers, it's pretty affordable, too, but these smokescreens and the constant demand for tips had just left a bad taste in my mouth. Perhaps not for the Western tourists who are vacationing for a week or two, but backpackers are a different breed. Almost all of them are operating on low budgets. This near-constant cutting and sniping had just worn me down.

Nonetheless, thank you, Lufthansa, for bankrolling my stay in Morocco. Sweet smell of victory!

18. TANZANIA: KILIN' ME SOFTLY

September 7, 2012
Kilimanjaro, Tanzania

Winner: "It's time to climb, baby! Are you ready?"

Loser: "- I'm not so sure. We are just coming off a 50 plus hour journey. Why did you have to fly to Frankfurt, Johannesburg, and Addis Ababa to get to Dar es Salaam? Couldn't you get a direct flight from Casablanca to Dar?"

Winner: "Good point. When you're using airline miles, you are not the chooser, remember?"

Loser: "- And that hip injury that resurfaced in Fez? That hasn't healed yet."

"We've been resting for more than 24 hours now. That's enough rest."

"- We've got a long way to go! This is not a day hike."

"I know, I know. Let's get going. Leave all the crap you're not gonna need, pack that sleeping bag and some food, and let's go."

"- Wait! Are we gonna sleep in that rented sleeping bag? In winter time, people don't even take showers when hiking Kilimanjaro."

"So what do we do? Sleep on the floor?"

"- I didn't say that. It just sounds like a bad idea. That's it."

"You think I don't know that? But there is no way I am going to carry a sleeping bag for the rest of the year just for this week-long hike."

"- Five days. I wish it was seven days."

"I wish we had the money to afford it. I read the same online posts you did, and I had to take the risk. This is twice our daily budget. The longer we take to hike, the more it hurts our wallets. You know that, don't you?"

"- Yeah, I know. But there is a higher chance of failure if we try to cram it into 5 days."

"Well, it's a risk worth taking."

"- All right, all right. I'm all packed up and ready to go."

"Good, good."

"- And what the hell is that? Are you going to hike in those rental shoes?"

"Why are we arguing about it now? We've gone over this before. Do you want to carry these heavy hiking boots all over the world just for this one hike?"

"- No, but those are shoes! How can you wear shoes used by God knows how many other hikers?"

"I never heard you complain when we went bowling."

"- Whatever. Let's just go."

*   *   *

End of Day 1

"See, we are the first ones to get here. There is nobody else here at the campsite. We are the first ones to check in."

"- Yeah, but this was the easiest part of the hike. 1800 meters to 2800 in 8 kilometers. Piece of cake. We started early, too. Remember?"

"You can't enjoy anything, can you?"

"- I'm just giving you a reality check."

"Ok. Well, the shoes are not bothering me much, which is good news."

"- I was a bit worried about those rental shoes. That's a big relief. We have a long way to go. Let's go grab some dinner. The guide stopped by 10-15 minutes ago."

Munch, munch, munch...

"Man, I wasn't even hungry. I still ate a bunch!"

"- Good for you. They say you lose your appetite at higher altitudes."

"Yeah, and it'll help me get a good night's sleep, too"

"- Hmmm...hold on. What's that noise? Did you hear that?"

"I did. Don't worry. For the past 48 hours, we've been stuffing way too many carbs in the name of scaling Kilimanjaro. It's probably just a bit of indigestion."

"- I think we're gonna have to make a run soon."

"I'm all wrapped up and comfy. I have no desire to go to the toilet in the cold. Let's just wait till tomorrow morning."

* * *

"- It's been a couple of hours, now. Things aren't getting any better. Gotta go."

"Man, that was a good call. Feeling relieved now."

"- We are not out of the woods, yet. I am fully aware of the churning in the stomach that you're trying to ignore."

"But you saw there was no sign of diarrhea. Why are you worried now?"

"- I don't know. Something feels wrong."

* * *

"- Gotta go!"

"Again? It hasn't even been an hour!"

"- I knew it. And see! It's diarrhea."

"Maybe it's just a minor thing. Everything will be all right by tomorrow morning."

"- I have a bad feeling about this one, but let's see what happens."

* * *

"- Hear that churning sound? Gotta go again."

"C'mon, man! Try to control it a bit."

"- It's not like I have a choice."

"It's just painful to go out, come back, and fall asleep every time."

"- Did you see what just happened? I told you I didn't have a good feeling about this one. It was all water."

"I still don't think it's that big a deal. But let's take a pill, just in case."

"- Ok, good. This one...anti-histamine. This one...antibiotic with steroids. This one...doesn't sound like an antibiotic, but doesn't sound like a diarrhea pill, either. Is that it? Don't we have any more pills?"

"Do I look like a pharmacy to you? Work with what you have."

"- What do you mean? Who goes to Africa without diarrhea pills?"

"Me. Just deal with it."

"- Wait. Say that again? Are you crazy?"

"I didn't check the pills."

"- What do you mean you didn't check the pills?"

"I just got it from my dad and put it straight in the bag. I thought we had diarrhea pills, but it looks like we don't. Plus, I still don't think it's anything serious. Just take that third pill and go to bed."

"- We don't even know what it does!"

"I'm not taking an antihistamine. I wouldn't mind the antibiotic, but I don't want to take the steroid mixed with it. You never know what it'll do to you at high altitudes. So this unknown one is our only option. Just take it. It's going to kill some germs, I'm sure!"

"- Your dad is going to be really proud of you. I told you not to eat that stale looking chicken at that stall where the bus stopped yesterday."

"All the Tanzanians were eating there. I wanted to know what they eat. Plus, that was more than twenty-four hours ago. It's unlikely that that's the reason."

"- Then it's got to be that big, fat pound cake you got at the super market."

"Could be. I bought it for all the carbs. If super market stuff is going to give us diarrhea, there is not much we can do about it. In any case, it doesn't matter. We have got to deal with it now."

*　　　　　　*　　　　　　*

Morning of Day 2

"- See, we lost a bunch of water in the morning again."

"Let's stuff ourselves up and keep walking. If we eat twice as much, I'm sure the body will retain something."

"- You know our golden rule. Starve yourself for a day and everything will be fine."

"Dude, we have to go 12 kilometers and hike up another 1000

meters today. Where is all that energy going to come from? Starvation?"

"- Not from food. It's all going to go straight out."

"Let's eat as much as we can and hope for the best."

"- If you say so."

*   *   *

Afternoon of Day 2

"Are you happy now? We made it up here with just one lunch stop."

"- Yeah, but we had to make a run there, too. We were lucky to have a toilet there. And that second pill we popped at lunch? I'm not sure it's doing much. I can still feel cramps in my stomach. I still can't believe you don't have diarrhea pills!"

"If everyone else carries diarrhea pills, it's fine that we don't have them. If things get worse, we'll ask someone for diarrhea pills."

"- What are you waiting for? We have another 9 kilometers and 1000 meters to climb tomorrow."

"I just want to wait out the evening to see if things get better."

"- Here we go again. I need to make another run...and it was all water again. I'm not sure how many of those carbs we are retaining. But once we run out of those – and at this rate, I'm sure we will – we are down to proteins, man. We don't have much fat left. So it's straight down to proteins."

"Here. Eat a power bar. It's got a lot of proteins in it."

*   *   *

"- Another run...some more water. Forget about proteins. I'm feeling weak and I'm worried about getting cramps in my feet now. Need some calcium and potassium."

"Here you go. Finish that packet of Gatorade powder."

"- Are you going to ask for pills now? It's not even dinner time and we've made a couple of runs already."

"I can't just go knocking on all the doors asking for pills. Wait until everyone comes out for dinner."

*   *   *

Night of Day 2

"- Ok. We're here now. Ask that couple sitting to our right."

"Blah, blah, blah, blah, blah – Oh, you are from Belgium! – blah, blah, blah, blah blah."

"- What the hell, dude? Just ask if they have the pills. I'm about to make another run here."

"Shhhhh! I can't just ask them if they have medicine. Give me a minute for some small talk."

"- If you don't ask in the next minute, I'm off to the toilet."

"Blah, blah, blah, blah, blah – Oh, by the way, are you carrying any medicines with you? ...Oh great. It looks like I have diarrhea, but I can't find my medicines...Oh nice. I think Imodium should do it. I don't think I need antibiotics yet."

"- Good lord! Finally!"

"This is going to do the trick."

"- Well, we just lost a whole lot of water again. Screw the proteins, carbs, and calcium. I'm just worried about water retention now. Where's the water bottle?"

"Here it is. Just hang in there. We have the right medicine now."

"- Dude, I'm suffering from indigestion, too. We've been stuffing ourselves with thrice the normal amount of food. The system is completely overloaded, now. Are you sure you would like to continue? It might be worth turning around."

"Not happening. I'm not going back because of diarrhea."

*   *   *

"- Here we are again. It's been an hour since we took Imodium and we are going back for another run. If the Imodium was meant to work, it would've worked by now. We are either going to have to take the antibiotic or just call it off tomorrow."

"Easy, boy!"

"- You realize there is nothing left in our body, right? We are running on empty and still getting those nasty burps because of indigestion. My feet are getting cold, too."

"Just hang in there. Wear this third pair of socks."

"- Maybe I should wear them inside out, so we can hide the smell. We haven't changed socks in 48 hours now."

"Who cares about smell here? Nobody has taken a shower and nobody has washed their feet. Everyone is in the same boat. Just wear the fresh pair on the inside."

*   *   *

"- Feet are still cold, dude. The third pair didn't help."

"Just wear the shoes then, and get in the sleeping bag."

"- Say what?"

"You heard me right. Wear the shoes and get in the sleeping bag."

"- These dusty shoes? In the sleeping bag?"

"Do you want frostbite instead? We are at 3800 meters already."

"- Why the hell did you not bring some woolen socks?"

"We are not traveling to hike Kili. We are traveling around the world, remember?"

"- Yeah, whatever. But still, these boots in the sleeping bag?"

"The sleeping bag is rented anyway."

*   *   *

"- And here is another run. I'm positively out of this hike, man. I'm even tired of getting out of this sleeping bag every hour or so to make a run. Spare a thought for this couple we are sharing our hut with. They are trying to sleep here and we are disturbing them every hour."

"What sleep? They are both passing gas like there is no tomorrow. Don't get me started now. They know I can hear it, but they don't care. And it's fine. Altitude does all kinds of stuff to the body. Maybe they are suffering from indigestion, too. It's all about climbing the mountain. Not about showers, smelly socks, or a good night's sleep. Just get up and go. We'll take another Imodium when we are back."

*   *   *

"- You are out of your mind, man. I need water first. Lots of it. There is no water in the system anymore."

"Take this whole bottle and take another Imodium with it."

*   *   *

"- Another run, man. This is our ninth or tenth run in the last 24 hours. I've lost count by now. Let's just call it off. Do you want to go down the mountain on a stretcher tomorrow?"

"If this doesn't work, we can try antibiotics tomorrow morning. Just wait for the second Imodium to kick in."

"- Have you checked the pulse lately? It's pushing 100."

"Yes. I've been keeping an eye on it. It was actually 120 when we got here. It's moving in the right direction. It should be back to normal by tomorrow morning. Now, if you will just go back to sleep."

"- You know I'm trying my best. It's just not going anywhere."

*   *   *

Morning of Day 3

"How was it?"

"- Looks like the second pill worked. Things are much better now. I think I can retain some water. The burping has stopped too, but we have to load up on all the lost nutrients, now."

"That's not a big problem. We've been overeating for the past 3-4 days. We'll just keep doing that. The pulse is back to 60. Feeling fresh. Rock and roll, baby!"

*   *   *

Afternoon of Day 3

"- We are officially the last ones to get to these huts. Have you checked the pulse? It's 110, pushing 120."

"Well, we are recovering from diarrhea. So I'm not surprised we are the last ones here. Just like last night, the pulse will be back to normal overnight. We didn't grow up at 4800 meters. It's going to take some time for the body to get used to this low oxygen."

"- Forget about growing up in these conditions. We've never ever been this high. How the hell do you know the pulse is going to come back to normal?"

"That's not true. We did Paso de Agua Negra. That was about the same height."

"- The most idiotic thing we've ever done. Going from sea level

129

to 4800 meters in a day, riding a motorcycle on a dirt road! You should feel lucky that nothing happened."

"The bottom line is that we did it. We are gonna be fine here, too. I'm not feeling dizzy. I don't have a headache. It's just the pulse rate."

"- We don't even have the whole night. We have to start the final ascent at midnight."

*   *   *

"Ready for action? It's the last 1000 meters. We're going to make it."

"- The pulse rate hasn't changed a bit. We are still pushing 120."

"What are you going to do? Turn around now? There is just no way I would do that. It's not like we have a heart condition. It will be fine."

"- Your heart has been beating at 120 since we got here. That's like doing low-intensity cardio for 9 hours. Who do you think you are? Lance Armstrong?"

"At least I'm not doping!"

"- Maybe you should have. They say diuretics help when you are at high altitudes. It's not like we are hiking Kili for the Olympics!"

"It's too late now to change our mind, anyway. Let's go!"

*   *   *

In the middle of the night on Day 3-4

"- I'm done, man. My tank is positively empty. I can't take even one step further. We've barely walked a kilometer. We have six kilometers to go before we reach the summit. At this rate, it'll take us forever."

"Let me make a phone call."

"- Who are you going to call at this ungodly hour?"

"Hello? Is Adrenalin there?"

"Yeah, dude. Need some help, here. Almost 5000 meters above sea level. Another 1000 or so left. We've tried our best, but it's a pretty steep dirt road full of gravel...I know, I know. I thought about it, but I didn't want to bother you. I could manage on my own until here. You're my ace of spades. Didn't want to waste it unless I absolutely had to."

*   *   *

"- It helped a bit. Another 100 meters, maybe? But it looks like we are back to square one. Running on empty."

"Let's take another break and regroup."

"- You realize that the last break was less than 20 steps ago, right? It's time to wrap up and go back."

"But it's not like we're feeling dizzy, or having a headache. I don't even feel like I'm going to collapse. It can't be altitude sickness."

"- Does it really matter? The truth is we can't even take a single step anymore. And I can already feel my toes freezing. The longer we sit, the worse they are going to get."

"It's just another few hours!"

"- I understand. But we set out to see the world. Not to hike Kili. What's the point in torturing ourselves to get to the summit of this random mountain? Maybe it is because of the diarrhea or altitude sickness, but the fact is that we have no energy to move forward. If we keep going, I guarantee you we will have to be evacuated or airlifted from here. Grow up, man! We have another 30 odd kilometers to walk before we can get out of this park. If we had come well- prepared, I would've understood, but that's not the case."

"All right. If you say so."

*   *   *

Morning of Day 4

"- The heart is still beating at 120 odd beats per minute. Turning around last night was the right thing to do."

"Yeah, I'm ok with it now. It wasn't meant to be. Maybe some other time. Live to fight another day."

"- That's the spirit. Remember that couple from yesterday? They had to turn around at 5600 meters because of shortness of breath. Just 300 meters from the summit! They probably felt worse than we did. Now let's start the long walk back down."

*   *   *

Evening of Day 4

"Whoa! What's that all about? Looks like we have uninvited guests in our shoes."

"- Yup. They're blisters."

"Precursors to blisters. Not full-blown yet. It's just 8 kilometers left tomorrow. Maybe we can just plough through."

"- With our rented shoes, I'm not surprised this is happening. It's always on your way down. But why do you want to plough through now?"

"I don't want to take the rescue van just for the last few kilometers."

"- So, you want to go back and nurse your blisters for the next week?"

"No, I didn't say that!"

"- But that's what you are implying. I asked the guide and we are gonna have to walk 3-4 kilometers before we can get to the rescue van anyway. What's the difference between walking 60 kilometers in 5 days and 64 kilometers in 5 days?"

"The difference is the rescue van."

"- And how old are you again?"

"All right. Do whatever you want to do. We didn't make it to the summit, anyway."

Loser wins the day.

*   *   *

The winner in me has a bad habit of taking outlandish risks. Mostly because of sheer luck, most of the bets have paid off. Today, it was the loser's turn to win. So we lost the battle but, in the process, we managed to win a million little skirmishes. You see, mountain climbing, especially the high altitude kind, is such a primal sport that it brings out the best and the worst in you. I started out worrying about the hip injury that had resurfaced in Morocco and hadn't healed completely. In a mere four days, I went from worrying about the hip, to a rented sleeping bag, to rented shoes, to showers, to smelly socks, to carbs, to proteins, to calcium, all the way down to water. Just water. And in those final moments, when we decided to turn around, even water didn't matter. All I was trying to figure out was how to take the next step and where to find the energy to do that. Even when my mind was telling me to take the next step, my body refused to listen. Making me forget all those inconsequential things is the true victory of mountain climbing. There is something so raw about the feeling of being completely drained of every bit of energy that, at that point, nothing else matters. There were no signs of injury or muscle fatigue or a twisted ankle or a broken bone, but there was nothing left in my core anymore.

On my way to Tanzania, the long flight from Frankfurt to Johannesburg helped me catch up on some movies. In a way, it was a weird feeling because I had never gone for more than a month or so without watching a movie. On that flight, it was just fun to watch a movie, any movie, after a four-month stretch without watching a single movie. One of the movies I watched was *The Best Exotic Marigold Hotel.* It's that movie about a few elderly British people vacationing in India for the first time. The movie is not spectacular. It explores a lot of predictable clichés about India. But there is one line in the movie that has stuck with me. About halfway through the movie, the female protagonist poses the question "Have you traveled far enough to let your tears fall?"

Without even shedding a single tear, when I reached 5000 meters on that dark, cold, fateful night, only to realize that, in spite of all my determination, I couldn't even put one foot forward, I knew I had.

*   *   *

Lost in Paradise

September 14, 2012
Zanzibar, Tanzania

After a bumpy three-day safari, and a bumpier 12-hour bus ride from Arusha to Dar es Salaam, I was more than ready for Zanzibar. For some reason, I had imagined it being a tiny island-town. When I finally got a chance to look at the map, that myth was shattered immediately. This is a good 100km long island, just off the coast of Dar es Salaam, full of palm trees and sandy beaches. The more interesting aspect of the island, though, is its complicated history. But after two weeks of hectic traveling, my brain blocked all my attempts of learning anything new. First stop,

Jambiani.

Even before I had found a hostel, the first glimpse of the Jambiani beach was enough to convince me that I had entered paradise. I have never been on a beach with sand whiter than this. And the turquoise color of the water is to die for! Fortunately, this town is so small there is nothing else to do here other than hanging out on the beach. One dusty road with some 30-40 huts on both sides of it. An occasional stray dog looking for food. School children in uniforms, running around in groups, looking at us curiously and yelling the local greeting, "jambo." Local women offering everything from massages to handmade jewelry and local fabrics. A switched-off cell phone, no internet, intermittent electricity. That's it! We found a basic, yet surprisingly clean and cheap hotel on the beachfront. Thus began my perfect beach day of doing nothing.

The hotel had strategically placed cots: In the shade and right on the beach. When I was in Egypt, I had picked up the English translation of *The conference of the birds*, one of the most revered works of Persian poetry. But the non-stop sight-seeing, traveling, and writing had left me no time to catch up with reading. This was going to be the day.

Poetry is not my domain. We are not even in the same area code. When it comes to the Middle East and South Asia, I've read a bit of Khalil Jibran and Mirza Ghalib. Growing up in India, Gulzar's verses were a part of my life. But it's more like scratching the surface. I had no idea who Farid Attar was until I picked up this book from the book shelf of the Cairo hostel. I have always been vaguely interested in Sufism, the sect of Islam Attar allegedly belonged to. Perhaps it is their reputation as wanderers, explorers, and mystics that I find attractive. But the fact that this man traveled from Iran all the way to China in the 12th century and wrote a five thousand line poem made me pick it up.

In my idyllic surroundings, it didn't take me too long to realize why this is considered one of the best works of Persian poetry. When it comes to literature, I'm not a big fan of English. It seems like a workman-like language, often failing to capture the wide range of human emotions. The quality of this poem seems to permeate effortlessly through the stiff language barrier. Kudos to the poet and the translator!

What is surprising to me, though, is the central theme of the poem. The entire poem is about a group of different birds getting together to decide who their leader should be, a metaphor for people from different walks of life searching for God. And one of those birds keeps arguing that there is only one way of seeking Him (or Her). Sitting here in this corner of the world, where Arabic, Persian, African, and Indian traditions are so seamlessly integrated, it was hard to fathom how someone who had traveled extensively and experienced different ways of life, could advocate only one way of searching for the truth. Sure, Islam was in its glory-days when the poem was written. But the more I travel, the clearer it becomes that religion and God are just made-up concepts. How is a local African tribal God better or worse than, say, Brahma? And why would a person following one be better than the other or have a Fast-Pass to attaining Heaven? Do we have a metric for evaluating Gods? In the absence of any metric, it is all just arbitrary. In the history of humankind, no one religion has ever dominated all the other religions for too long. And in today's world of separation of church and the state, it is becoming increasingly unlikely. After traveling to all the exotic and faraway lands, how could Attar foresee such a monolithic world?

As I walked into the hotel reception area to make my way to the restaurant, the remnants of Attar's dream were on full display, with all the bells and whistles. The owner of this hotel, a middle-aged guy of brown skin, perhaps of Omani descent, was a devout Muslim. No matter what time of day it was, if you walked into the reception area, you would always see a white cap on his head and hear Islamic chants in the background. Forget about Zanzibar, judging by his appearance, it was hard to believe he had even left that small village of Jambiani. Truth be told, if you are on this beach, why would you even bother leaving this village? Learn a bit of English, own a successful small business, pray five times a day, enjoy the beautiful tropical weather, and hope that you will go to heaven after dying. Even if there is no heaven, you've lived a great life! An impressive one, actually, considering the hotel owner's partial blindness, something that took me half a day to notice. The ease with which he was navigating his Jambiani world was astonishing, to say the least. More impressive than anything I've ever done in my life!

So, here we were. A guy who had traveled extensively and couldn't stop extolling the virtues of God and stressing the importance of seeking Him/Her, another avid traveler who doesn't believe in God, and a third guy who has most likely never traveled beyond Jambiani, but seems to be a devout Muslim. Socrates had said that an unexamined life is not worth living. Which life is less worth living here? The one that, after traveling from Iran to China, concludes that there is only one God? The one that, after getting the same kind of opportunity to travel, concludes that there really may not be any purpose to life? Or the one that is devoted to God without much examination? I obviously don't know whether the hotel owner has ever examined his belief in God in any way, or whether he even feels the need for it. His demeanor seemed to suggest that he was unencumbered by any such thoughts. Nonetheless, his examination would most likely be different than that of a traveler. Atheist-type scientists, like us, keep hoping that someday, we will have conclusive proof that God doesn't exist. But we don't have it yet. And even if we get it, it is possible that people may not buy into it. And who decides what is an examined life, anyway? After examination, if we conclude that there may not be any purpose to life, what is that examination worth?

Oh well! That fresh fish the hotel owner has just served is looking really good. Sit back, relax on the balcony, enjoy the fish, and go to bed!

*　　　　　*　　　　　*

A Tale of Two Countries

September 19, 2012
Dar es Salaam, Tanzania

Tanzania is supposed to be one of the most peaceful countries in Africa which, given all the chaos in Africa, is a pretty big deal. And it shows. It is one of the top tourist destinations in sub-Saharan Africa. Some basic infrastructure is in place at the tourist hot-spots, cell phones and internet are reaching the small towns and villages. There is at least some semblance of law and order. And walking around late in the night doesn't seem like an adventure here.

As I started talking to the locals, they attributed the lack of ethnic tensions to the first President, Julius Nyerere's, tireless efforts to bring everyone together. Like a lot of other African countries, there is no dearth of diversity in Tanzania. There are close to 120 tribes and myriad languages in this country but, thanks to Nyerere, they all live in peace and harmony. The booming tourism industry is the peace dividend they are enjoying.

That's not the whole story, though. Other than the main national arteries, paved roads are still a pipedream. A train line going from Dar es Salaam to Moshi, built in the mid-1900s and sitting in a state of neglect, hasn't been repaired even after two decades of bureaucratic "discussions." They are nowhere near having uninterrupted power or drinking water. Traffic in cities, big and small, is as chaotic as it can be. A Dutch doctor volunteering in a Tanzanian village told me health care in small-town Tanzania is barebones, at best. When the sole x-ray machine there broke down, they had to open up people with broken bones without any x-ray! And sanitary conditions in the operating rooms were dismal. The reason for all this: corruption. Nyerere's policies ensured that the chieftains of various tribes, who derived power mainly from their ethnic identities, would not hold sway in national politics. While this strategy led to a national political discourse devoid of regionalism and factionalism he, unfortunately, maintained a one-party system in Tanzania for the first few decades of its existence. Power tends to corrupt and absolute power corrupts absolutely. Ethnic peace was achieved, but corruption led to economic stagnation and divided the country into the haves and have-nots. As a result of the apathy and sense of resignation, every local person asks for your email address or phone number, as soon as they realize that you are a tourist. Escaping Africa seems to be on a lot of people's minds. In a way, it reminded me of my days as an engineering student in India, in the 90s, when leaving Indian shores for greener pastures was an important part of an Indian engineer's psyche.

The island of Zanzibar, on the other hand, seems to be a different story. For the past 600-700 years, it has never really been a part of mainland Tanzania. The Omanis landed on this small strip of land in 1698, after defeating the Portuguese in Mombasa, and ruled it for a few centuries. Around 1888, the Germans and the British came in and made it their trading outpost. To understand this historic quirk, it is important to understand the concept of a "dhow" and the monsoonal wind patterns in the Indian Ocean. Before the Europeans took to ship-building and dominating the world with their outsized navies, the entire rim of the Indian

Ocean, stretching from the east coast of Africa to the Middle East, and all the way to the west coast of India, was a booming corridor of economic activity. The 10-15 meter long wooden boats, known as dhows, were the means of transporting people, animals, goods, cultures, and ideas all along this rim. The northeasterly monsoon winds would move things from Africa to the Middle East and India. And the southwesterly winds would move things the other way. Zanzibar, more so than Tanzania, ended up becoming a major hub of all this activity. The effects of this exchange are visible in almost all aspects of life here. Unlike mainland Tanzania, which is a battleground for the Christianity-Islam turf war, Zanzibar looks solidly Islamic. It's not just the everyday prayers coming out of the megaphones, but also the architecture and the long kurta-type shirts and white caps the men wear. Compared to the mainland, there are also more shades of brown in the skin colors here. The island folk seem to be a bit more prosperous and you don't see too many people asking for your phone number and email address.

The most interesting influences, though, are related to language and food. The language here is peppered with Arabic, Persian, and Indian words. Jackfruit is called "mphanis". Remove the "m" and it sounds like the Marathi "phanas" or Oriya "panasa." Just like us Indians, they use hot milk and turmeric powder to soothe their strained vocal cords. They use lemongrass and ginger to spice up their tea, just like the Marathis do when making "gauti chaha," or lemongrass tea. Turmeric paste is used to make the skin softer and shinier. The pulav (or pilaf) served here, made of basmati rice, tastes like it's straight out of an Indian kitchen. When people eat pineapple, they do it with a side of a salt-and-chili-pepper mixture. Everyone knows about and eats some form of chapati, roti, or rotla. The list goes on and on.

And how can one forget the most famous son of Zanzibar, Farrokh Bulsara, also known as Freddie Mercury? After Gautam Buddha and Mahatma Gandhi, he is probably the third most famous Indian, but I am not sure how many Indians have heard about Freddie. Born to Parsis from Gujarat living in Zanzibar, he was educated in India. Lata Mangeshkar, the nightingale of India, was one of the most influential personalities during his formative years. During the uprising of the 1960s in Zanzibar, his family moved to the United Kingdom and thus began his journey to the top of the musical charts as the lead singer of Queen. Bohemian

Rhapsody...progressive rock at its best! They probably hadn't even coined the term "progressive rock" back then.

All these cultural influences are fairly well-entrenched in Zanzibar and the mainland. When it comes to politics though, they don't see eye to eye. Through some complicated political arrangement set up in the 60s, Zanzibar was annexed to the mainland, as part of Tanzania. Zanzibar still has its own President and Vice President and the islanders are supposed to have some say in the central government on the mainland. But, as usual, this complex bureaucratic system has never worked, leading to resentment among the Zanzibaris. Their distinctly different cultural identity and the fact that they send more tax Dollars to the mainland than they get back have given rise to a strong independence movement. And, to everyone's chagrin, that independence movement has been co-opted by a group of religious leaders with their own hidden agenda. Talk about history repeating itself! As if that weren't enough, they also recently discovered some oil reserves off the coast of Zanzibar. If the perpetual turmoil in oil-rich regions of the world is any indication, lasting peace is a pipe dream. Good luck, Zanzibar!

Just when I was getting cynical about the prospects of peace in Zanzibar, and Tanzania in general, in came this young guy; sharply dressed, well-groomed, curly hair, with an iPad in his hand, and speaking perfect English. He has a master's degree in business and is helping his elder brother with a tourism-related business. After exchanging pleasantries, we got into a lengthy discussion about the situation in Zanzibar. This guy, clearly years younger than I, said he wants to be the President of Zanzibar. I felt like asking him "Wait, how old are you?" but instead, I kept the conversation going. He told me how he had started a group of Zanzibaris supporting Obama's candidacy in 2008 and how they had organized a huge rally in Zanzibar on Obama's inauguration night in the United States. He talked about how he had been selected as one of the young African leaders to visit the White House in 2010, as a part of America's attempts to reach out to Africa. He told me about all the social causes he is championing and the funds he is raising to improve healthcare in Zanzibar. All the while, I was sitting there, my mouth agape, trying to remember what exactly I had been doing when I was his age. Accumulating academic degrees without even knowing why? I guess so!

It is young people like these who keep challenging the cynic and the detached observer in me. When I asked him about independence for Zanzibar, he demurred, giving me a measured response by telling me the pros and cons of being a part of Tanzania. Maybe it was a sign of a budding politician or maybe it was a sign of his maturity.

But no matter who wins the Tanzania-Zanzibar dispute, if there is one thing that binds their people, it is the daladala. This vehicle can be anywhere between a 10-seater and a 20-seater, but the designated number of seats doesn't really matter. They manage to cram at least twice as many people into these taxis. For amounts that don't even enter consciousness in the Western world, you can travel for tens of kilometers in them. They are not just taxis, but they are a microcosm of Tanzanian life.

On the mainland, when I reached Moshi from Dar es Salaam late at night, I took the last daladala leaving town to go to a tiny village nearby, which was my final destination. I was planning to start my hike to the top of Kilimanjaro from that village. The young guy sitting next to me in the packed bus from Dar to Moshi decided to come with me in the daladala. I never asked him to join me, but according to him, it wasn't all that safe to go to the village after dark. There was no place to sit in the daladala, so we had to stand in the narrow strip next to the four rows of seats. Since the minibus was barely five feet tall, standing was an exercise in leaning. For the next 90 minutes or so, we were grabbing whatever we could find – seat handles, broken lamp shades, window panes, even grooves on the ceiling – just to keep ourselves from falling. I was leaning on top of at least a couple of people, but they didn't seem to mind at all. Just like a rush-hour local train experience in Mumbai, I learned how Tanzanian bodies smelled after a hard day's work. As a bonus, I had to read all the text messages the guys sitting below me were sending. I had no option. In a way, I was glad I didn't understand Swahili!

Halfway through the ride, a hand came out of nowhere, asking for money for the ticket. How the hell are we going to reach our wallets while standing in this precarious position? My friend asked me not to worry about it. The girl sitting next to his pocket reached into his pocket, pulled out the exact amount of money for two tickets, and shoved the rest back into his pocket. A few minutes later, the cell phone in his pocket started ringing. The same girl promptly sprang back into action. She took the phone out of his pocket, held it to his ear while he spoke, and put it back again. No big deal.

In Zanzibar the vans were bigger, but they also served a larger purpose. In the evening, the top of the daladala was loaded with supplies for convenience stores in some remote corners of the island. In the morning, it was loaded with fresh catch from the ocean going to the main town. The gooey liquid from the baskets of fish on top was dripping down the side straight onto my neighbor's shirt, but he didn't seem to mind. The daladala kept stopping at random places, handing out parcels to people who somehow knew the time and place of delivery. It wasn't just the ticket collector who was handing out parcels. Even passengers could request random stops and deliver money, food, or pretty much anything on the planet to their relatives magically waiting for them on the roadside.

In spite of the daladala being completely packed, two women managed to crowd-surf their infants in and then managed to squeeze themselves in. While they traveled standing, strangers who had seats were taking care of their infants. Another infant whose mom had the luxury of having a seat started crying, and his mom managed to breast feed him amid all that chaos. A guy covered with dust and without any footwear came in and sat right next to a guy wearing a nice button-down shirt, clean trousers, and polished leather shoes. The young guy sitting next to me had one of his butt-cheeks practically on my lap, crushing the sunglasses in my shorts pocket. But that was a small price to pay for this invaluable experience.

As Tanzania becomes industrialized, these daladalas will disappear one day, taking away a certain sense of community from the Tanzanians and a vital source of amusement from travelers like me. Before that happens, crowd-surf the daladala. If you survive the ride, you can walk away with an Ashok Chakra or a Medal of Honor.

19. SOUTH AFRICA: NATION MANDELA

September 26, 2012
Cape Town, South Africa

As I hopped on a plane from Dar es Salaam to South Africa, I habitually started drawing parallels between the young Zanzibari leader's youthful exuberance and international affairs. First came the earliest civilizations in all parts of Africa and Asia, fighting amongst themselves to establish their supremacy. Then came the Mediterranean kingdoms, trying to conquer the world and spread their gospel. Then came the young European nations, with ambitions of dividing the entire world amongst themselves and teaching the "uncivilized" world to become more "civilized." Their destruction in the two World Wars, and subsequent war weariness, gave rise to the American Empire. And now, we have an old civilization reinventing itself in strange ways, trying to regain its once-dominant position in the world. On issues big and small, the world seems to be in a constant struggle between "old worlders," emphasizing the importance of status quo, and the "new worlders," willing to imagine a new world. It's just the actors who keep changing. Hindus would mark the four stages: rise, prosperity, decadence, and decline. The circle of life goes on!

The plane thudded down on the Johannesburg airstrip and gave me a glimpse of the newish world. This is supposed to be the most developed economy of sub-Saharan Africa, but almost everyone who knows anything about South Africa had warned me to skip Jo'burg. The crime rate here is supposed to be ridiculously high.

Cape Town, here I come!

As I made my way from the Jo'burg airport to the bus station and then down to Cape Town, it was easy to see all the development around me. Perhaps due to the recent football World Cup in 2010, the airports, bus stations, roads, and even the rest areas along the highways were so good they would rival those in the developed world.

Tourism-wise, Cape Town is supposed to be the jewel in the South African crown. The Cape of Good Hope, the views from the Table Mountain, wine country, penguin beach, a good surf; you name it. Before hitting any of these destinations, in my first hour in Cape Town I learned that safe was a relative term here. On my flight to South Africa, I had a guy from Jo'burg tell me emphatically that Cape Town really was safe. I took his word for it and decided to walk the five kilometers from the bus terminal to the hostel. It was a bit cloudy, with a hint of drizzle in the air, but it was 2 PM. Broad daylight! Surely nothing to worry about.

Within the first half kilometer, someone came up behind and tried to snatch my iPad out of my hand. *All right, stop acting like a dumbass, flaunting your iPad around!* But the neighborhoods got progressively worse, until I reached an alley full of people just hanging out and giving me "What are you doing here?" stares. A couple of them tried selling me drugs. *Clench your fists, look straight ahead, and keep walking!* The creepy areas lasted for a good 4-5 blocks before things started getting better. As I reached the hostel, with no bruises or burns or stolen valuables, I was greeted with expressions of incredulity when I told them I walked my way there. Lesson learned. Cape Town is not safe!

When it comes to tourism, this country is as well-developed, and perhaps even more developed, than Tanzania. But if Cape Town is any indication, these two countries are a study in contrasts in a lot of other aspects. Walking around here after dark is a no-no, but that's just the start. Twenty years after Mandela's historic victory in ending apartheid, resentment among blacks and whites lingers on under the surface of happy co-mingling in this rainbow nation. As I opened the local English newspaper, which is a luxury when the local language is changing every week, I found it was full of stories of the recent killing of miners in the north and existing racial undercurrents. There are some allegations of racism against black cricketers in the selection of the national cricket team. Even the black communities don't seem to get along well with each other. There are reports of tension between the native black South Africans and migrant black workers from other African countries.

The incidence of rape here is way above the world average. I took a minibus back home after dark and when a local girl noticed that the bus was full of men, she was hesitant to board it. The driver asked her boyfriend, who was there to see her off, to take his picture on his cell phone. If something went wrong, her boyfriend would be able to track down the driver and the bus. When I asked the locals about it, they said rape is condoned, and sometimes even considered a sign of manliness. Apparently, it has something to do with the allegations of rape against Jacob Zuma who, in spite of the allegations, was the sitting President of South Africa. Such allegations, even if unproven, would preclude you from becoming the head of state in several other countries, but not South Africa.

While the Tanzanians seem to be generally happy with their President, South Africans grab every opportunity they get to criticize Zuma. With four wives, charges of rape, and allegations of widespread corruption against him, he seems to be intent on reversing the gains of the last two decades. Other than the tourism industry, things seem to be moving backward here. According to one study, 25% of the workforce here is employed by the government and there is talk of nationalizing the mining industry. Whereas young Tanzanians seem to be interested in exploiting the peace dividend, young South Africans talk about widespread unemployment and corruption. The young, charismatic leader of the African National Congress, instead of being the rising star of this young nation, has just walked out of jail; winning a protracted political witch-hunt by Zuma. Standing in front of Nelson Mandela's tiny prison cell, in which he spent most of those dark 21 years, I couldn't help but wonder whether his dream was unraveling.

But this prison tour to the nearby Robben Island was certainly the highlight of my pit-stop in South Africa. I was debating whether I should take a detour to Durban and visit the train station where Mahatma Gandhi was thrown out of the train. Just to stand there and take it in. But I'm glad I stayed back and did the prison tour. One of the ex-prisoners was our guide and he took us around the entire prison complex, narrating in minute detail the anti-apartheid movement, his personal journey as a guerrilla warrior,

144

training all over Africa, and traveling in and out of South Africa to keep the underground movement alive, Mandela's own struggles in the prison, the smuggling of his writings out of the prison, and the culmination of it all in Mandela's election as the first black president in the first-ever non-racial elections. It's not just about Mandela's epic battle and his statesmanship. It's also about these tremendous acts of graciousness and burying of the past by people like this ex-prisoner, that help nations heal. And here we are, cribbing about inconsequential he-said, she-saids! Forget about forgiving and reconciliation, how many of us could even survive 21 years in prison? As I was leaving Africa, the young Tanzanian leader and the old, yet cheerful, ex-prisoner served as timely uplifting stories.

Oh well! Wake up at 4 AM, drive a couple of hours, get on a boat, put on your wet suit, get in a cage, take a deep breath, immerse yourself in the ice-cold Indian Ocean water, open your eyes, and then? The 4-meter-long great white shark opens his jaw just ten feet from you. It clears your head and drains your adrenalin glands. After enjoying the surreal experience of shark cage diving, pack your bags and move on!

ASIAN
WONDERS

6

20. CHINA: THE LAND OF CONTROLLED CHAOS

October 20, 2012
Xi'an, China

As I landed in Beijing, the first thing that hit me was people; the sheer number of people. It started right at the airport. Parts of Tanzania and South Africa were crowded, but not "Asia" crowded, with hordes of people being carted around with an incredible amount of discipline. In a nutshell, that's China for you.

For as long as I can remember, which is not a whole lot considering the histories of these two countries, India and China have had a pretty schizophrenic relationship. On the one hand, as countries in which most of the Eastern philosophies originated, India and China feel a certain sense of kinship toward each other. While the Indians and the Chinese both secretly love the United States, they both think their long histories and the richness of their cultures make them superior to the Americans, and Westerners in general. On the other hand, there is a lot of mistrust and fierce competition among these Asian neighbors. The lack of trust can be traced back to the 1962 war. Nehru's India declined permanent membership on the UN Security Council and handed it to China. Mao's China returned that favor by invading India and gobbling up a big chunk of India. As if that were not enough, China's pivotal role in propping up the Pakistani nuclear program, in the '60s and '70s, further widened the trust gap.

On top of that, the explosion of these two economies over the past 2-3 decades has created a sense of intense competition that is growing by the day. Going by the top two-three cities, though, there is really no competition. China has left India behind. Big time!

Beijing is all about history and politics. The most interesting aspect of visiting the Forbidden City, Temple of Heaven, summer palace, and a bunch of other historic sites was the nomenclature. When these monuments were built, it seemed like things had to be heavenly, magnificent, eternal, celestial, or something along those lines. The structures were all about peace, tranquility, harmony, permanence, or some similar desirable quality. You can choose any of these nouns, add one of those adjectives, and voila! You have just named a historic building in Beijing. However, standing in front of the *Hall of quintessence* made me wonder whether they had stretched it a bit too far. What are you supposed to do or gain in this hall?

Architecturally, these pagoda-like historic sites start getting repetitive after awhile. There are, however, some symbolic differences. The blue structures are places of worship and the green ones are houses or palaces of the royals. The number of tiny animals on the roofs indicates the position of the person in the political pecking order. Beyond that, the slanting roofs and the facades look fairly similar, unless you understand the complex symbolism. However, the most impressive thing about Beijing is what is outside these historic sites. It is the cleanliness and a certain sense of order they have managed to impose on this gigantic city. Perhaps due to the Beijing Olympics, the impressive metro system, garbage collection, street cleaning, and orderly traffic; everything seems to work. I made the mistake of landing in Beijing during the Chinese national holiday week. In this national capital, it translates into millions of tourists crowding every corner of the city. Walking out of the Tiananmen Square metro station and visiting the Forbidden City, on the day of the military parade, was as crazy as walking into the Chhatrapati Shivaji Terminus in Mumbai during rush hour. Even then, everything was working remarkably smoothly.

If Beijing is awesome, Shanghai is even better. As the center of the Chinese political universe, Beijing still retains some of the symbols of Maoist communism. His embalmed body, his photos around the city, communist red flags flying atop government buildings. Shanghai has quietly bid good-bye to all that. People's Square has a huge, glitzy mall, in the basement, selling all things Western. When it comes to neon lights, People's Street here beats Times Square and the Las Vegas strip combined. The French Concession area, where the first meeting of the Communist Party of China was held under Mao's leadership, is packed with outlets of top European and American fashion labels. On a clear day with blue skies, the skyline of Pudong, which was a swamp land less than two decades ago, beats Manhattan hands down! When you walk out of the charming Yuyuan Gardens, Ronald McDonald, the colonel of Kentucky, and everyone in between welcomes you with open arms. Even in the non-touristy areas, the tall apartment complexes of the Shanghai suburbs look much more diverse and colorful than the monotonic communist-era concrete blocks of East Berlin. Overall, on a smog-free day, this city rivals whatever you consider to be the best city in the world.

Hong Kong was no different. It's probably a bit smelly, but clean, nonetheless. One might argue that Hong Kong wasn't, and still doesn't consider itself to be, a part of China. But the gigantic city of Shenzhen next door is all Chinese. With so many people peddling prostitutes, it could get a bit sleazy here. That is mostly related to all the business conferences and conventions held here on a regular basis. You start seeing an occasional alley with garbage thrown all over the street. But by and large, the transformation of this village into a concrete jungle with wide roads, a brand-spanking-new metro system, and basic city infrastructure, in a mere decade, is nothing short of astonishing. If the top three cities are any indication, China serves India a smack-down on a golden platter.

The inordinate amount of time I spent on Chinese trains was a good way to get a glimpse of the other China. The trains themselves are a good starting point. The 300km/h bullet train from Beijing to Shanghai is world-class; maybe even better than its European rivals. The Shanghai to Hong Kong ride was a pleasure, although it was not as mind-blowing as the bullet train. Things became progressively worse as I moved to the interior of China. Bathrooms weren't as clean anymore, and people had no qualms about smoking in the vestibule between two coaches, effectively subjecting everyone to second-hand smoke. Still, the conditions were decidedly better than those in Indian trains, mostly because they have an attendant for each coach. If people are unwilling to develop any civic sense, China has decided to deploy armies of employees to impose it on them. Platforms and train stations were much cleaner than their Indian counterparts, too. The Chinese efficiency at moving millions of people in and out of this enormous train system is astonishing.

But the other cities I visited, like Guilin, Xi'an, and Chengdu, were still in the "site under construction" mode. The civic sense of not spitting in public, not littering on the streets, not smoking in public places, and obeying traffic rules hadn't reached these cities yet. As I was looking out the window of my train, it felt like the Chinese government had undertaken some sort of a generational "city upgrade" plan. If you spot a bunch of unfinished concrete structures and lots of cranes, that town has been selected by the powers that be for an upgrade. If your town isn't lucky enough, it looks almost identical to a small town or village in India. Dusty and unpaved roads, shacks or huts made out of bamboo, rice paddies, two-wheelers with three people packed on the tiny seats running around town; the uncanny similarity to the Indian countryside – made famous by cheesy Bollywood movies – made me feel nostalgic. For a minute, it felt like India was not too far behind in terms of development.

Just like any other country, China is full of contradictions. The Chinese culture is as idiosyncratic as any other culture in the world. Whereas the politicians and military leaders seem to be shrewd or borderline cunning, people on the streets of China seem incredibly honest and harmless. No matter how late it was in the night, safety on the streets was never an issue. During my one-month stay, except for one late-night taxi driver in Beijing, no one else tried to rip me off. With the stiff language barrier, there were times when it was difficult to understand how much street food was selling for. But more often than not, I would keep a bunch of Chinese Yuans – coins and notes – in my hand and extend my palm. They never took anything extra out of my hand. Maybe because of the Olympics in Beijing and the World Expo in Shanghai, clearing your throat and spitting in public had disappeared from these cities. However, in smaller cities, both men and women could be seen spitting with abandon. It got even worse on the trains. Two middle-aged men, sitting five feet away from me, were spitting on the floor and clearing it out with their foot-ware, as if that made it acceptable!

The language barrier made it difficult to interact with everyday Chinese, but it was the vast train network that helped me bond with them. On the long train ride from Xi'an to Chengdu, because of my last-minute plans, I had to travel with the cheapest available option, the hard plastic seat with no cushion. A 20-hour journey in a hard seat sounds pretty bad, but it turned out to be a blessing in disguise, mainly because that is how the vast majority of rural China travels. As soon as I boarded the train, five people around me – a young lady and her old father, an energetic young guy, a contemplative middle-aged man, and an old man with a wrinkled face – started bombarding me with questions in Chinese. After a five-minute bombardment, they realized my brain hadn't registered a thing. Even my humble "No Chinese" didn't seem to cross the language barrier. While it toned down their enthusiasm, it didn't affect their curiosity about me. I pulled out my cell phone to play some music. The energetic guy sitting in front of me leaned over and started staring at my cell phone screen. I was taken aback for a bit, but then I realized that all he wanted to know was what language it was. When he realized it was English, or something that he didn't comprehend, he retreated to his seat. A few minutes later, he pointed to my earplugs and asked "Hindu la?" or something like that. Finally, I managed to pick up one word that vaguely made sense. I was planning to play some rock music, but changed it to Hindi music and extended my earplugs to him. He listened to it for a bit, returned them to me with a smile on his face, and told the others something about me. They all nodded in unison. Now the old father wanted to hear the music, too. After listening to it for a while, he happily extended his bag of peanuts to me. I took a couple, but it looked like I managed to offend him with my modesty. He took a fistful of them and laid them in my lap! *All right, sir. I'll eat them all!* After observing them engaging in an animated discussion about something, I pulled out my iPad to work on my blog, but that attempt was thwarted immediately. They all wanted to touch and feel the iPad. I opened my photo album and shared my journey with them, showing them pictures from other parts of the world. Writing my blog post had to wait.

During dinner time, they took ownership of my bowl of noodles and showed me the right way to heat up instant noodles with hot water. After dinner, the contemplative guy bought a bottle of local liquor – 50% alcohol – and offered it to me. I smelt the bottle's contents and immediately declined, but he insisted on sharing it with me. A guy who smells the bottle before drinking probably knows his alcohol! He embarked on a ten-minute mission to cut a plastic bottle in half, to make a glass out of it, and served me a stiff drink. I took a sip and almost spit it out, but I didn't want to offend him. I went to the hot water tap near the vestibule, poured half of the liquor down the drain, replaced it with hot water, and returned to my seat. By the time my drink cooled down to room temperature, he had run through three quarters of his bottle...straight! And by the time I finished mine, he had finished the whole bottle. So this was the source of his contemplative demeanor!

The hospitality didn't end there. Even in those cramped conditions, they found a place for me to prop my legs up on the seat in front of me, making the ride a bit more comfortable. They didn't hesitate to grab my legs and put them in the empty space. Then, when the young lady and her dad disembarked at some ungodly hour, they woke me up and offered to let me lie down first, making the night much more bearable. In the morning, breakfast was offered, too, which I had to decline. By that time, I didn't hesitate to hand over my iPad to the contemplative guy to take care of, before going to the toilet. Alcohol bonds run deep! On and on it went...

In that 20-hour span, our verbal communication started and ended with "Hindu." But verbal communication is rarely, if ever, the most interesting exchange of information.

*   *   *

The Chinese Challenge

October 27, 2012
Beijing, China

The people and the culture of China give you plenty of food for thought, but a month in this country challenges you at several levels. It hits you a lot deeper than almost every other country.

The language is the most obvious challenge. This language

family is so different from all the other languages that even the basic stuff tourists tend to pick up in a week or two is a Herculean effort here. Once I started picking up the basics, I started noticing some amusing things, such as "she" is yes and "she she" is thank you. As a native Marathi speaker, getting used to saying "poop" when you want to say "yes" and keeping a straight face took awhile. The first time I heard "ni-ga," I was a bit shocked by the ease and frequency with which the word was being used. But then I learned that it means "that" in Chinese. After learning that, even the way street vendors were selling Snickers became mildly amusing.

It was all fun and games until I lost my way and needed a vocabulary that went beyond the hi-byes and ordering food. In Xi'an, my inability to understand what the locals were saying at the bus station led me to take the wrong bus and I landed in a neighborhood in which nobody understood any English. They didn't even understand the question, "Do you speak English?" That's because they have a Chinese word for the English language that I obviously didn't know. My dumb-charades style sign language attempt at telling them I was looking for the Terracotta Warriors was easily the highlight of my linguistic escapades here. After building a resume of visiting 35-40 odd countries, my utter failure at being able to convey anything was a disconcerting experience. Think about it. How would you tell someone that you were looking for the Terracotta Warriors if all you had was sign language? I tried the sword-fight and bow-and-arrow gestures. With my hands, I tried arranging virtual statues in rows, in the air. I tried digging underground to indicate that it's an excavated sight. Historic sight. Lots of tourists. Foreign tourists. Nothing! If anything, they looked a bit concerned when I was making the sword-fighting gestures. I quietly boarded the same bus back to the main station, chased down a couple of English-speaking people, and managed to get there three hours late. And they say this is "simplified" Chinese!

That brings us to Mao's legacy. As the architect of the Cultural Revolution, he was the instigator behind the development of simplified Chinese. But that is the silver lining, at best. As I was traveling the length and breadth of this country, I managed to learn some basic facts about Mysterious Mao. At first, I was worried that if I tried to access unbiased information about him online, the

Great Firewall would block my internet access. But somehow, that didn't happen. As I found out later, there is actually a concerted effort these days, by the powers that be, to de-emphasize Mao's legacy. Still, reading about the life and times of Mao put a lot of things in perspective.

When I was in Germany, I was appalled at seeing the WWII sites. In terms of atrocities, Mao apparently beat the Nazis, by far. During the Great Leap Forward, he decided to pay down the national debt by exporting as much food grain as he could, which resulted in the infamous famine (Looks like Ceauşescu of Romania got his idea from Mao!). After the Great Leap Forward, Mao orchestrated systematic purges of political opponents all the way till the end of the Cultural Revolution, putting the tally of people who died directly or indirectly at some 40 million. As a city, Berlin has probably seen more turmoil in the last hundred years than any other city, but as a country, China probably leaves all other countries behind. Perhaps it explains a certain degree of stoicism among the older people here. Even when dancing in the central squares, which seems to be a routine weekend activity across the country, these people seemed to dance with straight faces. Huge crowds gather in the central plazas of all the cities every Saturday or Sunday, and one could see people performing waltzes, square dances, and even tangos. Maybe this is some kind of community-building activity. But after the traumatic events of the last century, maybe they have become immune to their own emotions.

The silver lining is not limited to the simplification of the language. Education, and belatedly, English education, seems to be a major focus of this new Chinese society. I was surprised by the number of English teachers I met in one month, all coming from the United States, Canada, and the United Kingdom, teaching in remote towns and villages hidden from public glare. Even a small town of some 30,000 people just outside of Xi'an had a huge, 4000-student-capacity school with three English teachers from Canada.

Additionally, women were a visible force in all aspects of life here. All the government offices and private businesses I went to were well-represented by women. Their presence even extended to taxi and bus driving. On metros, unlike India, there was no concept of a women's coach here. Women and men traveled together in crowded trains. Local women steadfastly declined to take the seats I offered them. Think what you may, but even the act of women spitting and smoking in public was a sign of their liberation. The communist party leadership here seems to be dominated by men but, in daily life, China seems to be light years ahead of India, and even some Western countries, when it comes to women's liberation.

However, this current state of affairs makes you wonder where this society is headed. Is democracy really the inevitable destiny of this most populous nation on earth? Having spent all of my life in democracies, I can't imagine living in a managed society like this for any extended period of time. But one has to be democracy-agnostic to honestly assess the situation here. All said and done, democracy is counter-intuitive when we look at the whole animal kingdom. Almost all the other species work on the might-is-right principle and have strict hierarchies in their colonies. The main reason humans find it attractive is because it is intellectually appealing to those advanced mental faculties, like logical thinking and deductive inference, that evolution has granted us. Even in the context of human history, democracy is still a nascent social experiment. American democracy, when it started, was limited to white, male land-owners. Women were left out, which brings the participating members down to 50%. Men belonging to minorities were left out, which, assuming 10% minorities, brings it down to 45% or so. Even a generous 50% land ownership at the dawn of America means democracy and voting rights were limited to the most privileged 20-25% of Americans when they started their experiment. I'm sure the communist party membership in China is somewhere around 20%, at least. It took America almost two hundred years to empower all her constituents. The People's Republic of China, on the other hand, was established less than a hundred years ago. Plus, when you look at countries like Russia, India, Pakistan, Egypt, and Iraq, that suddenly woke up to democracy, the results are decidedly mixed. So, what gives?

And then, as they say, all politics is local. The Chinese people have endured so much in the past century. Mo Yan, the Nobel literature prize winner from 2012, apparently survived the famine by eating tree bark. Perhaps some semblance of political stability and security can be a good substitute for your yearnings for democracy.

I can't say that I'm a fan of the Chinese model. Their human rights record, media censorship, clamping down on the Internet, and many other such things, are suffocating for me. Even if they are the second-largest economy by GDP, their per-capita GDP, the real indicator of material human development, is comparable to that of Uganda. They'll have to have 3-4 times the GDP of the United States to be comparable in that regard, but their leaders have used poverty and a bizarre version of state-sponsored capitalism to rig the entire system in their favor. Instead of encouraging risk-taking, entrepreneurship, and a free exchange of information, they have decided to trade cheap labor for intellectual property developed elsewhere. To see how they are using their pile of cash to buy up all kinds of assets around the world, all you have to do is look at the trips Timothy Geithner, the former US treasury secretary, made to China during the height of the 2009 financial crisis, and all the sweeteners China got out of the back room deals in that period, to prop the American financial system.

Regardless of how you feel about all this, it is possible that, over the next fifty years, China will keep playing this game on their terms, get up to speed with America in terms of economic indicators, and then transition to democracy on its own terms. We will all be sitting in the arena, clapping our hands grudgingly, whispering, "Well played, well played."

21. THAILAND: OF FLY LICE, 7/11 TOASTEES & LADYBOYS

November 7, 2012
Pai, Thailand

Scuba diving was easily the highlight of my stay in Thailand. The island of Koh Tao is supposed to be one of the cheapest places in the world to get your scuba diving certification. And boy was it fun! I've always enjoyed swimming and snorkeling, but this is WAY better than both. In some ways, it's intriguing, too. Before doing our first dive in the ocean, we spent about 3-4 hours in the swimming pool, to learn all the scuba diving skills. More than the body, it was intriguing to learn how agile the human brain is. For as long as I can remember, I've always consciously made an effort to keep my mouth shut and breathe with my nose while working out. But with the oxygen tube in my mouth, as soon as I went underwater my brain knew my nose was not an option anymore. I didn't have to make any conscious effort to breathe with my mouth. More intriguing was the alacrity with which we all learned the underwater language. Faced with adversity, and when the margin of error is razor thin, our brains learn all the hand gestures necessary for survival underwater at lightning speed.

But in a way, that is all beside the point. I can guarantee you that, the first time you dive in the wide open ocean will be one of those unforgettable moments of your life. In the classroom sessions, they tell you that some 60-70% of the species in the world live underwater and that we should all strive to experience that world. No matter how many videos you have seen on the Discovery Channel or how many you see during the classroom training, the first time you put on your cylinder, insert the regulator in your mouth, and let yourself sink in the ocean, you will be filled with a sense of wonder like never before. It's like being a kid again; going to Disneyland for the first time, maybe. As rookies, we were diving in pairs. After seeing the corals and the schools of fish in their natural habitat for the first time, my buddy and I immediately looked at each other and started inventing hand gestures to convey our sense of amazement. Our brains, once again, had no problem understanding those gestures because there is no way anyone can escape that crazy feeling. Great Barrier Reef, here I come!

After spending six long months on the road, I've finally started embracing the true spirit of backpacking. When I boarded the Thai Airways flight from Beijing to Bangkok, I was pleasantly surprised to hear the instrumental version of the Hindi chartbuster song *Kal Ho Na Ho* on the flight, and I started wondering what other aspects of Thai life are influenced by India. Beyond that, I had no idea what the hell I was going to do in Thailand. I was thinking about doing a Thailand-Malaysia-Singapore-Vietnam-Cambodia loop and then spending a couple of weeks sight-seeing in Thailand, but that plan changed as soon as I landed in Bangkok and heard about the Halloween Full Moon Party in Koh Phangan. 30-40,000 people on a beach! I had to do it. I had bought a train ticket from Bangkok all the way to the Malaysia border, but abandoned the train halfway through, hopped on a ferry, and took a full-moon detour.

The revelry was unplanned and I was still considering getting back on track to Malaysia, until I realized how hot and humid it was in southern Thailand. Malaysia is south of Thailand. Sweating it out in Malaysia didn't sound like a good idea. It was time to get my scuba diving certification done and head north. Clock-wise Thailand-Cambodia-Vietnam-Singapore-Malaysia would put me in Malaysia in December instead of early November. It would have cooled down by then.

After embracing the underwater world, I embarked on a 26-hour ferry-bus-train trip from Koh Tao to Chiang Mai in northern Thailand, without knowing why travelers go there. The main attraction there seemed to be the park in which you can pet tigers, play with the cubs, and take pictures with them. But some say the tigers are drugged to the point where they are docile, which dampened my enthusiasm for that. At the hostel, I also started hearing that Pai is much more beautiful and less touristy than Chiang Mai. When we had a good group of eight people ready to go to Pai, I finally opened up a map to see where the hell I was and where I was headed. After Chiang Mai or Pai, I was thinking about going to Cambodia. When I looked at the map, though, I realized there was no easy way to get to Cambodia from either Chiang Mai or Pai. There is this big country called Laos in the middle!

Instead of worrying about reaching Cambodia, I decided to focus on the next few days. After two days of relaxing in Chiang Mai, and listening to some surprisingly good jazz at the North Gate Jazz bar (highly recommended for jazz lovers), I was ready to just go with the flow. I was hanging out with nice people and it made sense to head to Pai with them.

Pai didn't disappoint at all. Tucked away in the northern jungles of Thailand, this sleepy town is a backpacker's haven. It has the basics like cheap hostels, street-side food joints, hole-in-the-wall dive bars and such. But the mountains, rivers, waterfalls, and jungles around Pai provide endless opportunities for outdoor activities. The people I was hanging out with - two Canadians, an American, two South Africans, a Norwegian, and a Spaniard - made the whole experience all the more exciting. It all started in Chiang Mai, when we rented five mopeds and named ourselves Heaven's Devils. A gang of mopeds sounded a bit foolish, but hey, it's a lot less foolish than opening up the map in Chiang Mai and realizing that Cambodia is a long way away. In the backpacking world, stupidity is all relative. So I decided to play along with Heaven's Devils.

A late-afternoon to late-night ride on some of the most winding roads I've seen took us to Pai. Two waterfalls, a canyon, and hot springs later, we should have left Pai with smiles on our faces, but our youthful exuberance had other ideas. On the last day, with a 6 PM bus to catch, we all decided to start a 12km waterfall hike at 2 in the afternoon. Three kilometers per hour is totally doable, right? No, it's not, especially when you are hiking through a thick jungle and crossing the river every five minutes. Our young blood discounted such facts and kept going. The Spanish guy was the first one to drop out. After an hour or so, he realized that he preferred going slowly and smelling the roses along the way. I was the second one to call it quits. With only one pair of shoes, I didn't want to get them wet, so I decided to hike barefoot through the jungle. So innovative! After another half an hour, I realized that it was impossible to keep up with people wearing shoes. And on my way back, I managed to jump on a slippery rock in the river, and get my passport and the all-important shoes wet. Kudos to me!

The Spanish guy and I were waiting for the others to come back, when one of the Canadian guys showed up with a football-sized ankle, desperately looking for ice. He had managed to slip in the river, too. Others showed up just in time to catch the bus. Needless to say, nobody made it to the waterfalls. Some made it to a tiny waterfall less than 2 meters in height. The real one was apparently 20 meters high, a critical piece of information we didn't have until we came back. But hey, it's not about the destination. It's about the journey, right?

As beautiful, green, and mosquito-infested as Thailand is, the real attraction here is the food. This is a street-food nation, another reason backpackers call it their home. For a Dollar or two, you can have a tasty, satisfying meal here. In the traditional dishes like Penang curry, red curry, green curry, yellow curry (and whatever other color you can imagine), they generously pour ginger, garlic, basil, peanuts, chilies, and a host of other spices routinely used in India, making Indians like me feel at home. A lady at a restaurant in Koh Tao even dared me to eat the "ring-of-fire" spicy chicken she cooked, which I gladly accepted. The most hilarious aspect of this Indian side of Thai food, though, was the ordering process. Some of these street-food vendors, especially the ones in smaller towns, had a hard time understanding "fried rice." It is interesting cognitively because they don't seem to have "R" in their language. But that's not the most interesting part. If you don't want to repeat your order, try "fly lice" and they get it immediately. Given the kind of stuff they eat in this part of the world – grasshoppers, worms, cockroaches – a lice dish wouldn't have surprised me. Nonetheless, Heaven's Devils had a blast ordering fly lice for every other meal.

The Western side of Thai food is something called the 7/11 toastee. I don't know what bond 7/11s share with Thailand, but they are like Starbucks in New York. If someone tells you "Just go around the corner and your hostel is right next to the 7/11," you would be compelled to ask "Which one of those four 7/11s are you talking about?" But for backpackers, this is great news. No matter which 7/11 you walk into here, you can always find two tiny toasters and three options for hot sandwiches or toastees. For non-foodies like me, there is the ham and cheese toastee for breakfast. For foodies, they can step it up a notch and serve you a tuna toastee. And for hungover people stumbling into the store, they have a sausage toastee. All for one Dollar. If you are a backpacker, you cannot leave Thailand without trying this gourmet treat!

And finally, a trip to Thailand cannot be complete without a ladyboy story. In the United States, I've noticed a few of them in Vegas and New Orleans. In fact, I once had a hard time recognizing one in New Orleans. In India, they flock to the big cities but sadly, they are treated as social outcasts. When you land in Bangkok, this curious social phenomenon is hard to ignore. On the one hand, the seamless integration of ladyboys in this Buddhist Thai society speaks volumes about their social tolerance. Don't be surprised if you find them manning ticket booths, food stalls, or grocery stores. The unusually high numbers of ladyboys in Bangkok is also surprising, but sometimes, when people can't recognize them, it leads to some humor, albeit of a darker shade.

After a hectic day of sightseeing in Bangkok, we were all sitting around in the hostel lounge, sharing travel stories. One girl started narrating an incident from the previous night. A group of friends walked into a bar in Bangkok and one of the guys started chatting up with a local girl. He bought her a few drinks and before he even noticed, he had spent two hours talking to her. His friends, who knew him well, took him to the side and asked him whether he had checked if she is a ladyboy. He told his friends that he was confident she was not a ladyboy, but his friends still advised him to confirm it.

He went back to the girl and confronted her. She took his hand and dragged it under her skirt. The guy was clueless, nauseated, and felt like throwing up. He dashed to the bathroom, kicked open one of the booths, and threw up, only to realize that he had thrown up on a guy occupying the booth. At that point, he was even more clueless. He knew the guy he had puked on was not exactly thrilled about the whole situation. So he decided to punch guy he puked on in the face and knock him out. But he was a nice guy. He decided to keep the booth door open so that someone else could notice him and help him out. What's next? Grab your friends and run for your life!

Oh Bangkok! No wonder *Hangover II* was shot here. This city is crazy like that! Sometimes, reality is, indeed, stranger than fiction.

22. LAOS: NUMBER OF THE WEEK: 80 MILLION

November 12, 2012
Luangprabang, Laos

I'm talking about eighty million bombs. No matter how much time you spend in Laos - a day, a week, a month - if you leave this country without learning how many unexploded bombs and landmines this country still has, you are talking to the wrong people.

This country, smaller than the state of Maharashtra in size, has the dubious distinction of being one of the most heavily bombed countries in the world. During the Vietnam War, communist leader Ho Chi Minh was apparently using the road going through Laos and Cambodia – now known as the Ho Chi Minh trail – to supply arms to the communists fighting against Americans in south Vietnam. And the Americans resorted to indiscriminate bombing all along this trail to blow up this supply route. This resulted in a country that has some of the most pristine, untouched natural landscapes, riddled with cluster bombs, land-mines, and everything in between. Given the number of tragic land-mine accidents occurring in Laos every year, it almost makes you wonder whether these unexploded bombs are the real reason behind the country's untouched natural beauty.

That's not the only bizarre, unfortunate thing about this country. This is still a communist country, with single-party rule. In a throwback to the Soviet era, they have less than 3%

unemployment, but per-capita income that's nowhere on the world map. Almost all of the Mediterranean and Asian countries run on their own timetables. There is mañana-time in Spain, Indian Stretchable Time, and Bangkok time in Thailand. But time pretty much stands still in this country. Traveling around, you feel like the Lao people have found the secret of being in perfect harmony with each other and with the surrounding natural beauty. There is no chaotic traffic, nobody is rushing anywhere, and nobody seems to have any agenda. This makes it an ideal country for backpackers.

The chilling out started as soon as we entered the country at Huay Xai, a tiny border town on the Thai side. The Heaven's Devils boarded a boat and cruised along the Mekong River for two days to reach Luangprabang, one of the top three cities in Laos. A hippie from San Francisco with a ukulele was exactly what the doctor ordered to make the passing lush green scenery even more intoxicating. Backpackers roaming around with no agenda don't need an invitation to sing along. As if that weren't enough, the captain of the boat walked out of the cabin with a bottle of Lao rice whiskey, and the "Boat Band" stepped it up a notch. As people started disembarking in Luangprabang, everybody wanted the boat ride to last a little longer.

What was waiting for us there was even more fun. The waterfall just outside this city is easily one of the most beautiful ones I have ever seen. And the tilapia grilled on a stick, 25,000 Kip or $3 in the food alley, is to die for. The specialty liquor of Laos has a snake or a scorpion in the bottle, something I was too creeped out to try. But Laos is not just about these semi-touristy things. It's cities like Luangprabang and countries like Laos that define all things off the beaten path. Backpackers beat the hell out of such paths and after a few years, they become part of the mainstream. Perhaps because of the lack of commercialization here, it offers things that only backpackers can find amusing and enjoyable.

In Luangprabang, almost like clockwork, backpackers reach a bar called Utopia after dinner. If there is a backpacking "institution," this is the one. There are mattresses and pillows on the river-front and the decor is all based on empty bomb shells and hollowed out rockets. In Laos, maybe empty bomb shells that cannot kill you anymore can qualify as utopia. The weirdness of lying on those mattresses, surrounded by rusty rockets, overlooking the river, and sipping your drink are a quintessentially backpacker experience. But wait! There is a midnight curfew in town. The entire city shuts down by the stroke of midnight. So, at midnight, the entire pack goes to the only club, just outside the town, and ends up in a bowling alley – yes, a bowling alley – at 2 in the morning. Drunk bowling continues for as long as people can stand and the next day gets wiped out.

Further south in Vang Vieng, in addition to an eclectic breakfast menu of Italian, Mexican, English, and American fare and comfy mattresses to lie down, backpackers can also choose from a TV menu of *Family Guy*, *Friends*, and *South Park*. Finish your breakfast, get your sunscreen on, and it's time to go tubing. The thing to do in Vang Vieng is sit in a tube and float down the river for a good 2-3 hours and just enjoy the mountains passing by. With backpackers came millions of bars all along the river. People used to stop by, play some stupid drinking games at each bar, and get back on their tubes again. The current is so weak that your tube is floating down the river at a slower pace than walking. Even then, in the last year alone, some 20-30 backpackers got so drunk or high (or both) that they drowned, which led authorities to shut down all the bars along the river. So now, in addition to the beautiful mountains, you have a string of abandoned bars dotting the scenery.

After nightfall, an old dilapidated suspension bridge becomes a party venue. Backpackers are sitting on the bridge, probably waiting for it to collapse so they can add another stupidity feather to their caps. *If you don't let us die by way of getting high while tubing, we will find another stupid way!* The bizarre nature of all of this is charming in its own way.

And then, it was time to say good-bye to the Heaven's Devils. Everyone had their own schedules to follow and it was time to part ways. Having now spent a few weeks in South East Asia, one with Heaven's Devils intersecting Thailand and Laos, it's easy to see why this part of the world is backpackers' favorite stomping ground. With cheap accommodations, food, and sight-seeing, you can survive here on less than $25-30 a day. More importantly, you come here and get to experience the true essence of backpacking. Most of these people are lone warriors, everyone with a story to tell about how and why they got tired of the 9-to-5 grind. It's incredibly easy to make friends. And since most of them have no fixed travel schedules, things like Heaven's Devils are pretty common. Meet a few people, form a group, travel together for a while, add them to Facebook, and move on. Before you know it, you walk into a restaurant and know more than half the crowd, at least superficially, or maybe superfluously. That's because most of them are on roughly the same schedule you are and are visiting the same sights. Some people find love, some satisfy their lust, some find travel buddies, some get drunk and fight, some travel together for a few days and then fight, some people patch things up, and some don't. Backpacking is like life on steroids. Or life in fast-forward. Most of the 9-to-5ers have to hit their 50s and 60s to realize their time on earth is running out. Backpackers don't wait that long. If you look under the microscope, I'm sure the backpacker's DNA will have "Time is running out" etched in it. And that is why they love Laos, a country in which time stands still.

23. VIETNAM: WAR IS RAW. STILL RAW

November 21, 2012
Ho Chi Minh City, Vietnam

It's the American War, stupid. The rest of the world knows it as the Vietnam War, but the Vietnamese call it the American War. With a death toll of more than 4 million, 3 million of whom were civilians, and the effects of Agent Orange and Phosphor bombs still lingering, you are never too far away from the wounds of war in this country. Even now, more than 3 decades after cease fire, there are some 8 million children born with birth defects considered to be directly related to all the chemical weapons the Americans used. While most of the other wounds of the brutal 20-year war have healed, the propaganda, significantly toned down, lives on.

My first stop in Vietnam was Hanoi, the erstwhile capital of north Vietnam. They have the symbolic mausoleum of Ho Chi Minh, with his embalmed body, and the house he used to live in when he was fighting against the Americans. A trip to the prison museum here gives you the first glimpse of the atrocities committed during the war. A lot of it is heavily biased, of course. The contrast between the depiction of the way the Vietnamese prisoners were tortured, in French colonial times, and the way American POWs were treated by the Vietcong, is perhaps the best example of the fact that there is no single side to a story.

It would've been easier to understand things if the war here had just had two phases: The independence war against the French and the subsequent American take-over of the war. The history of war here is hopelessly complicated. Over the past few centuries, the Vietnamese have had to fight the Mongols, Chinese, Japanese, French, and American armies. And at different times, depending on the war, the Vietnamese army has been propped up by the Chinese, Japanese, French, and the Soviets. Go figure! I'm sure Henry Kissinger would love to teach the history of Vietnam as a classic case of Realpolitik. In international relations, there are no permanent friends or enemies. And war, after all, is good business for the prevailing superpowers. For them, suffering of the local people is collateral damage.

The prison museum mostly focuses on the 1955-75 war. The section dedicated to the role of Vietnamese women in the war is quite enlightening. It took a massive cultural revolution for Chinese women to break all the social barriers. Vietnamese women, on the other hand, seem to have been active in all aspects of life here for a long time, including the war. The inspiring stories of all the brave women fighting in the war reminded me of the iconic final scene from the movie *Full Metal Jacket* in which the American soldier finally finds the courage to pull the trigger. After visiting the prison museum, it is easy to understand why Kubrick decided to choose a young Vietcong woman soldier as the victim for that scene.

The signs of war, shrines mourning the loss of soldiers, and monuments celebrating famous victories, keep popping up at regular intervals, as you make your way from Hanoi all the way down to Saigon (or Ho Chi Minh City). The most hard-hitting symbols, though, are in and around Saigon. The war museum in Saigon is Exhibit A. It's not huge. You can finish it in 2-3 hours. It's the rawness, not the quantity of exhibits, that leave you uncomfortably numb. Back then, they didn't have embedded journalists recording the war and beaming it straight into people's living rooms. Still, brave photojournalists of the era couldn't have done a better job of capturing the soul of the Vietnam War. The pictures of massacres, families being torn apart, destruction of jungles using chemical weapons, and the effects of Agent Orange on humans are truly heart-breaking. The human capability for wartime cruelty is mind-boggling. As you walk out of the museum thinking that you've had enough, you notice that all the American warplanes, tanks, and other tools of mass destruction, are neatly arranged like war medals. Resentment and anger against the Americans is all inside. Pride of winning the war is proudly displayed outside.

To get a step closer to feeling the war, you have to go to the Vietcong tunnels, also known as the tunnels of Củ Chi. Over a period of 20-30 years, the Vietnamese soldiers built 250-odd kilometers of underground tunnels, to frustrate the American soldiers with guerrilla warfare. As a part of the tour, you get to see all the grisly booby-traps employed by both sides. But the feeling you get while crawling through the three-tiered tunnel system dwarfs anything else you feel in the museums or at any of the monuments. These tunnels were actually widened after the war to make them accessible for tourists. Even the 100-150 meters of the 250 kilometer long tunnel that is open for tourists will leave you dumbfounded. How could any human being survive in these claustrophobic conditions for months? The Vietcong didn't just live here. They were fighting a war from here against one of the best armies in the world. Sure, it was an elaborate tunnel system. There were organizational meetings on the first floor, dining halls on the second floor, and living quarters on the third floor. But it's still underground! No matter how you feel about the war, a 100-meter crawl through these tunnels will make you admire the tenacity of the Vietnamese soldiers.

But this is all for a history buff. That's just a small part of what Vietnam has to offer. As monochromatic as the depiction of the war is, the length and a little bit of the breadth of this country are full of ethnic, geographic, and cultural diversity. The town of Sapa, all the way to the north along the China border, is the rice bowl of this country. The minority communities around Sapa, that grow rice in the picturesque rice terraces, have started to embrace commercialization, but they still have a few years to go. The waterfalls around Sapa are not really spectacular, but the rice terraces are worth ruining your shoes for. There is no escaping the muddy roads, especially on a rainy day like the one I got. Still, this 20-odd kilometer walk is absolutely worth every step of it.

Then there is Ha Long Bay, to the east of Hanoi. With millions of tourists visiting the bay every year, the water is dirty, and you can spot dead fish as you start kayaking through the teeny-tiny tunnels in the bay. The weather, once again, stubbornly refused to cooperate, but a cloudy night in Ha Long Bay has its own charm. I picked up my blanket, went to the upper deck of the boat, and decided to sleep under the misty sky. My playlist that night was pretty eclectic: Lucky Ali's *Na Tum Jaano Na Hum*, Asha Bhosale's *Katra Katra*, Dire Straits's *Brothers in Arms*, Norah Jones's *Come Away with Me Tonight*, Duke Ellington's *Prelude to a Kiss*, among a bunch of other stuff. What would your playlist be if you were falling asleep with the silhouettes of beautiful mountains jutting out of the ocean, smeared by the cloudy night sky? The mountains themselves feel like poetry; set to the mystic music of the thick cloud cover.

The entire country of Vietnam is full of such natural or historic treats. The water puppet show in Hanoi blends an ancient story-telling custom with traditional Vietnamese music, to narrate the mythological beginning of the Vietnamese people. Apparently, a dragon mated with a beautiful bird, who laid some 100 eggs. You guessed it right! The first 100 Vietnamese people came from those 100 eggs. And this story is supposed to explain the existence of all the different tribes in this country. I love mythology. So illogical and yet so omnipresent.

As you make your way south toward Ho Chi Minh City, the influence of India is on display. In central Vietnam, it's on the devotional dance form called "Lakhon Bassac," which is a Vietnamese version of the Indian Raam-leela. Apparently, there was some Indian king named Cham who ruled central and south Vietnam, and telling mythological stories of the Hindu epic, Ramayana, through dance forms was quite common in those days. The Hindu king is gone, but the dance form lives on.

Halfway down in Hue, the ancient capital of the country, the palace in the city center was undergoing restoration. However, the architecture and the surroundings of the summer palace outside the city made it worth visiting. Hoi An is not necessarily a beautiful city, but it was fun to go on the river in the night and enjoy the ritual of releasing lanterns in the water. Further down, in Nha Trang and Mui Ne, typical beach towns, the Russian influence on daily life was visible everywhere. As a language, Vietnamese has French influence in the north and English influence in the south. In the middle of all this, there is this tiny island of Russian. Some say it's a hold-out from the Soviet era when this was a communist military outpost. Others say it's because of the Russian oil companies still active off the central coast. Nonetheless, it was mildly amusing to walk around a town that had everything written in Vietnamese, English, and Russian. Hotels, guest houses, restaurants, karaoke songs. Russian galore!

To enjoy the real Vietnam though, look no further than the sidewalks of Hanoi or Saigon. It is safe to say that Vietnamese life starts where the street ends and ends where the sidewalk meets the building. Walking along these sidewalks at any time during the day is like running an obstacle course. At six in the morning, it is crowded with tea and coffee vendors, populated by the early commuters. Around 8 or 9 in the morning, the breakfast baguette stalls pop out of nowhere. In the afternoon, it's the turn of the noodle soup or pho vendors. At the end of the workday, it's the men and women selling lemonade, fresh fruits, and a whole lot of local food. A couple of hours after the end of the workday, the same sidewalks become playgrounds for badminton and sepak takraw players. These Vietnamese sidewalks are like revolving doors. Vendors keep changing all day long, but there is always action on the street-side. As I was walking along one of the sidewalks, a lady threw a bucketful of water, perhaps to clean up the mess left behind by the previous stall. Half of it went up my flip-flops and my feet. She looked up apologetically. I just gave her a big smile and kept walking. On Vietnamese sidewalks, the people walking are encroaching on thriving businesses. All in a day's play! Don't be surprised if you occasionally find some semi-permanent establishments, like a barber shop or a travel agency, selling all kinds of tickets on these sidewalks. I'm sure they get a special permit from the city to stay there all day long. In Vietnam, a sidewalk is prime real estate!

But amid all these contrasting scenes of beautiful landscapes, chaotic sidewalks, intriguing cultural diversity, and images of war, I managed to meet someone special. When you backpack for eight months, you are bound to meet interesting women. Most of them have left the "normal" life behind, which makes them interesting in my eyes. Among them, a French woman, an Egyptian, an Australian, a Brazilian, a Swiss, a Colombian; at least a handful of these girls stand out. No Indian girls. Forget about meeting interesting Indian girls, I haven't met any Indian backpacking girls. Period. It's almost like an oxymoron. In any case, after a certain age, nationality is just a tag. You are mostly looking for that spark.

In Saigon, I went on a day trip to the Mekong delta. The minibus stopped at another hostel to pick up some more people and she hopped on. All day long, we kept playing the body language game. She kept walking a couple of steps behind her friend, waiting for me to say something. Small talk, small talk, small talk. At the end of the tour, we decided to go for dinner together.

At my age, I'm jaded beyond recognition when it comes to the outcome of such dinners and drinks. And the backpacking world can sometimes be predictable and boring, especially when people are introducing themselves. Where are you from? When did you start traveling? Where are you coming from? Where are you going? How long are you going to travel? What's your favorite country so far? A few weeks ago, I jokingly said that every backpacker should wear a badge with all this basic information, so we can start the conversation with more substantive stuff (All backpackers are either on a one-year trip or are planning one in the near future. It's not that special.). At one time, some of us backpackers even came up with a list of questions we would ask a new backpacker, if we were not allowed to ask the same old questions. So I wasn't expecting anything out of the "backpacker-ordinary" from this. But this one was different.

She showed up with her friend at nine in the night and we headed to some random roadside food joint. In the backpacking world, a fancy restaurant and a fat dinner bill are definitely not necessary to impress a girl. Everyone is on a budget and everyone else knows it. After dinner, we went to a bar selling the cheapest beer in town. By eleven that night, her friend was tired and went home. They both had an early morning flight to catch. For the next six hours, this girl and I kept talking, talking, and talking. Halfway through, maybe around three in the morning, the bar lady kicked us out. This girl, sitting across the table from me, asked the bar lady whether there were any other bars open in town. Hmmmm!

The end of the story is pretty anti-climactic. A friendly hug and a long walk back home with the realization that I will most likely never see her again. But the eight hours we spent sitting across the table from each other were magic. In the dating world, people from different walks of life are mostly looking for some common ground. Something to talk about, some life experiences that both of them share, something both of them enjoy doing, something, anything. After a while, this predictable game becomes boring. And then, out of nowhere comes this interesting girl. You share so many things with her that pretty soon you realize that perhaps you've been living parallel lives, thousands of miles apart from each other. Eight hours is more than enough for that! Oh well, before you know it, it's bar time again. She has her own travel and life schedule. I have mine.

But there is hope! Hope that it'll happen again! Next time, in a different country, with a different girl, and a different outcome, maybe?

24. CAMBODIA: SAME-SAME, BUT DIFFERENT

December 20, 2012
Angkor Wat, Cambodia

The unplanned detour to Laos and all the extra time spent in
Vietnam meant I had to rush through Cambodia. A couple of days
each in Angkor Wat and Phnom Penh were all that I could manage.
At a superficial level, beauty and the beast is the phrase that comes
to mind. First up, beauty. It may sound a bit ironic that the biggest
Hindu temple is outside of India. But this is not just one temple.
It's a temple complex, built over hundreds of years. Over the years,
I have seen a lot of places of worship, including the ones in old
Jerusalem, the Sistine Chapel, the mosque in Casablanca, and a
whole bunch of Hindu temples in India. But in terms of sheer
expanse, I don't think anything can beat Angkor Wat. It just goes
on and on and on. In the precious little time I had, I managed to
see just four main temples, which were each bigger than most of
the temples I had seen before.

All the temples are in varying stages of disrepair and there are
huge restoration projects underway. Still, it is easy to see how
majestic it all must have been in its heyday. With a small lake full of
beautiful lotuses right in front of it, sunrise over the main temple is
a must-see. And then, there is the *Tomb-raider* temple, with trees
intersecting and penetrating all the ancient walls. More
interestingly, Angkor Wat stands as a witness to the Hindu-

Buddhist turf war of olden days. In India, people jokingly say that, given the generally pacifist teachings of Hinduism, Buddhists are the only people Hindus can be the aggressors against. Angkor Wat is probably the best example of that. For generations, Hindus and Buddhists took turns desecrating each other's idols, burying them, and installing their own idols. In one of the temples, archeologists have found 250-odd Buddha statues buried under a Shivalinga!

I wanted to see some of the other temples, but I had to wrap it up in a day. When you take a step back and look at the bigger picture, "same same, but different" aptly describes the entire region of South East Asia. The phrase is used and abused throughout this region to describe everything from the mundane to the profound. If you walk into a store and point to two sarongs of different colors with the same price, the owner will say "same same, but different" with a big smile on his face. In Thailand, thank you is "kopankhaap" and in Laos, it is "kopchailalaai." If you find someone with reasonable knowledge of these languages, they will say "same same, but different." It can even be found on t-shirts and mugs all over this region. However, the phrase is not just clever marketing. This pop-culture phrase perfectly captures the heritage of this region.

As you go from Thailand to Cambodia to Laos and Vietnam, the influence of Sanskrit on the local language fades away, only to be replaced by Cantonese. The airport in Bangkok is called "Suvarnabhoomi", a Sanskrit word meaning, literally, the golden land. A bus or train "station," called "sthaan" in Sanskrit, is called "sathaani" in Thai. The influence of Sanskrit is easily detectable in a lot of the street names and in people's names. By the time you get to Laos or Vietnam, you start detecting more and more Cantonese. "hello" becomes "ni hao" and rice becomes "mi fan." Even the scripts in Thailand, Cambodia, and Laos resemble those of Bangla. With the strong French influence, Vietnamese script is more anglicized and is a bit of an exception here. But the pronunciations are quite similar to Cantonese. In a way, South East Asian languages are to Cantonese what Scandinavian languages are to German. Cantonese and German both sound pretty dry. South East Asian and Scandinavian languages all have that sing-song kind of feeling to them.

Food goes from being more curry-and-spice-based in Thailand to blander and more noodle-based in Vietnam. God-wise, the temples of Ganesha and Shiva can be found scattered all over Thailand. By the time you get to Laos, Ganesha is mostly gone, but every once in awhile, you can find a Shiva temple. In Vietnam, Hindu gods are mostly gone. Skin color goes from brown to yellowish-white. Facial features gradually become more and more Asian. Even the traditional dresses go from resembling a sari in Thailand to the hats made out of cane and long-sleeved woolen dresses in northern Vietnam. No wonder Vietnam, Cambodia, and Laos are collectively called Indochina. Culturally and linguistically, these countries are "same same, but different."

But that brings us to the sad part of my stay in Cambodia. Going from the beauty to the beast. Phnom Penh has all the trappings of a capital city. A central district with wide boulevards, huge government buildings, and some interesting monuments. Motorcades occasionally whizzing past your tuk-tuk, perhaps carting politicians around. Once you go past these neighborhoods, though, it is a fairly impoverished city, even more so than Vientiane. And a visit to one of the infamous killing fields helps you understand this state of affairs.

During the prolonged conflict in Vietnam, the communist forces managed to establish a strong presence in the northern and eastern parts of Cambodia. After the ceasefire in Vietnam in 1975, emboldened with their victory, they managed to take over Phnom Penh and impose communist rule over the entire country. In their post-war euphoria, they decided to eliminate the entire educated class in Cambodia and start from scratch. Highly educated teachers, businessmen, intellectuals, and their families, including kids, were sent to killing fields established all across the country for extermination. And schools were converted into prisons. Cities were considered breeding grounds for intellectuals and village life was considered more basic, more virtuous. In an attempt to downsize the cities, those who were a bit more fortunate, perhaps because they were a little less educated, were sent to the countryside and forced to become farmers.

I wish it were just a sequel of a bad movie, but the killing field in Phnom Penh is a testimony to the cruelest aspects of this attempt at social engineering. After the two-decades-long Vietnam War, both superpowers were financially and militarily exhausted, with little appetite for engaging in another conflict. The Khmer Rouge, the communist party in Cambodia, took advantage of that

178

and killed 3 to 4 million people in a span of 2-3 years. With no generous supply of weapons from the Soviets, the soldiers decided to use sharp edges of the leaves of cactus- and pine-like trees to cut people's throats, and dumped their bodies to rot in mass graves. Some unfortunate kids weren't even granted that courtesy. A plaque next to a big tree says that the heads of kids were smashed against the tree and the bodies dumped in a mass grave right next to it. Overall, the extermination program was so elaborate and widespread that some killing fields in the countryside remain undiscovered or unknown. The most astonishing fact of this story is that, after committing such heinous crimes, the Khmer Rouge was declared as the legitimate representative of the Cambodian people in the UN!

After visiting a place like this, comparisons with Auschwitz are inevitable. A part of me was telling myself not to indulge in any comparisons. The histories, the reasons, and the nature of these conflicts have nothing in common. More importantly, these are all sites of remembrance for the loss of innocent lives. There is no reason to compare the loss of one innocent life to another. But if human minds were so rational, they would cease to be human.

For better or worse, the killing field in Phnom Penh doesn't seem as raw as Auschwitz. There is a tower at the entrance of the killing field that houses a few hundred skulls recovered from the mass graves. And there are a few glass cases in the field, where shards of bones and pieces of torn clothes are neatly kept. But maybe it's just the sheer number of clothes, suitcases, utensils, shoes, and empty cans of Zyclon B in Auschwitz that have a deeper impact. On the other hand, there are still parts of the killing field where fragments of bones and clothing of victims come to the surface every monsoon season. Standing next to one of those graves will definitely send chills down your spine.

In a lot of ways, such comparisons are superficial and foolish. The sad truth is that, in spite of the tremendous advances in psychology, sociology, and technology of the past few decades, such mass killings have been occurring with unnerving regularity. Rwanda? Somalia? Sudan? Taking advantage of the war-weariness of the United States, the sole superpower, the Syrian regime has managed to kill a quarter million people in full glare of the internet, cell phone videos, and social media, with no apparent end in sight. If there is a silver lining to any of this, maybe it's the fact that the number of innocent lives being lost to such events is steadily decreasing. As information flow becomes cheaper and easier, dictators are finding it increasingly difficult to commit such crimes and stay away from the international spotlight. But as you are finishing the tour of the killing field, the audio guide plays a Western classical song as a tribute to the Cambodian victims. As the song hits the high notes, you can't help but ponder the inherent cruelty of human nature and wonder whether it's all just "same same, but different."

DIPPING
IN
OCEANIA

7

25. AUSTRALIA: THE ART OF SPORTS

December 26, 2012
Melbourne, Australia

I just attended the first day of play of the Boxing Day Test at the Melbourne Cricket Ground (or just MCG for cricket fans like me). This is perhaps the only tradition in cricket, a sport met with gazes of ridicule or yawns of boredom by the majority of the world. 20-25 degrees Celsius, a sunny day, bouncy pitch, lush green outfield, and no clouds on the horizon. A cricket fan cannot ask for anything more. Even after a 10-hour flight from Bangkok to Sydney, 3 hours of sleep in Sydney, and a 6:50 AM flight from Sydney to Melbourne, I watched all 8 hours of cricket without feeling tired for a minute.

This great day of cricket took me back to the day of tennis I had enjoyed a few months before, in Shanghai. I had an extra day to kill and the Shanghai Masters was on. With Nadal out, the top four seeds – Berdych, Murray, Djokovic, and Federer – were scheduled to play some lesser-known opponents. It was my first time watching live tennis, another sport I have followed religiously for as long as I can remember. Today, I feel like writing about tennis and cricket.

When it comes to sports, badminton is my first love; cricket and football (soccer for the Americans) probably close seconds. I can't choose one over the other. But tennis is arguably the most complete individual sport. Badminton is way faster, in terms of reflexes, and is harsher, in terms of the impact on your body, but maybe doesn't drain your body as much as tennis does. Marathons, triathlons, and such are all interesting and probably need more endurance. However, they don't require as much anticipation and understanding of your opponent's game as tennis does. Tennis seems to be perfect for testing of your anticipation and endurance. Unlike other sports, you don't even need endless angles and replays to appreciate the players' craft.

Sampras and Agassi were the Connors-McEnroe when I was growing up. As much as I respect Sampras's skills and humility, it was the rebel in Agassi that I was naturally attracted to. Plus, Sampras never got his career grand slam. And then came Federer! He announced his arrival by beating Sampras at his own game. At Wimbledon. He hasn't looked back since. It was great to finally see him live in Shanghai when he was still the number 1 player in the world. Djokovic will regain the top spot soon, and it is unlikely Federer will ever dethrone Djokovic again. I don't think he cares, though. Just like Sachin Tendulkar, the God of cricket who, incidentally, is his good friend, Federer has broken the last record he wanted to break, which was being number 1 longer than Sampras. Sure, he never won all four majors in one year, but that has more to do with the new era of tennis than anything else. Without taking anything away from Rod Lever, tennis in his era was not as physically and mentally demanding as it is today.

Sampras never had the patience for the clay court game. Agassi was terrible at serve and volley. McEnroe was way too temperamental. From what I've heard, Borg and Federer are in a legends dead-heat, but Borg has been through some personal issues that Federer hasn't yet, giving Federer the edge. Sure, Nadal, Djokovic, and lately, Murray, have all beaten him several times now, but most of the time, they were the challengers. With their tenacity and physical style of play, they have forced everyone to respect them. Federer is different. Federer arrived on the scene and said "OK. Who wants to beat me?" And the others kept chipping away; finally frustrating him with solid defense. For most of the last ten years, though, Federer was the one to beat.

So it was great to walk into the Shanghai arena to finally see some of these guys live. Nadal was out, due to an injury, but he probably has his own physical style of play to blame. First up was Berdych, playing against one of the top 20 players. His work ethic is admirable, but I was mostly focusing on other mundane stuff.

Just getting used to watching the sport live. On the light blue surface, the green ball was looking beautiful. When they served, though, the ball was nowhere to be seen. It went like a bullet and I only saw the service return. The actual width of the court is much larger than what you imagine on TV, and the fluorescent rackets, t-shirts, shorts, and shoes, running up and down the baseline, are a treat to watch.

Next up was Murray. His opponent withdrew at the last minute and he came out just to hit around and entertain the crowd. Oh well! Tsonga was playing on court No. 1 and I made my way there. By then, I had gotten used to the pace of the ball and the game. With most of the crowd hanging out on the center court, I managed to get a first row seat for the Tsonga match. And that demystified these tennis players for me. They have the same two hands, same two legs; they are all just twice the size. Or maybe even thrice, if you are Tsonga! When they serve, the extent to which they arch their backs and bend their legs is just mind-blowing. And in follow-through, one of the legs goes way above the waist. I'd probably pull a muscle if someone asked me to just repeat the serving action 15-20 times, even without the ball! And those two-handed backhand cross-courts? I have no idea how these guys keep twisting so much and hitting them, day-in and day-out.

In terms of temperament, Tsonga is my kind of guy. He has an opinion about every point and feels the need to voice it after every point. Sometimes even in the middle of a grueling rally! You see a sense of triumph, relief, ecstasy, sarcasm, disbelief, helplessness, rage; in a span of an hour, you will see his face run the whole gamut of emotions. TV crews focus on his face only when it is extremely animated, but every facial muscle of his follows the ebb and flow of the entire match. It would be intriguing just to record his facial expressions for an entire match. You wouldn't even need to see the ball to predict the score.

Enter Djokovic! I remember waking up at 3 AM and watching the entire five hours and fifty minutes of the epic 2012 Australian Open final he won against Nadal. This was, for Djokovic, what the epic 2009 Federer-Nadal Australian Open final was for Nadal, which made Federer cry. For the last half hour of that Djokovic-Nadal final, I was getting nervous just watching them play, waiting for one of them to collapse, and for paramedics to cart them out of the arena on a stretcher. And when Djokovic won the match, I remember emailing my brother "Move over Nadal and Federer, Djokovic has arrived." Seeing him play live, even against a not-so-fancy opponent, is no less awe-inspiring than seeing him in epics like that Australian Open final. Off the field and after the match, he might be known as the Djoker. When he is playing a match, it seems like there is some kind of glass wall around him. You can tell that the only thing he sees is the tennis ball. Having spent most of his career on the losing end of semi-finals and finals, mostly because of losing a few crucial points, he has learned the value of every point the hard way. Even when he is playing an opponent who has no realistic chance of winning, even when he is a break or two up and his opponent is serving, he doesn't want to lose a point.

All the unforced errors of Tsonga were gone and every point was like a match point. I can imagine how frustrating it must be to play against him. In the '90s, Michael Chang was the ultimate defensive player. Playing against Djokovic is like playing against two Michael Changs. He won't just get the ball back. He will hit winners from the most awkward defensive positions. You would have to hit at least three winners and then the last one would go past him, finally getting registered as a winner in the official statistics. I think the ATP should seriously consider multiplying your "winner" statistics against Djokovic by three.

Once your sense of respect for Djokovic has subsided, make some room for the greatest of them all! Even in China, not necessarily a tennis-crazy country, Federer elicits a standing ovation. He is like the Michael Jackson of tennis. Everyone around the world knows him. For most of his life, and against most of his opponents, he has played against his own idea of his game. Am I being the best I can be? Do I need to be the best I can be? Nadal had to double the size of his muscles to beat Federer on non-clay courts. Djokovic had to wait in the wings for a long time and switch to a gluten-free diet to be mentioned in the same breath as Federer and Nadal. All along, Federer has just been Federer. At his peak, victory was a foregone conclusion. The only question was whether it was a Federer master class or a scrappy, error-prone victory. Perhaps that's where some of his apparent cockiness in press conferences comes from. He can make statements like 'I think I played really well today' or 'Tennis is not everything in your life' without them feeling uncalled for.

Federer is just waltzing around to the beat of the ball. He uses his superior anticipation and his understanding of his opponent to decide which ones he needs to chase and which ones he doesn't. You would rarely see him lose his footing, easily the biggest reason for his longevity and his legendary status. With their grinding defense, Nadal and Djokovic will get under your skin. Federer is already in your head. He just knows where you are going to move after every stroke. Like a Gaudi or a Gehri, he constructs every point. That's when a sport transcends the physicality and moves into the realm of art. It's not about seeing your ten and raising it. It's about knowing that you are going to bet ten on it.

And that brings us to cricket. I was on the plane from Bangkok to Sydney when Sachin Tendulkar made his surprise announcement to retire from one-day international cricket. For about two-thirds of the world, cricket is a pesky insect or a strange sport that seems to go on forever. And Sachin Tendulkar sounds vaguely similar to their Indian friend's name. As the famous refrain goes, a cricket match can go on for five days and still end in a draw. There are shorter forms of the game; one that lasts about 8 hours and another that lasts just 3 hours. But for those who consider themselves purists, the five-day version is the ultimate strategy test. It's not just about knowing the opposing team. It's about the weather conditions, the quality of the wicket (or the track) on which the match is played, the gradual deterioration of the wicket every day, immense concentration and fatigue, how new or old the ball is, when you declare your innings, and on and on. I'm not sure why other cricket-playing countries love it, but for the famously argumentative Indians, love of this complex game just flows naturally. The more the variables and the more complicated the strategy, the more ways to argue the heck out of it. Americans indulge in Monday-night quarterbacking. Indians do next-week coaching.

So, there I was. An Indian attending the Australia-Sri Lanka five-day cricket match. Why do I care? With a capacity of 100,000, this is one of the biggest cricket stadiums in the world. The attendance? A little over 67,000. There is the rowdy Australian camp, bang opposite the all-dressed-up Members' End. And there is the jolly Sri Lankan camp, 90 degrees from the Aussie camp; trumpets, drums, and all. The Aussie camp was on a drinking binge and the Lankan camp was a carnival. But I was more interested in the cricket. When Bird, the debutant, or Mitchell Johnson bowled one of those 145-150km/h deliveries, it was impossible to see the ball. When Sangakkara hit a perfect cover drive, it was hard to see the ball before it crossed the 30-yard circle. When Warner hit a six, I saw the ball only after it landed in the crowd. But live test cricket is not about seeing the ball. Even the group of ten-year-old Aussie kids sitting next to me knew that. When the bat made the perfect, cracking noise that echoed throughout the stadium, the kids would reflexively say "shot!" It didn't matter whether it crossed the boundary or went straight to the fielder. When Sangakkara and Jayawardene were trying to rebuild the battered Sri Lankan innings, it was easy to feel the pressure in the crowd. When Warner made a 50 in 30-odd balls, there was a palpable sense of euphoria in the crowd. When the Aussies lost three quick wickets, the crowd nervously cheered "Clarkey" when their in-form captain, Michael Clarke, walked out of the pavilion. This is what you go to the MCG for. Not to see the ball swing or to appreciate the incredible fielding attempt that you rarely notice.

Sri Lanka didn't last too long and Warner started the Aussie innings with a bang. He is the Aussie Sehwag. He does not care whether he is playing a test or a one-day or a T20. He is just playing his own game. But when three quick wickets fell, Clarke walked in. Test cricket is a sport that separates the boys from the men and Clarke, maybe a legend in the making, didn't disappoint. With Michael Hussey, he hunkered down and rode out the storm. End of day's play. An absorbing day of satisfying cricket!

In this absorbing day of cricket, Mitchell Johnson crossed 200 test wickets and Sangakkara crossed 10,000 runs. When he scored his 10,000th run, the big screen flashed a statistic: Sangakkara is one of the three fastest to cross 10,000 runs in test cricket. The other two? Brian Lara and Sachin Tendulkar. 195 innings. Sangakkara, maybe another legend in the making, is in good company. But I couldn't help but think about Sachin. He hadn't retired from test cricket, but his surprise announcement of retirement from one-day cricket was the beginning of the end for him.

If cricket is your religion, Sachin Tendulkar has to be your God. Or at least one of your Gods, if you're not Indian. When God decides to hang up his boots, even atheists like me are bound to feel a bit uneasy. Name a sportsperson who has dominated his or her sport for 23 years. From the age of 16 to 39, Sachin has toyed with all kinds of oppositions on home grounds and abroad. He has had 2 or 3 lean patches, but even if you take away those 4-5 years, we are talking about a solid 18-year career. Tiger Woods is the only other one who comes to mind. But his scandals have probably tainted his legacy a bit.

After Tendulkar announced his retirement from one-day cricket, I spent 30-40 minutes watching his top 10 one-day innings online. It didn't even include my personal favorite, the one against the Aussies in Sharjah; the famous desert storm. Sachin coming down the pitch to Kasprovich, hitting him for a six, and Tony Grieg sitting in the commentary box screaming like there is no tomorrow. And his 200 in the Gwalior one-day? Some of the players he was playing with and against weren't even born when Sachin started playing international cricket! And we are talking about 200 runs in a one-day. It's like Tyson knocking out his opponent in the first thirty seconds; just 22 years after he started KOing on the international stage!

I can go on and on about Sachin. They say he is, or at least was, so fast he could think of 2-3 shots for the same ball and choose one. From the moment the ball leaves the bowler's hand, the batsman has only 600-700 milliseconds to hit a shot. How can anyone think of 2-3 options and choose one in such a short time span? His way of pacing his innings is almost unmatched. His ability to soak in the expectations of a billion people and stand and deliver? Unparalleled! Even the legendary Don Bradman didn't have to deal with that.

Beyond all the pressure and expectations, it goes back to anticipation. It is about getting into your opponent's head, not just under his or her skin. Federer crafts the point, Tendulkar has 2-3 options for his shot, and chooses one. With this rare natural gift, sport becomes some sort of abstract painting with strong, bold strokes across a canvas. It's hard to say why it's beautiful, but deep down, you can't deny that it's divine!

If there is one difference between Sachin and Federer, it is their attitude. Sachin lacks the cockiness of Federer. Sometimes I wonder whether he is truly humble or whether he is just cautious and knows that anything that comes out of his mouth will be beaten to death by analysts and the media. Nonetheless, hats off to a true legend! I'm one of those who would still choose Steve

Waugh, Bevan, or Dhoni over Tendulkar, if the team needs a match-winning knock in the second inning. But that's more like Federer finally losing to Nadal at the 2009 Wimbledon. That doesn't take anything away from these once-in-a-lifetime artists.

Roger, it's poetic justice that your finesse and precision in shot-making come from Switzerland. And Sachin, it's poetic justice that your passion for cricket is Indian. When you are gone, sports will return to what they used to be. Just sports!

*   *   *

Tamaso Maa Jyotirgamaya

January 20, 2013
Darwin, Australia

After enjoying a rare veal dinner on the plane because it was Christmas, I finally landed Down Under. This is Australia, the country that is the reason I'm on this round-the-world adventure. Some five years ago, around this time, I rented a motorcycle and traveled for six weeks in South America. When I started, I thought six weeks was a long time, until I started bumping into a bunch of Aussies (and Kiwis) who had decided to quit their jobs and see the world. I came back from that trip and told myself that I'd never be able to do it. But it was like a bug at the back of my mind. Can I really do it? Should I do it? And here I am, eight months into my trip, finally visiting Aussieland.

The first thing you notice here is tank tops. For men and women, shorts and tank tops are like a uniform, perhaps because it's summer time. Even jeans and a decent pair of sneakers are probably considered formal here. Melbourne is my first stop and Federation Square in the heart of the city is easily one of the most charming places for watching people. There are a couple of fancy restaurants in the square, where you can find people sipping beer all day long. Even in these swanky restaurants everyone, from kids to 60-year-olds, is in cargo shorts and t-shirts, at best.

What I am about to learn, after traveling up and down the east coast, is that lack of formality runs through the Aussie DNA. Tank tops and shorts were just the start. Don't be surprised if you find people walking around barefoot...by choice. Everyone here is your "mate." Everything here has a short form. McDonald's is Maccers. Sunglasses are sunnies. Even MCG, short for Melbourne Cricket Ground, is further shortened to "G." Every conversation ends with a "cheers," as if everyone is walking around with a beer can in their hands. Given the legendary Aussie tolerance for alcohol, it might as well be true. Baseball is America's favorite pastime. Drinking is the Aussie pastime. A lot of corporate offices here apparently have a fridge full of beer and, in some offices, weekend drinking starts at noon on Friday. God forbid, if you have to work late hours from Monday to Thursday, it's ok to open a cold one for some motivation after office hours. Germans are known for their love of beer, but these guys just hike it up a notch. However, that's just one aspect of Aussie life. Everyone here is a surfer, hiker, marathon runner, hunter, biker, or something along those lines. You can probably go to jail for being a couch potato. All in all, even America would seem formal compared to Australia. If California were to secede from the United States and become its own country, it would be Australia. Or maybe Australia-lite.

Aussies are extremely friendly. They don't seem to be overly curious about your heritage or culture, or history, and sometimes might even come off as being a bit insensitive to all of that. But they seem to be pretty helpful. If you are at an intersection, with a map in your hand and a puzzled look on your face, people will stop by and ask if everything is ok. If you walk into a bar, within half an hour they will buy you a drink, pat you on the back, and tell you their life stories. In my one month here, barring one airport incident in which a young white kid unnecessarily insulted a middle-aged South Asian about observing lines and got a mouthful in return, I found Aussies to be open, welcoming, and irreverent. They won't hold back when poking fun at anyone, including themselves.

But that's just the people. This vast land is blessed with a lot of natural beauty. I didn't get a chance to experience the rugged desert land of the outback, but this country seems to have something for everyone. In Melbourne, you can go to Philip Island and watch the little penguins come home at dusk from a full day of foraging in the ocean. This is a must-see for any nature lover. These guys are so tiny birds of prey can swoop in and pick them up. So they go to the sea before sunrise and come back home after sunset. When they come back, nobody has the courage to take the lead and cross the beach to go home. The first time they come out of the water, they come out as a group of 30 or 40 and go barely a couple of meters before wading back to the water. The next time, they go four instead of two meters before running back to the water. They do this at least five or ten times, inching forward at every attempt, before finally crossing the beach and going back home. It is as adorable as it is mind-boggling. You would think that evolution would take over at some point. Or the elder ones would have learned, over the years, to wait until it's fully dark. But to the joy of hundreds of tourists lining up here every night, they indulge in this "penguin parade." What a beautiful way to waste your time and energy!

That's just the start. The beautiful waters at Byron Bay, Whitehaven Beach off the town of Airlie Beach, where the sand is even softer than that in Clearwater Beach in Florida, and of course, the Great Barrier Reef in Cairns. All of this is extremely expensive by backpacker standards. Forget about sight-seeing and activities, even food is so expensive that I joked to a friend that these days, Subway is running through my veins. At 7.50 Aussie Dollars, there is nothing as cheap and as filling as a foot-long Subway sandwich. After eight months of junk food, a month-long Subway diet can't hurt, anyway. When you internalize the fact that this is an expensive country, you start focusing on the priceless things in Australia. There is no price tag on seeing the tiny, real-life Nemos rushing in and out of the coral reefs of the Great Barrier Reef. Then, there is a 1-2 meter long fish called Wally, who is so friendly you can play with his beard. Ok, I'm exaggerating. Fish don't have beards. But this species loves it when you scrub their chins. There are tiny little underwater flowers that can sense sounds. If you snap your fingers anywhere near them, they close immediately. And then, if you are lucky, you get to swim with some 2-3 meter long sharks. I really need to get an underwater camera. Finding Nemo probably does justice to the vibrant colors of the underwater world, but words can't do any justice to the beauty of this world. Just do me a favor and learn scuba diving! You have to see it all for yourself.

Besides natural beauty, this is really the first country, in my eight months of traveling, where I had to go searching for culture. There are some Victorian buildings in Melbourne and Sydney, but that's about it. In Melbourne, when I went out looking for culture, there wasn't much else apart from the aboriginal art museum. The other two museums were a film museum – an art form Australia hasn't contributed much to – and a t-shirt museum! Across the street from these museums, there is an alley full of all kinds of interesting graffiti. Some of it is pretty impressive, but graffiti generally comes from a counter-cultural impulse. Traveling along the east coast of Australia, it was hard to say what culture they were trying to counter. In Darwin, you finally get to see that thing called culture. Not the culture graffiti artists in Melbourne are trying to counter, but at least some culture. And it's mostly aboriginal.

It's not just one culture. It's a collection of tribal cultures. As in the United States, after the European settlers reached the Australian shores, they managed to wipe out most of the tribes in the south and the east. Their population went down from 3-4 million to around 300,000, mostly scattered around the sprawling desert of Australia. Hiking in the sweltering summer heat in the Kakadu National Park, you don't really get to see aboriginals going about their daily lives. However, you do get some glimpses of their beliefs and their customs. Some are straight-up superstitions, like a tall, distant mountain in the park that is considered evil because of a series of mishaps associated with the surroundings. But most of them are rooted in practical, empirical knowledge and are pretty intriguing. In the tropical jungles around Darwin, extensive knowledge of the local flora and fauna, and their use for daily consumption and medicinal purposes, is nothing short of impressive. Among the desert tribes, the venomous snakes are feared and revered, and perhaps rightly so. Petroglyphs dotting the landscape depict hunting, some stories of moral teachings, and some other aspects of cave life. To avoid incest, they came up with an elaborate system of "skin names," which dictated who could marry whom. Not necessarily foolproof, but interesting in its own way.

But these two worlds, the aboriginal one and the one with European influence, are worlds apart. Even after two to three hundred years of coexistence on the same island, they have struggled to find a common vocabulary. A few decades ago, in a bizarre attempt at social engineering and to "modernize" aboriginals, the government forcibly separated aboriginal children from the parents and raised in white, European-descent families. Instead of assimilation, this experiment managed to breed more resentment and misgivings among the communities, prompting a recent official apology to the aboriginals by Prime Minister, Julia Gillard. Traveling around this country, one can sense a state of uneasy equilibrium in which these communities live. They don't seem to be at war with each other, but they don't seem to care much about each other either. Most of the aboriginals seem to have itinerant lifestyles. And, unencumbered with any cultural or civilization history, the rest have wholeheartedly adopted a fairly irreverent version of the Western lifestyle, with virtually no sign of cultural assimilation with the aboriginals. After the failed experiment of trying to take aboriginal kids away from their parents and raise them in white households – infamously known as the "stolen generation" – the government has instituted several social welfare programs related to giving their land back to them, providing them with decent educational facilities, housing, healthcare; you name it. However, as my Couchsurfing host in Darwin was telling me, none of the aboriginals have been involved in either designing or implementing these programs. While the bureaucrats get to claim that millions of Dollars have been spent on such schemes, the money has been spent without any conscious attempt to understand their problems, brainstorming with them about potential solutions, or making them stakeholders in any of those schemes. The result is traumatic, yet expected. Results include high infant mortality rate, low life expectancy, lack of education, high unemployment and crime rates. For a country that claims to be developed, this apathy seems quite shocking, almost like the attitude toward Native Americans and African Americans in the United States.

A few days before leaving Australia, I learned that the aboriginals might have some Indian connection. Some recent genetic studies seem to suggest that their roots can be traced back to the southern part of India. If true, this would be pretty interesting. However, the culture wars of modern-day India are, in some ways, polar opposites of the ones in Australia. Australia seems to be struggling with the merging of the old and the new. And India seems to be struggling with moving from the old to the new. Throughout her 4000-5000 year civilization history, India seems to have done exceedingly well with cultural assimilation. Sure, we have the deeply entrenched caste system, which will take at least a century more to go away, but it is astonishing to see how a million different traditions coexist peacefully in today's India. For some reason, though, Indians are going through a social upheaval like never before. Some of it is related to the maddening pace of globalization. More than that, it is related to selective amnesia about India's own rich history.

Take the "khap panchayats" in the Indian state of Haryana. Just like the aboriginals, and perhaps even before the aboriginals, Indian society developed a concept similar to skin names called "gotra." People from the same gotra weren't allowed to marry each other because they were likely to be siblings. And the khap panchayats, or village councils, were in charge of enforcing these anti-incest rules. That might have been sensible a thousand years ago, but does it make sense today? After so many generations, the possibility of people from the same gotra being siblings has gone down significantly. However, the village councils are unwilling to give up their power, ordering honor killings if marriages happen within the same gotra.

It's the same story when it comes to female infanticide in India. The patriarchal nature of the society and the tradition of sons rather than daughters taking care of parents in their old age, have unnecessarily overemphasized the importance of a boy child. Even after banning the practice of in-utero sex determination, female infanticide is rampant in the underground world. It's not too difficult to connect the dots between a skewed sex ratio of 850-900 girls for every 1000 boys, and a sharp rise in the number of rape cases. The brutal gang rape of Jyoti Singh (also known as the infamous Nirbhaya case) in Delhi, followed by her unfortunate death, led to a social awakening and touched off large-scale protests against the government's apathy toward violence against women. But this has been going on for awhile. My sister briefly lived in Delhi a couple of years ago. As a homemaker living in a middle-class neighborhood of Delhi, she used to be virtually under self-imposed house arrest during office hours while her husband was at work. Reason? Almost daily reports of violence against women.

It's unfortunate that it took such a brutal act of violence against Jyoti Singh for society to find its pulse. The government seems to have moved quickly to amend the laws to strengthen the punishment for sexual violence against women. That's just the tip of the iceberg, though. The conversation needs to happen in a larger context. The prudish behavior and statements of the so called "moral police" in India do tremendous disservice to the rich and vibrant Indian culture, which has done an excellent job of exploring human sexuality. Some of the most famous Hindu Gods are polygamous. The five Pandavas, the five brothers in Mahabharata embodying desirable traits in men, have a polyandrous wife. When these men bet and lose their polyandrous wife in gambling and one of the Kauravas attempts to disrobe her in public, it is Krishna, well known for his flirtatious behavior and women fawning over him, who comes to her rescue. India has given the world Kamasutra and the Khajuraho temple, for God's sake! Before the self-styled members of the moral police start dictating the rules of engagement for men and women in Indian society, they should probably consider destroying the temple of Khajuraho and burning copies of the Kamasutra and other Hindu scriptures in public. If the generally tolerant society of India allows the self-styled moral police to destroy such rich Indian heritage, I will accept their legitimacy.

It is understandable that, if a cultural revolution like the one in the United States in the sixties and the one in China in the seventies, is not going to happen in India, the pace of social change is going to be slow. But how long are we going to wait to expand the conversation to have this broader dialogue? As the Australians look at their past and struggle to make peace with it, let us hope that Indian society looks introspectively at its own history and, instead of picking and choosing what is convenient, embraces it wholeheartedly. Given the raw wounds of the recent Jyoti Singh rape case, the sooner the better. As they say in Sanskrit, tamaso maa jyotirgamaya. Let us move from darkness to light!

26. NEW ZEALAND: THE MIDDLE EARTH

February 5, 2013
Queenstown, New Zealand

There is the Middle Kingdom, with a billion and a half inhabitants. And then, there is the Middle Earth, with hardly any. The Middle Kingdom is in the thick of it all, awe-inspiring for some, and fear-inducing for others. And the Middle Earth has found herself a quiet corner of the world, just on the edge of people's consciousness. She is like that quiet, shy girl, sitting in a corner in a coffee shop, solving crosswords and minding her own business. You are worried that if you approach her and say hi, she will start trembling in fear, drop her pencil, mumble a few words, and go silent. But when you actually talk to her, you walk away thinking "This is the most beautiful person I've ever met. Why did I not talk to her earlier?"

New Zealand is so far away from everything and everywhere that, until a few years ago, nobody had probably heard about it in their daily lives other than lamb aficionados, and maybe cricket fans. If you walked into a fancy restaurant and read "New Zealand" under lamb chops, you didn't mind paying a few extra bucks for the meal. And every cricket fan knows where Richard Hadlee, Danny Morrison, Daniel Vettori, and Shane Bond are from.

It all changed after Sir Peter Jackson released a million *Lord of the Rings* films. I haven't seen any of those, but I know that this story of hobbits has strong philosophical undercurrents and that the books are much more vivid and interesting than their screen

197

adaptations. I should at least read the books, right? Like the *Harry Potters*, I just couldn't get myself to care about them. I also know that I'm probably one of the last four (or five, maybe) people on earth who haven't seen the movies and if they could, they would put me in a zoo with a tag that says "One of the rare human specimens who hasn't seen *The Lord of the Rings*." But during my two weeks here, New Zealand brought me THIS close to watching them.

New Zealand has wholeheartedly embraced the status of *The Lord of the Rings* country. As I got on the Air New Zealand flight from Sydney to Christchurch, the safety instruction video was based entirely on the *Rings* theme, hobbits and all, with Peter Jackson even making a cameo. And in a lot of places around the islands, you can see people selling *Rings* tours and merchandise. It is kind of like the Swiss selling *Dilwale Dulhania Le Jaayenge* tours to every Indian visiting Switzerland, but we are talking about *Rings* here. They can sell those tours to the whole world.

Obviously, the story of New Zealand doesn't start or end there. What it does is set the agenda for your trip. The first three rules of New Zealand are natural beauty, natural beauty, and natural beauty. As we were touching down in Rotorua, my stopover on the North Island en route to Christchurch, there were hills draped with lush green vegetation for as far as I could see. As the plane hit the runway, I could see a horse farm right next to the runway, with horses grazing around, seemingly unperturbed by the noise of the airplanes. When we walked into the terminal, a Maori lady welcomed us by playing folk music on her native stringed instrument, which resembled a ukulele. A bit touristy, but it did a great job of giving the greenery some cultural context.

First up, nature taketh away. From the minute we landed in Christchurch, it was impossible to escape the consequences of the devastating 2011 earthquake that destroyed much of this beautiful city. You go to the city center and it looks like a war zone. You go to the public library for free Internet and there are flyers galore telling you how you can help rebuild the community. You go out in the night and the neighborhood bar is made out of trailers put together artistically. Every building has emergency evacuation procedures prominently displayed in every room. Everyone has a 9/11-ish story of what they were doing when the big earthquake hit. Everyone is talking about the time and effort required to bring back the glory days. The dark clouds of the 8-point-something quake and the two significant aftershocks still hover over this community.

But in a way, it has become part and parcel of life now. In the last year-and-a-half, the city has registered a mind-boggling 11,000 aftershocks! On my first night here, there was a 3-point-something aftershock which I failed to notice. On my third night, I was watching the Federer-Tsonga quarter-final of the Australian Open live and the entire room rattled for 5 seconds or so. I thought at first that somebody was probably jumping on the upper floor. The local guy sitting next to me asked nonchalantly, "Did you feel that?" I said yes and asked him, "Should we evacuate?" He pulled up his blanket again and said "Nah, it's just a minor one. Maybe a 4. We will find out tomorrow morning in the news." Guessing the intensity of the quake is like a betting game here. A bit unnerving, but hey, Federer was playing! No need to evacuate.

And then, nature giveth! Plenty of it! Once you leave Christchurch, you are transported into a magical world of unlimited natural beauty. I only had two weeks here and restricted myself to just the South Island. Even in such a short trip, this country managed to test the limits of how much beauty I could absorb on a daily basis. You have Mt. Cook and a handful of glaciers flowing down from the mountain range. Glacial lakes are brimming with turquoise water. There is a small cathedral on one of those lakes. The bus driver taking us along the lake told us this is the most photographed cathedral in the world. With the Vatican and Notre Dame still standing tall, it was a bit of an exaggerated claim, but I was too mesmerized to challenge it. Milford Sounds, a bit underwhelming compared to Ha Long Bay in Vietnam, was still pretty. Queenstown, with its imposing mountains looking down on a crystal clear lake, was so easy to fall in love with. The Abel Tasman National Park and its breathtaking shoreline! Arthur's Pass! The beauty continued unabated here. No wonder this country is one of the top destinations for European and South American students to "work-and-travel" for one year. If you are an American or European citizen under 30, you should seriously consider this option. It's very easy to get this one-year visa that allows you to work for a few months in New Zealand, make some money, and then travel around the country. Fruit-picking and farming-related jobs are pretty easy to find because this is primarily a farming country, by choice!

That's one aspect of this society that is intriguing. It's not as if the Kiwis are not keeping up with technology. Exports of lamb and dairy products are the main drivers of this economy. As you travel around the country, you can see they employ all the latest farming tools and technologies to run things efficiently. However, they don't seem to have any burning desire to enter the global rat race of tech leadership. New Zealand has a few tech companies with global reach, like Ninja Kiwi, the famous video game makers. They also have a handful of research institutes doing cutting edge medical research. But that's about it. With a tiny population and vast amounts of land rich in natural resources, they seem to know that farming is their strength and they seem to be comfortable with their position in the world. It doesn't mean they are not engaged with the rest of the world. If anything, it's the opposite. An export-based economy can't afford to be isolated from the world. Reading the local newspaper gives you a good idea of the forces of globalization in play. You open up the newspaper and there is one page for politics, one for business, one for sports, and two devoted to farming! It's adorable, in its own way, because in the United States, my home for the last decade or so, there is virtually no discussion of agriculture-related issues in national newspapers, and people living on the coasts jokingly call the huge expanse of central farmland "fly-by country." There is an article that talks about how demand for lamb meat plummeted in Europe and North America during the recession, and how China came to the rescue with increased demand of high-end clothing made from sheep's wool. Nobody is out of reach when it comes to globalization. And more often than not, China is everyone's savior.

Then another Kiwi told me about the recent rabbit invasion in the countryside. Apparently, an outsider introduced a particularly destructive species of rabbits on the South Island and, given their prodigious rate of procreation, their numbers quickly reached epidemic proportions. They started destroying crops with such abandon that farmers were struggling to make ends meet. The environmentalists were up in arms against their proposal to use a virus to eliminate the species. The issue went all the way up to parliament. Eventually, one of the farmers smuggled the virus in and introduced it among the rabbits. The rabbits were gone within five years and everyone noticed a big jump in farm yield. A cautionary tale about the perils of global trade, disturbing local ecosystems, overreach of environmentalists, how markets sometimes override other humanitarian concerns, and how all politics are local!

Stories like these make this land all the more quaint. The issues here are not cyber warfare, the next country trying to get nuclear weapons, the specter of corporate espionage, or the threat of blocking the export of rare earth metals. They are related to more immediate needs. People from a distant land are not eating as much meat anymore. But wait, with more disposable income, people from some other distant land are demanding more of those woolen clothes. Life here has all the trappings of a technologically advanced country, but the problems that grab headlines here are more "old world." A nice change of pace.

As they say, if everything is going right, you have ignored something. My two weeks in New Zealand were no exception to that rule. Well, nine out of those fifteen days. With good roads, beautiful scenery, and great camping facilities, this is road-trip country. Renting a camper van and driving around is the best way to enjoy the country. I met up with a 21-year-old Norwegian girl and her 37-year-old Canadian friend and we decided to do the road trip together. Successful and/or adventurous in their own right, they just weren't my kind of people. I had met the Norwegian girl earlier in Kuala Lumpur, but had never met the Canadian guy before. In the spirit of backpacking, I thought nothing would go wrong. However, from the minute we met to the minute we parted ways, it was a barrage of sarcasm, snarky comments, bombastic claims, and overall, a whole lot of negativity. Just didn't go the way I thought it would.

There were Heaven's Devils, the group of eight people I traveled with in Thailand and Laos. And then, there were these two travelers I met in New Zealand. As abuela, my Argentine friend's 70-something mom, says, if you want to know someone, travel with that person. That's the best way to know if you can live with the person. Within nine days, it was quite clear to me that beyond this trip, I had no intention of hanging out with these people. But in the backpacking world of anything goes and "Oh, I can get along with anyone," it was good to get a reality check and realize that there are some people I can't get along with. Words of wisdom, abuela!

SOUTH
AMERICAN
SAGA

8

27. BRAZIL: SWITCH OFF & CONNECT MORE

February 14, 2013
Inhotim, Brazil

It was just yesterday when I visited a contemporary art museum in a city called Inhotim, in the Brazilian state of Minas Gerais. It is easily one of the most magical places I have ever been to. It is a sprawling botanical garden spread over 100 or so acres, dotted with beautiful, modern sculptures and galleries with wonderfully creative exhibits. One such exhibit was a 22-minute movie called *The Last Silent Movie*. I walked into a pitch-dark theater and the movie started rolling. The screen was dark for the entire duration of the movie and the audio track was a collection of words and sentences spoken in languages that are now extinct. There were subtitles in Portuguese, which means I didn't understand much. With my basic knowledge of Spanish, I could tell that they weren't saying anything profound in those extinct languages. One person was talking about his life, the other was talking about his family, one more was reciting commonly used verbs translated in her dead language, yet another language was entirely based on whistling. If that last one had been my only language option, I would have been labeled an idiot!

In April of last year, I turned off my cell phone and set out to see the world. Barring a few times when I had to coordinate my schedule with a family member or friends hosting me, I managed to keep my phone off. The isolation I experienced during this yearlong trip has also helped me experience some genuine moments of ecstasy, agony, compassion, and universal understanding. And the absence of a phone to fiddle around with blocked that ubiquitous escape route and helped in letting those emotions sink in. I ended up connecting more by connecting less. Climbing Kilimanjaro for four days, only to turn around when I had barely 800 meters left to go. Visiting the concentration camp in Auschwitz to confront our own cruel history. Sitting on a secluded beach in Zanzibar and reading Farid Attar's poem *The Conference of the Birds*. Losing my way in Xi'an, trying to explain the Terracotta Warriors to Chinese people with sign language. I can go on and on.

Certainly no technophobe, I have always stayed abreast of the world happenings around me. As part of my professional life, I've had to keep up with the latest advances in science and technology. These advances are exciting, and happen fast! However, our brains are exquisitely tuned to filter out more than 90% of the information that hits our senses every second of every minute of every day. It is an evolutionarily-protective strategy to help us focus on what is most important. And here we are, bombarding our brains with more information every day. Texting, for instance, gives us the illusion of better connectivity. I have always found it to be a hindrance. A hindrance to the conversation I'm having at the moment or the document I'm writing or the movie I'm currently watching. Then, there are Twitter and Facebook. Wait! Maybe we want to cast as wide a net as possible when we download that latest craze "Bang with Friends." I want to have a one-night-stand, but I am not even willing to go out to a bar, find a person, talk to her, see it in her eyes, feel it in her touch, or read it from her body language. Out of fear of rejection, we are willing to outsource the job of our beautiful senses to the click of a mouse button. By playing on our primal instincts, technology has strangely detached us from our own senses.

Yet, there is still hope, there always is! Switching off my cell phone and traveling far and wide has made me see that ray of light. It's not just switching off the phone, though. I took a break from friendships and family relationships, as well. Sure, I have Skyped once in awhile and sent occasional emails to friends and family. Other than that, I've been successful at keeping the noise down to a bare minimum and my mind open to my immediate surroundings. Nobody is waiting for my phone calls or emails and I am not waiting for anything from anyone, either. Every chance one gets to do this is worth grabbing. If you are ever too scared or anxious about what would happen, think of it as a scientific experiment or some bitter pill you have to take because you are sick. In the end, it is always rewarding in more ways than one.

In hindsight, it turned out to be a blessing in disguise that I could not follow the subtitles in *The Last Silent Movie* down to the word. It made me reflect on the title of the documentary. The movie had sound, but without subtitles, it was as good as a silent movie. More importantly, it made me think about languages themselves. In the heydays of Latin and Sanskrit, no one thought these languages would someday go extinct. Today, these languages are restricted to certain church masses and Hindu religious ceremonies alone. Calligraphy, the art of beautifying Chinese script by incorporating images of everyday objects and landscapes, has been relegated as a tool to merely attract tourists. In this age of computers, the concept of handwriting is on its way to extinction anyway. Even signatures have gone electronic. The ephemeral nature of language itself – the tool that has helped humans communicate with each other and dominate other species – was thrown into sharp relief in that tiny theater. Sitting in that small, dark room, thousands of miles away from family and friends, and light years away from cell phones and the internet, listening to those extinct languages was a powerful experience. It helped me ponder the way we communicate. Writers love to say that everything we do and everything we say melts away into the ether. Written word stays forever. But how many of us have read any Latin or Sanskrit texts? Forget about our emotions, our ambitions, our dreams, and our hopes, even our language is so feeble it can't resist the tide of changing times. So what are you fighting about?

There is a Facebook kind of forced detachment that moves one away from one's senses and sucks one into the world of mouse clicks and keyboard hits. And then, there is a round-the-world-trip kind of detachment that moves one closer to one's senses and away from computer-generated reality. The choice is ours!

28. ARGENTINA: MARACANÃ? OR LA BOMBONERA?

March 7, 2013
Buenos Aires, Argentina

If you are a guy, any discussion of Rio de Janeiro and Buenos Aires has to start with women. Especially when your stay in Rio coincides with the Carnival. Like *The Guns of Navarone*, I think someone should make a movie called *Girls of Rio* or *Girls of Buenos Aires*. It's not as if every girl walking down the street is Gisele. But those who are beautiful are just stunning! Drop dead gorgeous!

Girls of Rio are a mix of everything. Native American, African, Mediterranean, Asian. It's a bit of history and a bit of culture. Because of the popularity of Hollywood movies and the fact that things happening in the United States garner more attention in my world, issues around slavery in the United States have always been in the news. When you come to Brazil, you learn that during the peak of slave trade in the 17th and 18th centuries, only about 10-15% of the slaves went from Africa to the United States. The rest went to Latin America, a huge majority ending up in Brazil. Then, there were the Germans, the Italians, and the Japanese who arrived in Brazil after the Second World War. Add the warmth of Brazilian culture to this immigration concoction, and voila! You get more than 50 shades of brown! With this diversity, the Brazilians can give the South Africans a run for their money when it comes to the "Rainbow Nation" tag.

Girls in Buenos Aires are the exact opposite. On a sunny Sunday, you can sit in a coffee shop on 9 de Julio Avenue and play the Spain-Italy-Germany game as modelesque women walk by. Spain, Spain, Italy, Spain, Germany, Italy, Germany, mostly Spain but with German eyes, Germany, but with Mediterranean dark hair, Italy, Spain, Spain, Germany. On, and on, and on. The brownest you can get is probably the Mediterranean olive skin. As friendly and happy as the Rio girls are, the Buenos Aires girls carry their model-ness with them everywhere they go. "Oh, I don't have time to look at you. There is nothing really interesting going on in front of me, but I'll still keep looking straight ahead!"

Rio takes the cake when it comes to the biggest party in the world. I've seen a few big ones around the world now. The Halloween Full Moon party in Thailand, assorted locations for New Year's Eve, Sydney, Istanbul, Las Vegas. However, nothing comes anywhere near the Carnival. For five days, everything in the city shuts down and the only things people do are drink and dance. Buses, trains, airports, streets, beaches, intersections; every 50 to 100 meters, there is a new kind of music and a new kind of party. For these five days, you can sleep whenever you want, although the city doesn't sleep at all.

Buenos Aires is not too far behind, though. Buenos Aires is a life-long party. There is something going on almost every night of the week. People have dinner at ten and go out after midnight. Monday is probably the only time things are a bit mellow in the night. You'll find a Milonga somewhere on a Tuesday night. Wednesday is the official "after-work party" day. Thursday is when you get together with friends and start planning your weekend. Then, there is the weekend! It all comes with a healthy side of haughtiness, of course.

Overall, Rio reminded me of Mumbai. In a New York minute, everything can change. In a Rio minute, just like in Mumbai, everything can change and go back to how it was. On a normal day, everyone is rushing somewhere, wading through the chaotic traffic. Run-down neighborhoods mesh into the swankier ones. On the promenade that goes along the Copacabana and Ipanema beach, you can see Porches, Mercs, BMWs, even an occasional Ferrari. On one of the side streets, you will find people looking for food in dumpsters or collecting empty cans and plastics for recycling. One day, on my way back to the hostel from the Carnival, I was on a bus and saw a motorcyclist passed out on the street, with blood oozing out of the back of his head. Buses, trucks, cars, and other motorcycles were all whizzing past the scene. Look out of the window, do the cross across your chest, and move on. Life here is so busy and rough-and-tumble that people don't have much time to stop and think. But at the end of the day, they somehow seem to be happy. And Carnival time? Double happy!

Buenos Aires is a bit of a mixed bag. The pretty girls think they are the best in the world. Other than that, there is a certain degree of stoicism in the air. It is every bit as rough-and-tumble as Rio, but they might have borrowed some of that Chinese stoicism. The Chinese are stoic because of all the political and cultural upheaval of the past few decades. The people of Buenos Aires seem to be a bit stoic, too, perhaps because of the economic issues they keep having every few years. The world goes through major economic downturns every 2-3 decades. Argentinean economic cycles are like the world on steroids. They don't wait for the world economy to collapse. They find ingenious ways to collapse their economy every few years. As one of the local guys told me, the current global recession doesn't feel all that bad because the Argentinean credit crisis in the late 1990s and early 2000s was so terrible there were Soviet-style long lines outside of grocery stores for food. Argentina follows its own recession timeline.

Rio seems to smile and take everything in its stride. Buenos Aires seems to be a bit philosophical about the fact that it used to be the capital of one of the richest countries in the world, but has since lost its pre-eminence. You can see it in the architecture, too. Rio is blessed with amazing natural beauty. The views from Sugarloaf Mountain, the iconic "Jesus" mountain, and the Copacabana beach are to die for. But architecturally, it is mostly a few ancient Portuguese buildings surrounded by concrete blocks and slums. BA, on the other hand, is not blessed with natural beauty. However, it makes up for this lack with its impressive mix of architectural styles. There is the old colonial architecture mixed with some Greek, French, and Italian styles. When Argentina was one of the richest countries, the government paid top Dollar to get famous European architects to come to Buenos Aires and build imposing buildings, making the city center more charming than Rio's.

Maybe that extends to culture, too. Brazil seems to be rich in street-culture. There is a guy on the street corner with a guitar singing bossa nova songs. There is a girl on the beach, casually juggling a football, who would put the best of American and Indian football players to shame. During the Carnival, there are people sitting outside in neighborhood restaurants, with their musical instruments, playing samba. People stop by, dance for a bit, hug each other, and move on. Buenos Aires has a bit of this street culture, too, mostly due to Italian immigrants. But this city is more about high-brow culture, the operas, classical music, theaters and book shops on Avenida Corrientes, the fancy sculptures in the sprawling gardens in Palermo and Belgrano. In a way, Rio says, "We may not have been the richest in the world, but we don't care." And Buenos Aires says, "We know we were the best in the world and we want the glory days back, but we don't know how to get them."

It is hard to choose one city, or even one country, over the other. Rio has its paõ du queijo, the Brazilian cheese bread, and Buenos Aires has its milanesa, the breaded meat preparation. Rio drinks Cashaça, made from sugarcane juice, and Buenos Aires drinks Fernet, the bitter Italian liquor. To Rio's samba, Buenos Aires replies with the tango. The Rio hand gesture is the Ali G style clapping with a single hand. The Buenos Aires hand gesture is the equally entertaining, basketball-style, three-pointer sign, held horizontal and moved up and down ad infinitum. The languages in these two cities are pretty intriguing, too. I love Spanish because of its oomph. Even with a paucity of words, the way they express the entire range of emotions in Spanish is incredible. Plus, a "cabrón" or a "la puta que lo parió" used at the right time in a conversation are lethally effective, but hard to translate into other languages. Portuguese is a totally different world. If Spanish is the language of love and hatred and everything in between, Portuguese, at least the Brazilian version of it, is the language of love. Every syllable in Brazilian-Portuguese is emphasized and extended so much it sounds like two lovers cuddled up, exchanging sweet nothings. I have no idea how you can fight or even yell at someone else in Portuguese!

Sometimes, though, it feels like Portuguese is trying to rub Spanish the wrong way. In Spanish, you enunciate Rio de Janeiro as Rio de Haneiro. In Portuguese, you would say Hio de Janeiro. In Spanish, "now" is "ahora," pronounced as aaora. In Portuguese, they spell it the same way, but call it aagora. *C'mon, guys! I only know a little bit of Spanish and I'm just trying to learn the basics of Portuguese here. Why do you have to make Portuguese so hard to understand? Poooorfavooooor!* Notwithstanding all this confusion, as an Indian, both languages have influenced India. Spanish "pan" for bread becomes "paõ" in Portuguese, "pav" in Marathi and Hindi, and "pau" in Bengali. Portuguese "caju" for cashew is the same word in Marathi and Hindi. Portuguese "batata" for potato is the same word in Marathi. Spanish "camisa" for shirt becomes "kameez" in Hindi and the Spanish "llave" for a key, pronounced as "shaave" becomes "chaabi" in Hindi and Bengali, and "chaavi" in Marathi. Funny how words travel, eh?

When all is said and done, any discussion of Rio and Buenos Aires has to end with fútbol for a guy like me! Sure, Europe is where all the money in fútbol is, but South America is where the corazón or the heart of fútbol is. Maracanã Stadium in Rio is easily the Mecca of fútbol. Wimbledon Center Court, the Lords, and Yankee Stadium all rolled into one. Imagine more than 100,000 fans watching the World Cup final in this stadium (which happened in 2014.) And millions more in and around Rio partying like there is no tomorrow. But even in this department, Buenos Aires comes up with a fitting riposte. In the gritty neighborhood of La Boca, which the earliest Italian immigrants called their home, La Bombonera, home of the Boca Juniors, stands out like a palace. As you walk into the stadium, they tell you the funny story of how the famous blue and yellow colors were chosen. With the founding members of the club unable to agree on the colors of the club jerseys, they decided to pick the colors of the first ship to sail into the bay, which happened to be a Swedish ship. Ergo, blue and yellow. With its strange shape, with one of the four sides just a straight wall with no seats for spectators, it resembles a Roman-era theater or reminds you of the Green Monster in Boston. The more interesting stuff, though, is outside the stadium. Posters and paintings of Maradona, the famous son of Boca Juniors, are plastered all over the neighborhood walls. Even the infamous Hand of God is boldly painted with pride on the wall of one of the nearby restaurants. Maracanã might be grand, but La Bombonera definitely has more character. It's like Pele and Maradona. If Pele is the elder statesman, Maradona is the equally gifted bad boy. Pele is classy, Maradona is flamboyant. Take your pick!

A local friend told me that Rio and Buenos Aires are like brothers who keep fighting, but who still know they are one family. It's like my brother and me. Other than our love for bacon, science, and all things sports, we have little in common. And while my brother's life has mostly gravitated around the United States and India, if Rio or Buenos Aires throws a good opportunity my way, I might just move there. Watch out, South America!

And when two brothers start fighting, big daddy has to step in as the arbiter. Perhaps it is poetic justice that the majestic Iguazu Falls are located roughly the same distance from Rio and Buenos Aires and are shared by Brazil and Argentina. At four times the expanse of Niagara Falls, these falls are beyond mind-blowing. Standing between Rio and Buenos Aires, it seems to tell the two brothers "Shut up, boys. Daddy is still in the hizzie!"

*   *   *

Aire Y Sol Y Solitude

March 19, 2013
El Chalten, Argentina

Patagonia! That outdoor-gear brand. In Argentina, it's half the country. This province in southern Argentina is all about gusty winds, bright sunshine, and a whole lot of nothing.

I started from Ushuaia, the southernmost city in the world. There is an Argentinean highway, Ruta 3, which keeps going south until it can't go any further. That point is called Fin del Mundo, or the end of the world. I was under the impression that it would be within walking distance of the city center of Ushuaia. It turned out to be a good 24km away from the city. A fellow backpacker told me I could hitchhike my way to the end of the world, but he forgot to tell me to start early in the morning. With a 3 PM start, I was asking for trouble. Cheap thrills, here I come! Out of the 48km round-trip journey, I managed to hitchhike for some 30-odd kilometers. I failed to find a ride for the all-important final stretch. An elderly couple dropped me off 4-5 kilometers from the end and I had to walk the final stretch. In a way, the end of the world was asking me to leave all man-made technology behind and use my own two feet to get there.

213

The scenery wasn't as spectacular as the Cape of Good Hope, but I wasn't going there for scenery. It's the idea. The idea of traveling as far south on this earth as the roads would let me. Sure, there is Antarctica down below. And if I had had the time and money, I would have loved to have gone there. But that's a sheet of ice; not land in the traditional sense of the word. So it was great to finally reach the spot where a sign board said there is no road beyond this point. Of course, there was a tiny church beyond that point. But what is the end of the world without a little bit of religion?

As I turned around and started walking back to find a ride back to the hostel, I realized this was the beginning of the end. At that point, I still had a little over a month to go. Then again, it was all just a matter of working my way up to the United States. A few more exciting stops along the way, but the direction of my travel was a bit depressing. It was getting dark, as well. Thankfully, an American tourist couple took pity on me and gave me a ride back to town; pulling me back from the end of the world and brightening my day a little.

I haven't even finished my trip yet and I'm already getting withdrawal symptoms. Slowly but surely, I've started thinking about my life after the trip. What would my next job be? Where would it take me? How would it feel to go back to "normal" life? How long would I last before I start another big trip? Or another gig?

Standing in front of the Perito Moreno glacier helped me snap out of those depressing thoughts. The guide told me this wasn't the largest glacier in the world, but it was one of the largest stable glaciers. Boy, was it large! Forget about the boat ride and the glacier walk that allow you to touch it and feel it and play with it. Just standing in the viewing gallery, looking at the length and breadth and height of this beautiful creation of nature, makes you feel so insignificant that all your depressing thoughts vanish before your jaw drops to the floor. And if that killer view doesn't solve your problem, there is always whiskey on the Moreno rocks! Yep, as touristy as it sounds, it was fun to have a shot of Jamison on glacial ice.

The grandeur of Perito Moreno set the tone for the rest of my stay in Patagonia. Two weeks really don't do justice to this part of the world. The soaring Andes and the Pampas lowlands, on the Argentinean side, can easily compete with New Zealand and

Switzerland as the most beautiful place in the world. For backpackers, the remoteness and ruggedness of this terrain make it even more exciting. Switzerland and New Zealand are equally beautiful, but you have all the amenities in the world to enjoy them. Patagonia is still underdeveloped, making it physically more challenging to experience it all. Wide open lands, semi-paved roads, steep hikes, the sun bearing down from cloudless skies; all in all, just like Perito Moreno, everything in Patagonia makes you feel pretty small.

The 1,400km trip north from El Calafate to Bariloche was no exception. These states in Argentina are so sparsely populated you don't see anything, not even passing cars, for 200-300 kilometers at a stretch. Other than the shrubs and bushes and an occasional distant mountain range, it's just flat, grassy land, as far as you can see. As another cheap thrill, I managed to hitchhike the 200-plus kilometers from El Calafate to El Chalten. After that, it was some long-ass bus rides. I noticed a pretty girl from Switzerland boarding the same bus and hustled my way in to grab a seat next to her. We decided to tell our life stories without exchanging the usual pleasantries or our names. She was on a much shorter trip – three months – to celebrate her graduation. She was planning to spend most of it in Argentina and we were both going to spend at least a few days in Bariloche. At the next stop, which was a shack in the middle of nowhere offering food and drinks that were ridiculously overpriced, I asked the owner for a pen and paper. I scribbled a note mentioning I would love to spend time with her in Bariloche and signed it as "The Bariloche Backpacker." If she was not interested, we would never know each other's names. And that is exactly how it ended. While boarding the bus again, I gave her the note and found a different seat away from her. The initial warmth was gone and for the rest of the trip, she was busy avoiding me. Oh well!

The solitude of sitting in the bus and staring at the nothingness outside the window naturally makes you look inward. The back-to-back 12-hour bus rides from El Chalten to Bariloche were more than enough for that.

Tick...tock...tick...tock.

On my way from Australia to Brazil, I had a one-day layover in San Francisco. I used the time to catch up with some old friends. These are some of the smartest guys I know. One of them was working for Google and the other had just finished interviewing there, as well. As we all met up, they spent about 2 hours analyzing the series of interviews. The main question on their minds was the "rank" of the interviewers. How many of the interviewers were level 5 and how many of them were level 6?

And here I was, between levels 5 and 6 of solitude in Patagonia. One day before getting on the bus, I shared a breakfast table with a girl from Belgium and a couple from England, all in their early twenties. The Belgian girl was three weeks into her 6-month trip to South America. The British couple was nine months into their trip of as-yet-undecided duration. In the backpacking world, it's called "until the money runs out." And I was 11-months into my year-long trip. At the end of that conversation, I remember telling myself that soon, I would be sitting around lunch and dinner tables, forced to listen to people's two-week vacation plans. Sigh!

As I was replaying the two conversations in my head, I couldn't help the wry smile on my face. There are people for whom jobs and careers become their lives. And then, there are people for whom jobs and careers are the means to enable their lives, which exist outside of their office walls. Different things work for different people. And as someone who thought he would grow up to be the former, I've started feeling an overwhelming force to be the latter. Marriage and raising a family have definitely become optional for me. And now, even my job and career will become means. Means for another one-year trip, writing another book, making a movie, going to an unknown country to learn a new language, learning to play the saxophone, or whatever else catches my fancy. I will go wherever my life takes me. If somebody asks me in a job interview, "Where do you see yourself in five years?" I'll be tempted to say "Definitely not in your chair and definitely not asking that question of another candidate."

29. COLOMBIA: NEVER SAY NEVER AGAIN

April 1, 2013
Leticia, Colombia

Bogota is a lot like San Francisco or Melbourne. The weather can change so quickly you will be experiencing all four seasons in one day. A beautiful, sunny day with 20-25 degree Celsius temperatures can suddenly turn into a cold, cloudy, and rainy afternoon. However, all that cold weather was gone as soon as I landed in Leticia. This small town is at the southern tip of Colombia, but it is bang in the middle of the Amazon jungle. In this part of the world, it's just hot and humid. Nonstop.

At first glance, the Amazon River and the jungle seemed like some sort of a combination of the wide open Nile in Egypt and the thick forests of northern Thailand. After spending a week in the Amazon jungle, I realized how much more than that it was. On my last crazy trip, the motorcycle adventure in South America, I had saved the best for the last. Machu Picchu! This trip is no different. I couldn't have found a better country to end my trip. The Amazon jungle is magical, impossible to describe in words. And to experience it all, you have to challenge yourself physically and mentally. Train the mind. Train the body. It's all about mind over matter.

The heat and humidity were just the start. I didn't grow up on the coasts. 35-40 degrees Celsius temperatures and almost 100% humidity are my worst nightmare. On our first morning in the jungle, we walked about 2-3 kilometers in exactly that kind of weather. The backpack was around 5 kilograms and wasn't that big a deal, but we had to cover our bodies to save ourselves from the mosquitoes. A pullover and slacks in 40 degrees Celsius heat and near 100% humidity are unimaginable. It reminded me of my younger days when I played competitive sports. I used to go to badminton practice with three t-shirts and return with two of them so wet they felt like I had dipped them in a bucket of water and forgotten to dry them. There is one difference though. There was no point in changing clothes in the Amazon. The weather is such that you'd have to carry 10-15 pullovers daily to keep yourself sweat-free. And the more weight you carry, the more you'll sweat. Good luck!

The battle with my own body resumed as soon as we reached the first stop, which was called a Malloca, a hut of one of the indigenous people. By backpacking standards, these stops are a bit touristy in the sense that they prepare food for you and have designated spots where you set up your hammock and sleep. Or try to sleep, at least. The guide served us lunch in the military-style metal bowls and plates we were carrying with us. When we were done eating, it was our job to wash them. There was no tap water in the middle of the jungle and the mineral water we were carrying was just enough for drinking. The guide led us to a nearby pond with still water, where I could see a nice layer of scum crowding the lakeshore. Diarrhea? Dysentery? Ha! For the first time in my trip, I regretted not finishing my Hepatitis A and B vaccination series. Wash your dishes, wish your body good luck, eat in the same dish again, and don't forget to wish your body good luck again!

After lunch, it was time for a nap. How do you take a nap in this kind of weather, inside a hammock with a mosquito net, while your entire body is covered in sweat and full-sleeved clothes? I lay down in the hammock and started breathing the heavy air. With the mosquito net killing whatever little breeze was around, I started sweating even more profusely, my body trying to adjust to the temperature. There was no way I was going to fall asleep! Sure enough, within 20 minutes or so, my body had gotten used to the weather and I dozed off out of sheer mental exhaustion!

When I had first visited Baja California in Mexico six years ago, my accidental introduction to backpacking, I told myself that pit toilets, with a cockroach or two crawling out, would be the lowest bar. I would never do it again. And here I was, walking into another one. No cockroaches this time, but plenty of fruit flies and mosquitoes droning around. How much insect spray are you going to use?

As if pit toilets weren't enough, I also had to deal with my fear of heights. For the past few years, I've slowly been trying to overcome it. Amazon, though, was like a pop-quiz meant to shock me to the core. Before we left, the tour guide had told us we would be sleeping in a tree house one of the nights. Sounded like fun. What he didn't tell us was the way we were going to get up there. If they had shown us photos, I would've said, "No way!" As we were standing under the 45 meter (135 feet) tall tree, one of the guides held the rope tied to a branch at the top of the tree, wrapped up the climbing gear around his waist, and went straight up. *Wait a minute. We're not going to go up like that, are we?* I thought we were going to hold on to the tree trunk...or something! No, the tree trunk is 3-4 meters away. You can't use the trunk for support. *No, dude!*

I decided to take the bull by the horns and went first. I took the two clamps, wrapped the harness around my waist, and started going up. *Don't look down, don't look down, don't look down.* I went up 5-6 meters and click-swoop, click-swoop. Once again, click-swoop. One of the clamps wasn't working. *Damn it! This should qualify as poetic injustice.* I was suspended in mid-air, hanging on to a rope tied to some random branch 45 meters above ground, I had a million mosquitoes hovering all around me, and then, I had to look down. In that state, I had to wait 10-15 minutes for one of the guides to come replace my clamp, so I could continue my inane adventure.

When I finally reached the top, there was no tree house. It was a 5 by 5 sq. meter bamboo platform, with rickety rails, supported by the branches of the tree. Sleeping here had never crossed my mind. Not even in my dreams. Not even in my nightmares! These branches better be strong. We have to sleep here!

And then came the mosquitoes, my mortal enemies. If there is even one mosquito in the room, it manages to sniff me out and target me among a crowd, buzzing around me so I can no longer sleep. For someone like me, going to the Amazon was like raising your hand to be a sacrificial lamb. I heard that if you take vitamin B tablets for a week or so, mosquitoes don't bother you because they don't like your body odor. The only problem was I found out about it a day before I started the jungle trip. Too late.

In spite of keeping my hands and legs covered at all times, and pouring a bottle of insect spray on my palms, neck, ears, and face, I started scratching my whole body like never before. I had never signed up for that! One of the guys took a photo of my back, as a souvenir, and told me the next time he goes into a jungle, he will take me with him. I was like a good insurance policy for him. Ironically enough, after a day or two in the Amazon, I actually started admiring the mosquitoes. These mosquitoes are so good they can bite you through your clothes. And they've gotten so resistant to mosquito sprays that they can easily crawl all over your skin and locate that one pore on your skin that you missed. How many times have you had a mosquito bite on the inside of your palm? Or where your fingernail meets the skin? Welcome to the Amazon and its mosquitoes!

I know I'm making it sound like it's a Herculean task to go hiking and camping in the Amazon jungle. However, hundreds of travelers go to the Amazon every year, walk the same trails, and sleep in the same "tree-houses." That's how I played the mind-over-matter game. If so many people can do it, so can I. The reward makes it all worth it. Attempting Kilimanjaro was exhilarating. Shark cage diving in South Africa was thrilling. The sight of Whitehaven beach was soothing. Perito Moreno was awe-inspiring. The Amazon jungle was just pure magic.

For most of the time, you walk through either layer upon layer of dry, rotting leaves or knee-deep mud, the stench of it mixing seamlessly with the aromas of the flowers to create a unique, heavenly blend. In the middle of the muddy trail, the guide somehow noticed fresh pug marks of a puma, less than 24-hours old. *What the hell am I doing here again?* Then he picked up a tiny frog and put it on my nail. It's called a crystal frog because it is almost transparent and you can see its heart beating. It seemed to be a bit scared and held onto my nail, as if it was holding on for dear life. How the hell does this species survive? How does this tiny frog find its brethren in this seemingly endless jungle?

It's not really about spotting animals, though, as much as it is about feeling like a stray dog or a cat walking through a city. Other than some species of monkeys, spiders, insects, and birds, you don't see much. You are the stranger and all those invisible animals are looking at you. In the city, it is the honking in the morning and the street lights in the evening. In the thickness of Amazonia, it is the million birds in the morning and the billion critters in the evening. As soon as the sun goes down, the frogs set the tone. It is like jazz. They improvise all the time. Sometimes, they get tired and the critters pick it up. Some distant monkey plays the lead, screeching for a while, then the howling owls do the aria, and the frogs pick it up again. In the middle of it all, your guide takes you on a night walk to see tarantulas, and you start walking to the beat of the frogs. The guide is clearing the waist-length grass below with his machete and marking crosses on the trees as we make our way through the jungle, so that we can find our way back. The grass below and the trees grow so fast that, even if the guide comes back in a couple of weeks, these trails and marks will have disappeared. So he has to create new ones every time he comes back. "What if this guide disappears or a puma attacks and eats him?" I wondered. I didn't have a map. Even if I had one, it would have been useless. It's just jungle for a few hundred kilometers in each direction! *Just block the thought and keep walking.*

I don't have arachnophobia, but when you see a spider as big as your palm, crawling 2-3 meters away, and the guide picks up a stick and starts nagging it, after telling you it's a jumping black tarantula, you ask yourself one more time "What the hell am I doing here?" You come back, lay down in the hammock, and it starts pouring. All of a sudden, the symphony dies down and you can hear a million small creeks flowing around you, desperately searching for the river. Listen to Ma Rewa by Indian Ocean, hear the rain pick up as the natural music dies down and man-made music reaches its crescendo, and you will experience ecstasy! No pills needed.

As we were cruising our way on the Amazon River and out of the jungle, I told myself, for the millionth time, that this was the spirit of traveling. It's fun to see the pyramids, the leaning tower, the Terracotta Warriors, and go to the top of the empire state building to enjoy the view. But every once in awhile, you get the opportunity to immerse yourself in nature and understand where you come from. Become one with the trees, the animals, the birds, the river, the mud, the morning sky, and yes, the mosquitoes. Not to see any sights or to admire feats of human engineering; just to go back to your roots. If the indigenous tribes living here do it every day, and if our explorer ancestors have done it with means far less sophisticated, so can you. Leaving the creature comforts behind and enduring the minor discomforts is our little tribute to them, certainly more fulfilling than visiting the graves of James Cook or Marco Polo!

*   *   *

Sometimes, Truth is Stranger than Fiction

April 13, 2013
Medellin, Colombia

Medellin happened to be my last stop of this crazy, yearlong journey. Three nights here, a quick stopover in Bogota, and then I fly back to the United States. No matter how many times I think about it, I still find it hard to believe the sheer number of things I've seen and done in one year. Medellin is everything the Amazon jungle is not. A bustling city with chaotic traffic, charming nightlife, and beautiful women. As far as beautiful women are concerned, Medellin would give stiff competition to Buenos Aires and Rio any day. There is a reason Colombia keeps winning international beauty pageants. The reason is called Medellin. But what makes Medellin even more intriguing is its notorious son, Pablo Escobar.

There are several tours that take you to the city center, the nearby mountains, the churches, and the historic towns nearby. As a foreigner, though, I found the Pablo Escobar tour the eeriest and most mind-boggling one. While I had heard about Colombia being the center of the drug universe and Medellin being the cocaine capital of the world, I hadn't spent enough time reading about Pablo Escobar, the undisputed king of cocaine during the seventies and eighties. For the handful of locals I talked to, the suffering has been immense. Also, nobody wants their country to be associated with drug lords and drug trafficking. Even more so, when you're a proud Colombian because in the twentieth century, this is one of the few countries in South America that hasn't had its democratic institutions trampled on by dictators. Former president Uribe came close to it, but never succeeded at it.

Nonetheless, as a foreigner, Pablo Escobar's story is a classic rags-to-riches story full of the near failure of democratic institutions, a twisted sense of morality, grandeur, pomp, unbelievable power, outsized egos, gruesome violence, and everything in between. There is a reason why, regardless of our sense of morality, we find Godfather-like personalities enigmatic and charming. To paraphrase a line from a Bollywood movie, these guys engage in illegitimate businesses with a sense of fairness that is sometimes hard to find in the world of legal businesses. Pablo was no exception.

The tour started with a documentary *The Two Escobars* that provided a background about Escobar's rise from being a petty thief in the poor neighborhoods of Medellin, to one of FBI's most wanted criminals, selling $500 million of cocaine a day. I found his life history astonishing at many levels. At one point, he was making so much cash he didn't know what to do with it or even how to store it! Legend has it that rats were eating away the piles of cash he made. He was schmoozing with Prime Ministers, Presidents, and celebrities from around the world and had 80 airplanes at his disposal. Even Frank Sinatra visited his ranch in Colombia. When the FBI put a $10 million bounty on his head, he visited the United States, took pictures standing in front of the White House, and released them to the media just to rub it in. At the height of his empire, when he started feeling the noose tightening around him, he was still so powerful he elected himself to the Colombian parliament and ensured the passage of a constitutional amendment to abolish the extradition treaty with the United States before he decided to surrender. Surrender he did, eventually. And how? He engaged in protracted negotiations with the government to ensure that they would build a five-star prison just for him. As someone who was angry at the government's neglect of the poor, he perfected the art of greasing the entire democratic machinery to build a criminal empire that set a new benchmark in terms of its size, scope, and influence.

And yet, in spite of this outsized power, he never forgot where he came from. He built hundreds of football fields in the poor neighborhoods of Colombia and acted as the godfather for a whole new generation of Colombian football players. He built schools for poor Colombians and, ironically, kept telling young kids to stay away from cocaine. When one of the slums in Medellin burnt down, he rebuilt the entire neighborhood, giving away homes to 300 devastated families. The neighborhood is called Pablo Escobar. To politicians and criminals all over the world, Pablo's word was Pablo's word. The guy who brought so much embarrassment to

Colombian citizens also gave them a sense of pride, and put Colombia on the international football map when the Colombian national football team qualified for the US football World Cup in 1994 and started as one of the favorites.

In the end, he got what he deserved, like we all do. When the Colombian special operations teams came looking for him, he escaped his five-star prison and, after a few weeks of hot pursuit, was killed in broad daylight. Or maybe he committed suicide, depending on what version you want to believe. Even after death, visiting his grave gives us glimpses of his split personality. His inflated ego didn't change his desire to be buried in a simple grave in the community he grew up in. This entire story sounds more like a fast-paced Robert Ludlum or John le Carré thriller, except for the fact that, as you are taking the tour, they stop by some of the buildings that are still bombed out and stand as witnesses to the carnage that was a result of his wars against the rival Cali cartel and then against the Colombian government.

But the real kicker on this tour is the last stop. After climbing one of the hills surrounding the city, you get to the house of Pablo Escobar's mother. She is long gone, but Pablo's brother, Roberto, still lives there. Roberto was a gifted athlete and won several cycling medals as a teenager, but was sucked into his brother's thriving business. He was the finance guy of the cartel and handled all the cash flow for their worldwide business. He managed to escape the five-star prison with Pablo, but apparently Pablo convinced him to turn himself in and escape near-certain death at the hands of the Colombian government. He got 22 years in prison and, according to the tour guide, learned medicine while in prison. When he was in prison, someone sent him a letter bomb and it blew up in his face. He somehow survived the bomb blast, but it disfigured and disabled him for life. They say multiple plastic surgeries were able to restore his face, but he has lost almost all of his vision and can't hear well, either. He was released after 11 years on parole because of his good conduct.

Seeing him in flesh and blood is a strange experience. He seems to be cordial and welcoming. He has been claiming, for some time now, that the money he makes by selling Pablo's memorabilia and souvenirs goes toward a charity helping HIV research. He also claims the research has led to development of a vaccine that has already cured 15-20 patients and that they are waiting for approval by regulatory agencies.

I have no way of verifying these claims but, unlike my fellow backpackers on the tour, I didn't feel the burning desire to buy any posters or bumper stickers of someone I consider to be a bad guy with a few shades of virtue in him. Roberto, on the other hand, turned out to be a bit of a moral dilemma for me. As someone who handled the money of the cartel, does he have a shot at redemption? Does spending 11 years in prison and partially losing his sight and hearing count as enough repentance? What if his claims about the HIV vaccine are true? Does that count for anything? After all, the difference between arguably morally defensible collateral damage and a cold-blooded murder is the larger context. If the death of an innocent bystander is part of a larger war to liberate an oppressed society, we are more likely to condone it. Then, what if Roberto's presumably charitable causes end up saving more people than Pablo's cartel killed?

As we were getting ready to leave his house, I asked him if he had the chance to change one thing in his life, what, if anything, he would change. Without even a second's worth of pondering, he said "Toda la vida." He would change his entire life. If you have to live the rest of your life thinking you would like to change everything in your past, is there any bigger punishment than that?

I have no clear answers to these questions, but on my way back to the United States, my mind kept going back to this improbable story of two brothers. Drug addiction, money laundering, murders, dizzying amounts of money, unchecked power and its corrupting influence, a sense of justice, and perhaps eventual redemption. Some stories have no clear winners and losers, just a bunch of characters who evoke tough moral and ethical questions. And, in a larger context, that is what my round-the-world trip has taught me. It is easy to sit in one corner of the world and pontificate about good and evil. When you actually visit different countries and try to understand their historic and cultural contexts, the situation gets a lot murkier and you learn to accept the world the way it is. The world is too morally complex for one person or one society to impose its vision on the rest of the world.

It's not all that hopeless, though. Beyond history, culture, and everything that plagues today's world, there is the individual. You, me, and every other person in the world. Taking a break from life as usual has taught me to find happiness within. Sure, you can keep striving for a better world however you want to define "better." And, like Martin Luther King, Jr. famously said "The arc of the moral universe is long, but it bends toward justice." However, it is important not to get disillusioned and disheartened by the world around you or the setbacks you might face in your pursuit of a better world. As Hindu philosophy says, true happiness lies inside. The world around you is just "maya," an illusion. If you're looking for happiness in things around you, you are looking in the wrong place. Look inside and it is right there.

WRAPPING UP

9

30. USA: RETURN TO NON-INNOCENCE

April 15, 2013
New Haven, USA

After almost one year on the road, I landed in the United States two hours after the Boston Marathon bombing. As I was standing in the long immigration line, all I could see on the TV was CNN reporters hammering in the early details, over and over again. My first thought turned to a Pakistani-American friend who was running the marathon that day. Within a few hours, I found out she had finished the marathon half an hour before the bombings and was just 2-3 blocks away from the finish line. Last May, my trip started in Egypt on a day that saw the death of 10-15 protesters in Cairo. And this April, my trip ended with the deaths of innocent athletes in Boston.

Beyond the well-being of my marathoner friend, there was no time to ponder the meaning of death. The first thing I had to worry about, immediately after landing, was filing my tax returns. Talk about excitement! Navigating that maze meant catching up with family had to wait for the next day. It was great to see them after such a long time, especially my niece, who can engage in proper, yet completely nonsensical, conversations. It is adorable in its own way. In one year, she has learned to make up stories on the fly, an indication that she is a fiction writer in the making. Other than that, it felt like we had all said good-bye just yesterday. After a day or two of storytelling, we were back to our old ways, pulling each other's legs and digging up the same old funny stories about each other. For a change, that sense of familiarity was comforting.

Almost everyone I meet keeps saying that nothing has changed. I look the same and act the same way. And yet, so much has changed! Sure, it was nice to sleep in the same, comfortable bed, take a long shower, and eat some healthy, home cooked food after such a long time. For the first few days, I kept using the same four t-shirts from my backpack, but it was nice to know there was a washing machine in the house and I did not need to wash my clothes every day. Within a week, though, I realized I didn't have the patience for driving and traffic anymore. In the whole year I was on the road, I drove a car only for the ten days I was in New Zealand. And those were wide open roads. The rest was public transportation, flights, and a whole lot of walking. I have learned to enjoy walking. I remember the first month of my trip, when I got anxious waiting for buses and trains, or walked a couple of miles to get to my destination. I used to feel like I was wasting time. Slowly but surely, I learned that waiting and walking were integral parts of the experience. Walk along, smell the roses, talk to people, observe how wide or narrow the sidewalks are and what the local people throw on them, peek into people's homes, and take in the smells of the side alleys. In the sterilized American suburbia, I miss all that.

In a way, I still haven't finished my trip because I haven't started working again. It is still fun to meet old friends and catch up with them. The real test is going to be the first few weeks of my next job. Maybe that is the reason why I am looking for something that will keep me outside of an office with four walls, and in the middle of the chaos called humanity. But for a few weeks, at least, it is fun to renew old friendships. People have moved up the corporate ladder. Some have gotten promoted, others have started their own businesses, some have completely switched tracks, some have gotten married, some have kids now, and some have them on the way. Then again, just like my fellow travelers had predicted, the things they complain about haven't changed much. And I haven't changed my habit of being a patient listener and nodding away. After this trip, I find myself so far removed from the day-to-day struggles of everyone around me that I don't even know what to say. What should I say? Go pack your bags and see the world. Learn about all the horrific things our parents, grandparents, and great grandparents have endured. Climb Kilimanjaro, scuba dive in the great barrier reef, go shark cage diving, breathe in the fresh air of Norway, enjoy the serenity of sitting by the lakes of New Zealand, talk to the young revolutionaries of Egypt, meet random strangers and fall in love with them. Just go out, embrace the world, and find out what you enjoy doing.

But I know they will all look at me with a fake smile and say "You're funny." Not really. Life is only as complicated as you want it to be. What if you are an innocent bystander who, unfortunately, meets his death tomorrow? Do you want to die happy? Or die complaining?

*   *   *

What is in a Starbucks?

June 2, 2013
Baltimore, USA

Thirty-six hours to go. A quick drive back to my home base to pack my bags and I'm off to India. A little over a year ago, I bid a temporary good-bye to the United States. Temporary because I knew that my round-the-world trip would end in the United States. I would have to finish my soul searching, come back, do some job searching, and then leave the United States for good. And now, that day is just one night away.

Most of my family and friends think this is going to be a temporary move. They all think the chaos, corruption, rigid social structure, and corporate culture of India will be more than enough to override my love for the people and food, and the unmistakable sense of irony and amazement that are everyday India. They have a point. More than anything else, I'm worried about the barrage of marriage questions I will have to handle on a daily basis. But I know that the chances of my returning to the United States are bleak. Given the kind of work I do, I guess I will keep visiting the United States. Those will mostly be business trips or vacations, though.

The ramp to the expressway is the second right, but I reluctantly take the first right. I have some unfinished business to take care of. I know this street like the back of my hand. I have driven up and down this stretch a million times. It's a pretty upscale neighborhood, the kind that still supports the quaint bicycle shop on the corner. A twist of fate made me live here for a couple of years, but I rarely took the left turn I was about to take. It is the turn for Whole Foods, a florist, a mom-and-pop bakery, and a Starbucks. What the hell is a guy like me going to do there? Buy flowers? Health food? Overpriced coffee?

More than ten years ago, the reason I came here that day was pure convenience. I was new to the city and didn't know any better. I took that left turn once again, perhaps for the last time. The Whole Foods was still there. On this uneventful weekday morning, housewives were driving their Beetles and Mercedes convertibles in and out of the parking lots, their brown bags full of flowers and organic goodies. In rich American suburbia, these things rarely change.

I parked my car, but the spot was now reserved for Whole Foods' customers. *Well, something has changed!* I drove around and found an unreserved parking spot. I walked up the four-five stairs and noticed that the railing against which I had been leaning on that day was gone. They had built a tiny patio and arranged some tables and chairs for customers to enjoy the sun. I stepped in and noticed that the table I was looking for was gone. In fact, all the small tables had been replaced by two big tables in the middle. The comfy sofas and La-Z-Boy type chairs had also gotten upgrades. The coffee counter had doubled in size. I took a deep breath and walked to the counter.

"A green tea, please."

"- Sure, what flavor, sir?"

"How about, umm…Zen?"

"- Sure, what size?"

"Small is fine."

"- We don't have small, sir."

"Yeah, give me a tall." *You stupid Starbucks!*

I paid for it, waited, looked around, grabbed my tea, and sat down at one of the two big tables facing the small table that used to be next to the window. I took a sip of the steaming tea. It cleared my sinuses a bit and I wiped off my runny nose for the millionth time. In the last ten years, even my physiology had changed from not having any allergies to being allergic to pollen in the spring. But mentally, I was still hanging on to something.

That non-existent table is where I had met the only girl I have fallen in love with…yet. Over the past decade, almost everything was gone. Sure, I probably won't fall out of love. I have a million things to say. And I think I always will. At the same time, I know there is nothing left to say. That realization came a few years ago, but this irrational fear remains. I kept thinking that I would never be able to go back to this coffee shop again, but after traveling around the world, this must be doable.

It was nothing, really. I looked around. A young girl was working on her assignment. Two men and a woman in business attire were discussing, well, business. Two Asian women were playing with their kids and catching up. For everyone around me, it seemed like just another day. For me, it was a small, yet important, milestone in my personal journey.

If there was a moment I could trace my craziness back to, it would be that moment on that table that has disappeared. Once you fail in love, you lose your fear of failure. And so began my journey toward risk-taking. Other than a vague sense of longing, there is not much left of my first love. But after such a long time, it is an interesting dilemma for me now. If anything had come of it, in all probability, I would've followed the standard path of getting a fat salary in some big corporation. I wouldn't have thrown caution to the wind to travel the world. I wouldn't have written that damn book about my motorcycle trip so early. I would've been risk-averse. I would've procrastinated. In hindsight, it is almost impossible to choose one path over the other. Perhaps it is fine the way it is. In any case, I was not the chooser. The safe choice was only my wishful thinking.

In a few minutes, I realized the stupidity of it all. I never drink tea or coffee. I go to Starbucks once in two years, or maybe even less frequently. I have to pack up my life and move out of this country in less than thirty-six hours. This country and this Starbucks, in particular, have given me a lot. A can-do spirit, a never-say-die attitude, rejection of dogmas, a non-judgmental worldview, skepticism about traditional institutions like marriage, friends from all around the world; there are a million things I can thank this country and this Starbucks for, but it is time to move on and embrace the next chapter of my life. Every once in a while, time teaches you lessons you don't want to learn. All you can do is be thankful for it.

I got in my car and turned up the radio. The first time I left this Starbucks, I had blasted *Raspberry Jam Delta* by Joe Satriani for its heady rush. This time, the Spanish radio channel was playing a mix of mellow Mariachi songs and Latin power ballads. My last few hours of enjoying Spanish music on a radio. I am a changed man. For better or worse? Time will tell.

ABOUT THE AUTHOR

Mauktik Kulkarni is an electronics engineer-turned-neuroscientist based in Mumbai, India. An entrepreneur at heart, he was a part of some successful start-ups before he began exploring his creative side. He is an author, film maker, public speaker, and traveler, who has backpacked through more than 50 countries. His first book, *A Ghost of Che*, a memoir based on his solo, 8000km motorcycle trip in South America, was published in 2009. It was followed by a whirlwind, round-the-world trip to 36 countries in one year. *Riding on a Sunbeam*, his first film as an executive producer and the male protagonist, was released in 2016, and is a backpacking film which explores the social, cultural, economic and religious contradictions of modern-day India. These days, he is co-producing the feature film adaptation of *A Ghost of Che*. He has delivered invited lectures on neuroscience, entrepreneurship, traveling, film-making, and anything else that strikes his fancy. He has also been a guest columnist for travel and sports magazines and is constantly looking for new adventures in life.

Made in the USA
Middletown, DE
05 June 2017